FRANK DUFF

FOUNDER OF THE LEGION OF MARY

FR. ROBERT BRADSHAW

Imprimatur:
    DR. HENRICUS FREHEN, SMM
    Ep. Reykjavikensis
    August 2, 1984

MONTFORTPUBLICATIONS
Ad Jesus per Mariam
26 South Saxon Ave
Bay Shore, NY 11706

MontfortPublications.com

©1985, Montfort Publications

ISBN 978-0910984263

THE MISSIONARIES OF THE COMPANY OF MARY
(Montfort Missionaries)
AD JESUM PER MARIAM

The spiritual legacy contained within the life and writings of St. Louis de Montfort is one of the truly great treasures of the Roman Catholic Church. The task of bringing the full wealth of that treasure to the faithful is the heart of the mission of the MISSIONARIES OF THE COMPANY OF MARY (Montfort Missionaries), the community of those priests and brothers who have been consecrated to follow in his footsteps. Since our foundation by St. Louis de Montfort, the missionary activity of the Company of Mary has grown to include active apostolates serving the needs of the people of God in nearly thirty countries.

MONTFORT PUBLICATIONS is a ministry of the Company of Mary through which we make available the writings of St. Louis de Montfort and resources to assist the faithful in understanding and living the full depth of his profound spirituality.

Montfort Publications	*631.665.0726*
26 South Saxon Avenue	*info@montfortpublications.com*
Bay Shore, NY 11706	*MontfortPublications.com*

Frank Duff

1	About this book
2	Foreword
4	Introduction
7	ROOTS
12	EARLY YEARS
17	SCHOOLDAYS
22	DISCOVERING A WHOLE NEW WORLD
27	ENTER JOE GABBETT
37	THE EASTER REBELLION 1916 – AND TROUBLED TIMES FOR IRELAND
42	"PURE COMMUNICATION WITH GOD"
47	THE PRICE OF A BREAKFAST
50	MOTHER
54	THE "TRUE DEVOTION"
59	MATT TALBOT – AND OTHERS
64	THE LEGION IS BORN
70	"SHALL HE NOT LEAVE THE NINETY-NINE?"
74	THE SIGN-LANGUAGE OF FAITH
83	ENTER MR. LALOR
87	THE MORNING STAR
92	THE UNEXPECTED GUEST
99	FIRST VISIT TO ROME
104	REGINA COELI

108	POOR OLD LIZZIE
113	ENCIRCLING THE GLOBE
119	AFRICA'S FIRST LEGIONARY
123	EDEL QUINN
129	A MAN SET APART
137	MESSENGER FOR OUR LADY OF KNOCK
144	MELLERAY REVISITED
153	LOUIS FROM MONTFORT
162	LOUGH DERG PILGRIMAGE
169	THE TRUSTY OLD BIKE
177	THE MIRACLE OF SOUTH AMERICA
183	NUNCIOS AND ENVOYS
188	"I'M NOT AFRAID TO DIE"
195	LAY OBSERVER AT VATICAN COUNCIL
203	CONQUEST FOR CHRIST
209	MAN, GREAT IS YOUR FAITH!
215	MOTHER RUSSIA
222	GOLDEN JUBILEE
232	TWILIGHT
240	FAREWELL
246	MAGNIFIER OF MARY
253	Pictorial Section
266	Thru the Years

Author with Frank Duff

About this book

Montfort Publications welcomes the opportunity to introduce its readers to Frank Duff, the founder of the Legion of Mary and one of the 20th century's great Marian apostles. Based on a close personal relationship spanning the last twenty-five years of Frank Duff's life and Apostolate, the author, Father Robert Bradshaw, a native son of Ireland himself, describes with a distinct Irish flavor Frank Duff the man, as he knew him. Such a deeply personal and warm approach, betraying on every page the author's admiration, not to say reverence, for his hero, his culture and his times, is a precious contribution towards the many biographies which will undoubtedly appear in the years ahead, as the genius and holiness of this spiritual giant emerge and become better known in the Church.

Having discovered St. Louis de Montfort's "True Devotion to Mary," while still a young man, Frank Duff was to center his whole spirituality and Apostolate around the Saint's motto: "To Jesus Through Mary." It is our hope that Father Bradshaw's life of Frank Duff may lead souls to a deeper personal commitment to Christ and to His Church, through Mary, the De Montfort Way.

Foreword
by W. Aedan McGrath, S.S.C.

It was with great expectations that I sat down to read Father Robert Bradshaw's Life of Frank Duff, founder of the Legion of Mary, and it is with enthusiasm that I recommend it, not only to legionaries but to all Catholics, both clerical and lay.

The subject of this book is one of the men I have most admired in my life. Frank Duff was always a modest, unassuming man. Yet Cardinal O'Fiaich of Armagh, in his sermon at Frank's funeral, forecast that "the day may come soon when the Church will declare him the 'Irishman of the Century.'"

Indeed he was more. His celebrity is as wide as the Catholic Church. His work and the work of the Legion he founded have been praised by five Popes and by innumerable cardinals, bishops and priests all over the world. At the Second Vatican Council, which he was invited to attend as a lay observer, when he was introduced by Cardinal Heenan, the 2,500 prelates rose to their feet and greeted him with prolonged applause. They were saluting the man who had anticipated by fifty years the teaching of the Council that, as members of the Mystical Body, we are responsible for one another, that the Church is essentially missionary, and that all of us by our baptism are called to be apostles to everyone with whom we come in contact.

Frank Duff had not only understood all this, he had lived it, he had propagated it. Under Our Lady's tutelage he had founded the Legion of Mary to spread it to the ends of the earth. But the "Apostolate of the Laity" had largely been forgotten in the Church, so he met at first with some misunderstanding, criticism and even hostility.

But he persevered.

This was the characteristic that most impressed me when I first met Frank in 1946, his deep faith and his trust in Our Lady. And when, at the behest of Archbishop Riberi, Internuncio to China, I found myself starting the Legion all over China just before the Communist takeover, Frank was my constant correspondent and advisor. Indeed his letters followed me in all my subsequent Legion travels in England, the United States and Canada, and the far eastern countries of Japan, Korea, Taiwan, Hong Kong, Malaysia and the Philippine Islands—always encouraging, challenging, sympathizing—and advising with a wisdom that was not of this world.

Impressive as Frank's letters were, conversation with him was an education. The many personal talks I was privileged to have with him greatly influenced my thinking, my activity and my life. For that reason I realize what a service Father Bob Bradshaw has rendered to us all by taping his conversations with Frank over a period of nineteen years. This book is a distillation of those tapes.

Father Bob brings another qualification to his work: his long experience and understanding of the apostolate of the Legion of Mary. In London I saw for myself his fruitful work in setting up many praesidia under the direction of Cardinal Heenan. Later during his years as spiritual director in Thurles Seminary he took every opportunity to attend the Concilium meetings and associate with Frank and the Concilium officers. For many summers now Father Bradshaw has led teams of legionaries to Russia and made fruitful contact with the young people of that country, and for several years he has been resident in Iceland engaged in the Legion's effort to restore the Faith there. Add to that his easy narrative style that makes every chapter a fireside chat, and you can understand why I so highly recommend his book.

I recommend it to priests and lay people who are reading about Frank Duff for the first time. I can't imagine a more pleasant introduction. And I recommend it to legionaries and others who want to know more about Mary's Legion and her heroic apostle. I am confident that they will find it, as I did, an inspiration and a joy.

Introduction
by the Author

I first met Frank Duff at a Legion of Mary Congress in my native Tipperary in the summer of 1955. I had just recently been ordained a priest and had been invited to celebrate the Congress Mass. After the Mass, we adjourned to a local hotel for lunch. I was seated next to Frank Duff at table. I remember being surprised that, when we engaged in conversation, Frank spoke to me not about Legion matters but about his own family and about himself. Among other things, he said to me: "My mother died a few years ago, and I was so attached to her that I still can hardly think about her without getting very upset."

I was quite fascinated by the humanness of the man.

It was six years later that I made my first recording of Frank Duff. It happened almost by accident. I chanced to visit the Legion headquarters in Dublin in connection with some Legion business. When I walked in, Frank said to me: "Father, you are just in time to hear a recording of Alfie Lambe making his Legion Promise; I received the record from South America today." As I happened to have my tape-recorder in my car outside the door, I asked Frank if I might make a copy of the record. Within a few minutes, I had my recorder set up. We both listened in silence as Alfie's voice came across loud and clear—and I got my copy tape.

Then, on a sudden inspiration—there was no premeditation about it—I asked Frank if he would have any objection to my recording his memories of the early Legion days. He had absolutely no objection, and there and then began a series of recordings that was to continue on and off for the next twenty years, right up, in fact, until almost the time of his death.

In appearance, Frank Duff did not immediately present an imposing figure. He was of medium height, slender enough in physique and modest and unassuming in manner. But when he spoke, you took more notice. His voice was soft and calm. He had an enchanting Dublin accent. His eyes were lively and full of kindness; and when he spoke, those eyes looked straight at you, they captured you, they made you feel you were someone who counted very much.

Frank's face was pleasant, and he had a lovely smile. I have often thought that the expression on his face was something beautiful, even remarkable. Sometimes, it seemed to me that his expression could be classified as gentleness personified. At other times, I felt it betrayed silent suffering. At other times, again, it conveyed the impression of some great inner strength. However, as the years went by, I began to realize more and more how real and how close the doctrine of the Mystical Body had become for Frank and, furthermore, how intensely he loved Mary, his heavenly Mother. He once said in a talk: "When Mary pours out on us her love for Jesus, He receives back through us the very love of Jesus." Then I couldn't help thinking that Frank himself had become a meeting-place, as it were, for the love between Jesus and Mary. At any rate, in the latter years, while I still wondered sometimes at the expression on his face, I ceased to be surprised by it.

For many years, my priestly and pastoral activities brought me a good deal into close contact with Frank. Besides, it was my good fortune to share many Legion holidays with him in Mount Melleray Abbey and the surrounding countryside. I cycled with him through Connemara. Whenever I said Mass in the Regina Coeli Hostel chapel in Dublin—which was quite often—Frank participated and joined me afterwards for breakfast. It wasn't simply that I enjoyed his companionship and the privilege of his confidences; more important was that I sensed, early on, the importance of our conversations, and I developed the habit of noting down everything of significance that he said to me as well as many items which were of no great significance but which were interesting nonetheless. My practice was to make my notes while a particular conversation was still fresh in my mind, usually in fact the same evening. I am glad now that I did so. Otherwise, the passage of time might have impaired my memory and rendered my account less accurate.

These notes and the many tape recordings I made of Frank Duff are the primary "source material" for this biography. In addition, I was fortunate to have been able to make recordings of people who were approximately the same age as Frank and whose contact with him stretched back to the early days of the Legion. Some of these people are now dead but they have made a valuable contribution. I also got valuable help from the Concilium officers and from others who were closely associated with Frank.

My reason in writing this book is twofold. Firstly, I believe that if my fellow priests and Religious get to know something of the religious outlook of Frank Duff, their lives will be enriched. If they can gain some insights into his extraordinary faith, his deep understanding of the Church, his enlightened and tender devotion to the Blessed Virgin Mary, if they can come to appreciate the Legion of Mary as he envisaged it, I am sure they will benefit immensely—and so will the people entrusted to their care.

Secondly, I am hopeful that this book will give to our very many legionaries throughout the world a greater appreciation of the marvelous helps the Legion of Mary offers them in their quest for holiness and the immense opportunities it affords for the evangelization of the world.

I owe a special debt of gratitude to Nora Buckley who corrected my manuscript and made many helpful suggestions. My thanks are also due to Donal Healy who did the research into my tapes. Gilda Cellini and Angela Kandolf were my dedicated and patient typists.

Most of all, I am indebted to the Legion of Mary itself which, by its ingenious systems and its marvellous spirit, has been a real inspiration to me and has helped, under God, to make the exercising of my priestly ministry a thing of sheer joy.

Robert Bradshaw.

1 Roots

Frank Duff's grandfather was Michael Francis Frehill, a retired schoolmaster from Co. Meath.

Michael Frehill had seen hard times. He was born in the early part of the 19th century, a time of great poverty and oppression in Ireland. It was a time of hardship particularly for Irish catholics who were severely deprived as a result of the infamous Penal Laws. Ireland was still under the British regime. It was a time of unrest and agitation when the Young Ireland Movement was gathering momentum and urging the youth to rise once again in an attempt to throw off the yoke of foreign rule.

But it was also the era of Daniel O'Connell, the Liberator, a time of new hope and fresh aspirations and united purpose. Earlier in 1829, O'Connell had succeeded in having the Catholic Emancipation Bill passed. This secured at least a measure of freedom for Irish Catholics. Later, the "Catholic Committee" was set up to organize and finance the campaign of O'Connell for full Catholic Emancipation. Catholics were asked to pay one penny per month to defray the expenses. This was known as "Catholic Rent" and Michael Frehill was proud of the fact that he was one of the collectors of this historic rent.

In 1847, the potato crop failed in Ireland and the great ogre of famine stalked through the land. At least one million Irish people died of starvation or disease. Another million sought refuge in England, America, Australia. Michael's own brother, Tom, emigrated to America and eventually settled in San Francisco.

By 1849 the food crisis had eased. The fever epidemic which had accompanied the famine was abating. And yet in that year the situation was still so bad that the number of people who had to be fed and maintained in Government-run "Poorhouses" reached the staggering total of 932,000.

FRANK DUFF

In that same year, the Model School in Trim, Co. Meath, was opened and Michael Frehill was appointed headmaster. He was the first Catholic to be appointed headmaster of a State-run school since the Penal Laws were enacted 150 years before. He realized the significance of his appointment.

He himself had received his early education in a "hedge school." These makeshift, rugged schools provided a rudimentary education and also kept alive the Irish language, culture and traditions which were threatened with extinction by the colonial overlords in Dublin.

His new position as headmaster was a challenging and responsible one and he was determined to do his patriotic best in forming the characters of his pupils and extending their mental horizons. But first he showed them where to find their inspiration. As they turned the pages of history, they met the men and women of mettle who gave the Irish nation its character, its moral fibre. These ranged from the great Irish missionaries of the 6th and 7th centuries, who rekindled the lights which had gone out all over Europe after the barbarian invasions, right down to the 18th century friends of Christ who endured "dungeon, fire and Sword," for love of their divine Master.

Many of Michael's pupils, having gone from "under his wing," acquitted themselves well in the school of life both at home and abroad, as laymen and priests.

On the fly-leaf of one of his books, Michael wrote the following entry: "According to the chronicles, the Frehills are directly descended from St. Colmcille's only brother." It would be impossible, of course, to prove the veracity of the chronicle, but at least the tradition appealed to him.

In the meantime, Michael's brother, Tom, had done very well in America. His initiative and business acumen brought him great wealth. He owned vast properties in San Francisco. When he died, his brothers in Ireland received a legacy of £100,000 — a huge sum in those days. With his share of the money, Michael bought a large tract of land in Co. Cavan and also invested a good deal in Railway Stocks. He was now in a position to build up a library of the best books and also acquire the most up-to-date scientific equipment. He had a special flair for science. In the poverty stricken Ireland of that time, he was the envy of many a headmaster. Equipped with a keen intellect and a first-class library, he gave himself generously to this new generation. He was hopeful for the future.

Michael's wife bore him three sons and one daughter. Susan, a gentle and affectionate daughter, was the apple of her father's eye. Besides doing her home lessons and helping her mother with the shopping and the cooking, she found time to take piano lessons. It was an additional joy to her father that she had, like himself, a special aptitude for science, and great was his pride when, at the age of eighteen, she was awarded the Queen's Prize for Science by the Department of Education in London. He then encouraged her to apply for a post in the British Civil Service. At that time, the British Civil Service covered Ireland as well as England. In the entrance examination, Susan obtained 2nd place. This was quite an achievement, as there were competitors from all the top schools in Great Britain and Ireland.

Soon it was time for her departure to take up her post in London. There was the packing of cases, the hurried goodbyes, the tears of parting, the last minute parental advice: "take care of yourself, Susan; write to us as often as you can; may God and His Blessed Mother protect you."

Susan spent two years in London. The excitement of life in a big city and the challenge of her work distracted her from feeling too lonely. Besides, one of her brothers lived in London and it was nice to be able to visit him. There were times, though, when deep down inside her she felt a great longing to be back in her lovely native Trim. If ever the Civil Service in Dublin opened its doors to women, she would be the first to apply for a transfer there.

Back in Trim, the years were catching up with Michael Frehill, who had reached and passed the retirement age. It was a hard break for him to leave the school he loved so deeply. Then he made a brave decision, he would move to Dublin and build a house. There he would be nearer to his family. Two of his sons already lived there and most probably Susan would be able to get back to Ireland for an occasional holiday.

Drumcondra was a large rural area just north of Dublin

FRANK DUFF

city. It was here that Michael Frehill chose to build his house. His, in fact, was the first house to be built in Drumcondra. When, in time, the area became developed, his house was "addressed" as 55 St. Patrick's Road, Drumcondra.

Michael's joy knew no bounds when he received a letter one day from his daughter to say that the Civil Service in Dublin (still under the British) was, at last, opening its doors to women clerks and that her application for a transfer to Dublin had been successful. It wasn't merely for his own sake that Michael was glad; he was especially glad for Susan's sake. He knew how much she missed Ireland. Besides, she was now a young lady and if she was thinking about marriage at some future date, he would like to see her marrying an Irishman.

Susan quickly adapted to the Dublin scene where the pace of life was more leisurely than it had been in London. Moreover, Trim was now within easy reach for a visit, now and again, to her former companions. The two framed pictures of Trim that hung in her father's new house in Drumcondra were a lovely reminder of the "good old days."

Dublin is too old a city to have the spectacular beauty of the large modern cities, but it has a character of its own which seems to cast its spell over visitor and native alike. Within a short time, Susan had come to love "Dublin's fair city" in all its glorious diversity—the picturesque Grand Canal with its grassy banks and graceful swans, the panoramic view of the Georgian houses of Fitzwilliam Street with the blue mountains in the distance, the sylvan beauty of Stephen's Green with its noisy duck-pond, the theatres, the crowded churches, Moore Street with its colourful fruitsellers, the horse-trams, the street balladeers and musicians, the friendliness and informality of the "salt-of-the-earth Dubliner" who, despite his poverty, had a jovial spirit and a ready wit; it was the gas-lit city immortalized by James Joyce.

Yes, indeed, Susan liked living in Dublin. Besides, it was in Dublin that she met John Duff, her future husband. The manner of their meeting was as simple as it was beautiful. It was Susan's own father who introduced them.

John Duff had also been a former pupil of Michael Frehill. The son of Lord Dunsany's chief steward, he lived on the landlord's estate in Co. Meath. He had done extremely well in all his examinations, and brought credit on the Model School of Trim. He was now in a good position in the Civil Service in Dublin. It was a chance meeting that brought John once again into contact with Michael Frehill, his former headmaster.

"John, you have to come and visit us; we'll be anxious to hear how you have been getting on these past few years. Besides, you must meet Susan, my daughter; you know her, don't you?"

Actually, John did know Susan but only by sight. He had never spoken to her, even though they both had attended the same school in Trim. Nevertheless, he remembered quite well the shy teenage daughter of the headmaster.

"Thank you, Mr. Frehill, I shall be delighted to come." And there was no hesitancy in John's reply.

A short time later, he was being entertained to tea in the Frehill home. The shy blushes of Susan and the discreet maneuverings of her father can only be conjectured. But of one thing John was quite sure: in the years which had passed since he last saw her, Susan had grown into a very beautiful young woman.

A year later John Duff married Susan Frehill. He was 26 and was her senior by two years. Their first child was born on the 7th June, 1889. He was baptized Francis Michael Duff.

2 Early Years

Some of Frank Duff's earliest memories were of his grandfather, Michael Frehill, as the old man, patriarchal looking, relaxed in his own special rocking-chair and reflected, looking back wistfully perhaps, on an era which was passing away. He knew he had a lot to be thankful to God for. True, he had seen hard days but he had also witnessed great changes for the better and he was grateful that providence had appointed him to do his share in forming the characters of many young Irish men and women who would, he was sure, build a new and a better Ireland. His own working days were over now and he felt his energy was ebbing away with each passing year. It was a great comfort to him to have his beloved daughter, Susan, giving him every attention in his old age. She was a rare pearl, that girl; and her husband, John Duff, was a gentleman if ever there was one.

The arrival of Baby Frank brought great joy all round: the incomparable sight of tiny fingers, the sheer helplessness of infancy, the teardrops glistening on tender cheeks, and then, with the passing months and years, the welcome patter of little feet, the ingenious efforts at climbing, the chatter and questions of a small boy. Soon it will be time for school. Michael Frehill immensely enjoyed his grandson. But the shadows were soon upon him: he died when Frank was only five years old.

• • • • •

God blessed John and Susan Duff with seven children. After Frank, came Isabel, Laetitia, Eva, John, Sara Geraldine and Ailis. Laetitia died in infancy.

John Duff was a dedicated husband and father. He was what the neighbours would call "a good family man." If he

Early Years

was rather over ambitious concerning the future careers of his children, it was because he recognized their intellectual abilities. He saw that Frank, the oldest, was exceptionally brilliant and he planned to put him through university to enable him to qualify for an administrative post in the British Colonial Civil Service. He could well afford to do this as he had a good salary, having reached the higher echelons of the Civil Service. His wife, too, had inherited a good deal of wealth from her father and the family lived in the style of the rich.

John was a man of great energy, spending a good deal of his spare time cycling and swimming. He initiated Frank into the healthy joys of outdoor life. It was a pleasing sight to see father and son—the young lad seated behind on the carrier—cycling into the highways and byways of the Dublin countryside. They also went swimming together and, in later years, Frank would take genuine pride in recounting how his father had once saved a man from drowning.

The Duffs were a close-knit family and the children were brimming over with the high spirits of a normal healthy Irish family. Of course, there was an occasional squabble and the usual childish bickering and noisy prattle. Mrs. Duff used to say: "Birds in their little nests agree: isn't it a pity that the children in a family should quarrel and fight?"

The family were usually together for their meals. Lunch mostly consisted of mutton, potatoes and vegetables. Rabbit was also on the menu regularly. On special occasions they had chicken. The Friday abstinence from meat was no exception. However, it transpired that the Friday dinner was the most popular one of the week as Mrs. Duff, the most kind-hearted of mothers, prepared the children's favorite dishes—potato cakes and pancakes, followed by a special dessert.

Mrs. Duff was an accomplished pianist and singer, and sometimes entertained the family in the evenings. Frank learned many lovely songs from her. More often though the children gathered round the fireside to hear their mother read stories. The large oil lamp hanging from the ceiling, the flames dancing in the open fireplace as the children listened spellbound, the girls in their graceful dresses and long flowing hair of the period, made a heart-warming picture.

FRANK DUFF

But during these times of recreation, the mother was also inculcating virtue in her young children, more by example than by word. Her great love for them revealed itself in her kindliness and unselfishness. As the children gathered round her, she divided a bag of sweets into portions, allocating a share for each child and one for herself. According to her rota system, each one had a chance to have his or her first preference on the dates indicated on the list. However, when her own turn came she never availed of the first preference but always took the last choice. Whenever a visitor called at night, the discreet and unobtrusive manner in which Mamma Duff vacated her fireside seat in favor of the visitor left a deep impression on the observant Frank.

On one occasion she was taking Frank to the hospital for a minor operation. They walked hand in hand. Then his mother stopped a moment, looked compassionately at her young son and said: "Frank, I wish I could undergo this operation in your place to save you the pain." The memory of that remark and all that it implied was treasured by Frank for the rest of his life.

But it was surely most of all by her genuine humility that Mrs. Duff won, by the grace of God, such wonderful blessings for her family, for she was indeed a person of great humility and simplicity. Though she was rather wealthy, she never considered herself to be superior to poor people. She was very talented and endowed with a brilliant mind, yet she did not seek to display it. It was only after her death, for example, that Frank discovered that she had, in her schooldays, been awarded the Queen's Prize for Science. During her lifetime she had never even mentioned it to her own children.

It must not be thought, however, that Mr. and Mrs. Duff were exceptionally holy people or that their home was a home of great piety. Frank described his mother as "an ordinary good Catholic woman." She taught her children their prayers, trained them in the virtues and ensured that they went to Sunday Mass. The Duffs were simply "honest-to-goodness Catholics."

The Catholic Church is like a vast garden of very beautiful flowers of many varieties. Each nation is a flower grow-

Early Years

ing there and each gives glory to God in a way peculiar to itself and contributes to the infinite variety which is the Church. Early Irish monasticism had set the tone for "Irish" Catholicism. It had grafted a certain amount of asceticism on to the relaxed and informal character of the Irish people. It had bred, too, a sort of supernatural outlook into their normal everyday lives. "The strong and persistent feature in them," to quote Frank Sheed, "is their utter and fundamental religiousness, a sort of instinctive awareness of God's presence as something actual and obvious, a taking for granted of the spiritual world." And of course the faith, in its Irish form, had been tested and strengthened through seven centuries of suffering. There were times in fact when practically nothing was left to the Irish people except their faith. God's providence was their sole refuge. In sickness or tragedy or difficulty their cry was: "May God's holy will be done."

The Duff family were heirs to this tradition. And so perhaps the most pleasing feature of their faith and religion was that, while it impregnated and influenced their whole way of life, it was nevertheless inconspicuous for the simple reason that it was so natural, so much taken for granted.

The nightly readings in the home developed in Frank a great love of literature. He became, in modern parlance, a book-worm. All his pocket money was spent on books. The magnificent library that Frank's grandfather had built up had been augmented by Frank's father. By the time he was ten years old, Frank had read a very great number of good books including most of the classical novels of Walter Scott and Charles Dickens. Even at that early age, he had also read Cardinal Wiseman's, "Lectures on Science and Revealed Religion," and "Reflections on the Eucharist," as well as many other books of a serious nature. Such reading at that age was surely indicative of a prodigious and brilliant mind. It is quite likely that it was in the same family library that Frank first became acquainted with Cardinal Newman's writings which were destined to exercise a profound influence on his own intellectual development later on.*

The family suffered a heavy blow when Frank was still

FRANK DUFF

young. Both he and his father were struck down with typhoid fever. They were nursed at home, in separate rooms. At one stage, Frank was so ill they thought he was dead. However, he recovered completely. His father recovered too, but the fever left a permanent weakness in his constitution.

When Frank was a little over nine years old, the family moved to 17 Clarinda Park East, Dun Laoghaire. This was a large mansion in County Dublin. The increase in the family, the wealth of the parents and the social status of the Duffs warranted such a move. The grandeur, but even more so the spaciousness, must have been very pleasing to Mrs. Duff. Quality furniture graced the rooms. Two maidservants were employed. It was a "select" neighbourhood. All in all, life had been good to the Duffs.

NOTE

*cf. "John Henry Newman and Frank Duff" by Finola Kennedy

3 Schooldays

Frank Duff never attended a national school. He first went to a local private school for boys. Such private schools were common at that time. Then he went to Belvedere College for a year or so. In 1899, when his family moved to Dun Laoghaire, he enrolled as a day-pupil in Blackrock College, which was in the charge of the Holy Ghost Fathers of worldwide mission fame. Here, shortly after his enrollment, he was prepared for his first Confession and his First Holy Communion.

From his very early years, he had a very delicate and precise conscience. This was not due to scrupulosity, nor to any vagueness about the exact nature of sin. Rather it seems to have been due to his extraordinary honesty of mind which insisted on truthfulness, regardless of the consequences. His First Confession illustrated this. Many years later, in a talk to the deacons of St. Patrick's Seminary, Thurles, he related the incident:

> "In the General Confession which I made the day before my First Holy Communion, I shaded off an offence which I confessed. On thinking it over, I became extremely worried in case I had made a sacrilegious Confession. Consequently, on the following morning, when the great mustering was taking place I had, to my great confusion, to ask for Confession. So let no one tell me that very young people do not realize their wrongdoing very precisely."

Well, it's very likely he was unduly sensitive. At any rate, the First Confession incident does reveal him, even at that tender age, as having a penetrating and precise mind and the moral courage to face up to a problem as he saw it.

The worry about his Confession did not distract him from appreciating the importance of his First Holy Communion. He had of course his basic religious training in his

FRANK DUFF

own home. In his school he and his classmates had their catechism classes. Then for a whole week before the Communion Day, there had been concentrated preparation for the marvelous event that was about to take place. In addition, each boy was invited to write out his special requests or resolutions on a piece of paper which was then sealed in an envelope and placed on the altar. Such a gesture was intended to impress more deeply on the boys the solemnity of the occasion.

However, in spite of all such helps, one does not normally expect a mature appreciation from boys so young. Nevertheless, when Frank Duff was an elderly man, a friend one day asked him:

"Mr. Duff, did you at the time of your First Holy Communion realize the value of it?"

Frank replied simply:

"Yes, I did even at that time realize the extraordinary value of it."

And, in fact, the Blessed Eucharist was to become the driving force of his whole life.

• • • • •

Decidedly, Frank Duff did not like school. On Sunday evenings he used to get a pain in his heart at the very thought of resuming school on the Monday mornings, and when eventually he finished his schooling, he was absolutely thrilled. He felt emancipated. But meanwhile he had to make the best of it, and he did.

He had a strong dislike for mathematics, believing he had no aptitude for that subject. He preferred history and languages, especially the classics. Shortly after his enrollment, he had come to be recognized as one of the school's most brilliant pupils.

Blackrock College was not without its lighter side, being renowned for its athletic and sporting activities. Frank, hardy and strong, revelled in these. He was an exceptionally good runner and cyclist. He was also very fond of tennis and cricket.

One day—he was 12 years old at the time—he was at wicket in the College grounds playing cricket. A cricket

Schooldays

ball hit him at the back of the left ear and knocked him unconscious. There was consternation, but Frank recovered quickly enough in the school infirmary and was allowed home. Unfortunately, damage had been done to his ear and his hearing was permanently impaired. This was to be a severe handicap to him later on.

He didn't play rugby very much but he took an interest in it. One morning an article appeared in the "Freeman's Journal," a prominent Dublin publication, describing a rugby match played between Blackrock College and another school. The article shocked the teaching staff in Blackrock because it not only described the allegedly hilarious celebrations in the College after their victory but it cast a number of the College "characters" in the most "impossible" roles. It was, indeed, a fine piece of caricature. There were raised eyebrows and red faces. There was consternation that the "Freeman's Journal," a responsible publication, should have published such an article. It could not be allowed to pass. The editor of the Journal was contacted. More raised eyebrows! The Journal had only printed what had been received in the supplied articles from Blackrock College. Supplied article?? Some of the College teaching staff promptly visited the offices of the "Freeman's Journal" where they were handed the "document." They were flabbergasted. The article was unsigned but they recognized immediately the handwriting of one of their twelve year old pupils, namely Frank Duff!

Presumably behind the scenes, there were threats of punishment, maybe even expulsion. But the fact was that Blackrock College was reluctant to part with this brilliant pupil. The "indignities" had to be borne in silence. The authorities chose to pretend that the culprit was undiscovered. However, not a word was said to Frank about it, or about his part in it. But when Frank's report-sheet was sent to his parents at the end of the term indicating his marks in the various subjects—usually 10 out of 10, or 9 out of 10— it ended up, like the proverbial sting in the tail of the wasp: Conduct 2 out of 10! Hitherto his lowest mark in conduct was 9 out of 10!

A couple of years after this, misfortune befell the family. Frank's father never enjoyed perfect health after his ty-

19

FRANK DUFF

phoid illness. There was gradual deterioration. His strength and energy ebbed. It was a hard and humbling blow to a man who had once been so strong and energetic. But he had to face facts; he was no longer able to work, so he resigned his post in the Civil Service. As he was only 42 years old when he retired, he did not qualify for a full pension. The pension he received was only a third of what his salary had been.

Unfortunately, too, his wife's inherited income was greatly reduced, due to a drastic devaluation in the Railway Stocks in which her father had invested his money.

The financial set-back meant that the family could no longer afford to maintain the big house in Dun Laoghaire. They moved back to their former home in Drumcondra which was still owned by Mrs. Duff.

It was decided to send Frank to Belvedere College; that was not so far from Drumcondra. The Holy Ghost Fathers, however, appealed to the parents not to take him away from Blackrock College. They even offered to keep him, free of charge, as a boarder. His parents yielded, but his mother would not consent to his becoming a boarder at Blackrock because it was her wish that he should be living at home with the family.

For the remainder of his schooldays Frank's schedule was as follows: At 7:15 a.m. he had breakfast. At 7:30 he set out from his Drumcondra home to walk the two miles to Westland Row Station. As yet he had no bicycle. Then a train journey and after that another ¾ mile walk to Blackrock College.

In the evenings there were home-lessons to be done. Pupils had to work hard. From the age of twelve or thirteen Frank was studying five languages, Irish, English, Greek, Latin, and French.

The time-table for classes in Blackrock College was, on the whole, set to suit the boarders. Hence some of the classes were held at times which were unsuitable for Frank. The Irish class, for instance, was held in the late evening. To facilitate Frank, the College authorities arranged private tuition for him. Twice a week he went to the tutor's house in Cabra for Irish lessons. The tutor, Mr. Denis Lynch, would sit at one side of the fire, the pupil at the other.

Schooldays

Frank had an inquiring mind as well as a prodigious memory and made great progress. He came to appreciate, too, the great advantage of the "participation by pupil" system over the "pure lecture" method. One day his tutor said to him: "Frank, you will have no difficulty in getting first place in all-Ireland when you do your examination." There was a special medal for first place. Frank was equally optimistic since, as he said himself, there was nothing he didn't know about the Irish language. But the medal evaded him. Another student beat him by half a mark.

Although he had great intellectual ability and was endowed with a marvelous sense of humour, Frank was nevertheless a very shy boy during his schooldays at Blackrock. On one occasion he was allotted a major role in Shakespeare's play "Twelfth Night." But, at an early stage in the rehearsals, he got stagefright and asked to be excused from it. On the spacious sportsfields in Blackrock College he excelled at athletics, yet he would never enter the competitions on the school's Sportsday.

This shyness stayed with him and mellowed in time into a gracious gentleness that was one of his loveliest characteristics.

At the age of eighteen he finished his schooling and crowned a marvelous academic career by winning, in his final year, a First Class Exhibition Award for Modern Literature.

4 Discovering a Whole New World

Generally speaking, health-wise, the Duffs were a delicate family. Laetitia, Eva's twin sister, died in infancy. Eva herself had never been very robust. She was 13 years old now, a beautiful girl with black curly hair and a rather pale complexion. She was bright and vivacious and very witty. Brilliant in school, she got first place in every examination and was, according to Frank, the real genius of the Duff family. Her school was the Dominican Convent in Eccles Street, where she was a great favourite with the nuns.

But it was her sanctity, her sheer beauty of soul, which shone out from her like a diamond of fine quality.

Maud Breen was Eva's school classmate and friend. One winter's day the two girls watched through the classroom window as the lovely snowflakes danced their way through the sky and wove a silky white carpet over the playing grounds. It was beautiful—and tempting! Out they went during the lunch-hour to enjoy themselves. In their excitement they hardly noticed the sharp cold air. The nun scolded them for their foolhardiness, and, sure enough, Eva caught cold. It was destined to be her last day in school. She became seriously ill and was sent into hospital for an operation. The doctors diagnosed tuberculosis.

During the six months illness before her death she manifested a remarkable holiness. Father McGrath, the local priest, used to visit her and bring her the Blessed Sacrament. He was so impressed by her saintliness that he

Discovering a Whole New World

brought Rev. Dr. Hickey of Clonliffe College to see her.

Even in the latter years of his life Frank retained a vivid memory of the day he was passing by the landing in his home. In front of him stood Eva in her dressing gown, her face pale and beautiful. He said to himself with a heavy heart: "She is not for this world." And, indeed, she died shortly afterwards.

• • • • •

When Frank left school, his first concern was to get a job. Because of his father's premature retirement, due to ill health, and the drastic reversal in family fortunes, a University career was now out of the question. Instead, he entered the Civil Service (having taken first place in the examination), and was assigned to the Department of Finance. He had rather suddenly become the breadwinner of the family.

Because of his dislike for mathematics, it was with a certain amount of concern that Frank viewed his assignment to the Department of Finance. But he realized his responsibilities and took them seriously. There was only one thing for it and that was to "get back to his books." He set about educating himself in higher mathematics and science. The magnificent library built up by his father and grandfather had practically everything he needed for his studies. The challenge was there and he relished it. Book after book was taken down from the shelves; day after day he applied himself diligently. The solving of mathematical problems, the interesting world of scientific data, the sheer mental effort, all this excited his mind and dispelled whatever dislike he had previously harboured towards these subjects. It was no longer mere dedication on his part, it was sheer enthusiasm.

His precise mind and his eminently practical approach to problems were decided assets to the Department in which he worked. When he was just twenty-one years old, he invented a system of calculus which attracted the attention of the Principal Officer of his branch of the Department. As a result, he was invited to London to demonstrate his system to the officials of the London Treasury. The Depart-

FRANK DUFF

ment subsequently adopted his new system. He took a genuine pride in his achievement and was pleased, too, about the rise in his salary.

Although hard work and dedication to duty were part and parcel of office routine, yet a marvelous spirit of fraternity and joviality pervaded the office in which he worked. As one colleague remarked: "The blooming place resounded with Duff's hearty laugh and humorous banter."

His busy work schedule didn't lessen Frank's interest in outdoor activities. Upon his "emancipation" from school he immediately joined the tennis club in Drumcondra. Tennis was one of his great loves and he excelled in it. Then he joined a second tennis club because it had hard courts and could be used all the year round.

Walking was not one of his favourite pastimes, unless it were in the nature of a challenge. For example, one day he heard his father say he had missed the train and had thereupon walked all the way to Trim. Well, "What father can do, son can do," thought Frank. So he set out on foot from Dublin and within twenty-four hours had walked all the way to Trim and back, a distance of 83 kilometres. The weather was so hot that everytime he was passing a roadside pump he put his head under it. To keep his head cool, he put grass under his cap, forgot that he had done so and then suffered embarrassment when he uncovered his head as he entered a chapel on the way. For the last six miles of the return journey, his right foot was badly blistered but he struggled on, nevertheless, determined to complete what he had set out to do. When asked later why he did such a "crazy" thing, he replied: "I wouldn't give in."

That stubborn determination emerged as a notable feature of his character. Once he had made up his mind on a course of action it was practically impossible to divert him from it.

Of all outdoor activities that he enjoyed, cycling undoubtedly took pride of place. When he got his first job, his father said to him:

"Frank, I'm not too well able for my bicycle any more; it's yours, you'll need it."

Frank got some adjustments made, and ever after that his "bike" was his travelling companion. He cycled to his

Discovering a Whole New World

office, he cycled for his messages, he cycled on his "outings." On Sunday mornings after Mass he and his pal would cycle out to Howth along the coast road; then in the afternoon they would cycle out to Bray or some other scenic place.

On the whole, the young Mr. Duff was having a very pleasant and exhilarating time. A number of his friends belonged to the "upper-crust" society and he acted as best man at many fashionable weddings. At the Department of Finance a bright future was predicted for the young mathematician.

Then an event occurred which drastically changed his whole life; Frank joined the Saint Vincent de Paul Society (referred to as S.V.P.). It was October 1913. He was just 24 years old.

• • • • •

Previously, Frank had been invited to join the S.V.P. but had declined, making the excuse that he was too busy! Then he was invited again, this time by Jack Callaghan who worked in the same office with him and for whom he had a great regard. He hadn't the heart to say "no." He joined the S.V.P. Conference of Our Lady of Mount Carmel and was deeply impressed by what he observed. When he attended the third meeting he was appointed secretary of that particular Conference.

The poverty at that time in Dublin was appalling. Great numbers were unemployed. Families lived in one-room tenements in the slums. Hunger, squalor and drunkenness were rampant. There was much religious neglect.

The aim of the S.V.P. Society was to relieve in some measure those in greatest distress, and at the same time to uplift those poor people spiritually. Frank noticed that sometimes, because the urgency to feed the poor was so great the spiritual aims were overlooked. But what undoubtedly made the greatest impression on him was the emphasis placed by the S.V.P. on Christ's words in the Gospel: "As long as you did it to one of these my least brethren, you did it to me" (Matt 25:40). Slowly but surely, the stark reality of that text dawned on him. In each and

FRANK DUFF

every one of these poor hungry persons, Jesus Christ was really present. Each dirty hand, each grimy face, each weary foot was a member of Christ's living Mystical Body crying out for pity and for help. It wasn't simply that they were reminders of Christ's words, nor were they simply poor people to be helped for Christ's sake. They were really and truly Christ's Body on this earth.

Frank realized now that his religion hitherto had been a mediocre affair, a comparatively dull routine. Without a proper appreciation of this doctrine, that the people of God—the Church—is Christ's continuing presence on this earth, it just isn't possible to realize the wonderful and thrilling adventure that religion could and should be.

In some of the hospitals, the conditions at that time were primitive and unhygienic. When Frank went to visit patients in the cancer ward of one hospital he was able to endure it and overcome his revulsion only by reflecting that it really and truly was Christ he was visiting. Likewise, later on, it was only by recalling the same sublime truth, that he was enabled to face horrible situations when he visited the slums with all their squalor and filth.

As a boy, Frank had never come into close contact with poverty. In his home there was abundance and cleanliness and refinement. He had, of course, seen poverty at a distance, had seen children poorly clothed, had seen drunken men on the footpaths and had recoiled in fear. But he had never really "rubbed shoulders," as it were, with the "down and outs" of society, had never experienced the conditions in which very poor people live. His membership in the S.V.P. now brought him into touch with grim reality, and probably his refined nature was hurt by what he saw and heard. But there would be no turning back. He had discovered a whole new world—the poor of Christ. He would come to love them with ardour and gentleness. He would serve them, or rather serve Christ in them. They were his new-found friends, and they would be his friends for life.

5 Enter Joe Gabbett

"In the heart of every right thinking Catholic, God has implanted the desire to become a saint." So wrote Frank Duff in 1916.[1]

We cannot know all the various factors which made Frank take his religion more seriously and set his sights on "the narrow gate that leads to eternal life," but two things in particular had a profound influence on him even at that early stage—spiritual reading and enclosed Retreats.

He had already begun to read spiritual books before he joined the S.V.P. Probably he got them in his father's library. When he joined the S.V.P., he became an avid reader of books about God and His saints. A number of his comrades in the Society—Sir Joseph Glynn, Ralph Callaghan, Tom Fallon, Matt Lalor, Vincent Kelly, Frank Sweeney and others—very strongly encouraged spiritual reading.

Frank was particularly interested in reading the Lives of the Saints. Though he was sensible enough not to attempt to imitate their great austerities, their zeal for God and souls spurred him on to be ambitious for holiness. "Once we accept," he said, "that holiness is the most important thing in the world for us, it will become the most natural thing in the world for us to strive after it."[2]

He read a great number of deeply theological books. In addition, his fluency in French enabled him to read all the most important books of the great French mystics.

Two months after he joined the S.V.P., he attended his first enclosed Retreat. It was conducted by Fr. Scanlon S.J. Weekend Retreats were conducted regularly at the Jesuit

FRANK DUFF

Jacob's biscuit factory nearby where they were employed. Gabbett decided that his little organization should have a title, so he called it, "The Guild of the Immaculate Conception," and he arranged in the largest room a charming altar suitably adorned. The centerpiece of that altar was a beautiful statue of the Immaculate Conception. Some of the money collected was used to purchase the statue. It was this same statue that was later used on the first Legion altar.

On the opening day, a number of the people who had been frequenting the proselytizing Centre changed over to Gabbett's Centre. And the numbers grew each week.

Frank became Gabbett's "right-hand" man and came along every Saturday night to help in preparing the Sunday breakfasts. He was fascinated with Gabbett's method of making tea. He filled a big vat with water and put into it a very large quantity of the strongest tea available. Then he put it on the fire and allowed it to stew the whole night through. "Talk about whiskey," said Frank, "you could get drunk on Gabbett's tea!"

Frank did the sweeping and the washing up. He cut and buttered the bread, "mountains" of it. And he stewed Gabbett's "tea."

While the people were partaking of the Sunday morning breakfast, Gabbett delivered a sermon to them about their faith. His language was rough and unpolished, but it was simple and they understood him. Whenever he was unable to be present, Frank took charge of affairs.

When the Great War of 1914 broke out, Gabbett extended his field of operation; he managed to get appointed as lay assistant to Father O'Loughlin, the chaplain to Portobello Military Barracks. And, of course, Gabbett took Frank with him. There were two thousand soldiers in the barracks. Gabbet and Frank moved around among them, encouraging them to be faithful to their religion. The number of "captures" among the lapsed catholics was incredible. They arranged that Father O'Loughlin would visit the barracks on the eve of the First Friday and hear Confessions. He came again on the First Friday mornings to administer Holy Communion. It was a wonderful piece of team-work between the priest, his lay-assistant and Frank — who was assistant to the lay-assistant!

Enter Joe Gabbett

Sometimes Gabbett would gather a number of Catholic soldiers into one of the large barrack rooms and conduct a Service for them. Gathered around a statue of Our Lady, they would sing a hymn. Then they prayed the Rosary, after which Gabbet gave a rousing sermon on their eternal salvation and the importance of the Sacraments. He would encourage them to use the Brown Scapular and the "Miraculous" Medal. Then he and Frank would give out the medals to the men. There was a considerable response to all that, and on one occasion they had a most astounding result: seventy soldiers gathered at a meeting point, and Gabbett and Frank lined them up in fours and they marched, in military formation, across the city to the Jesuit house at Milltown Park, where a number of priests were mobilized to deal with the "invasion" and hear the Confessions of seventy men.

Frank was captivated by Gabbett. Never before had he met anybody like this erstwhile soldier of a worldly army, now a warrior of Christ. This powerful man, like St. Paul, had put on "the breastplate of faith and charity and for a helmet, the hope of salvation" (1 Thes: 8). He was saturated with the love of God and of His Blessed Mother.

Gabbett was a high-class shoemaker and worked late hours. Most evenings, Frank, having completed his round of apostolic activities, called around to the cobbler's workshop and found himself a seat among the boots and shoes. It seemed an incongruous setting for religious conversation but in fact Gabbett, while stitching and hammering the leather, would talk away about God and about Our Lady. Frank absorbed it all with relish, truly a disciple at his master's feet.

He noticed that Gabbett wore a Pioneer badge. And Frank had a "thing" about badges; he disliked the idea of exhibiting one's religion publicly. He just couldn't wear a religious emblem of any kind.

The Pioneer Total Abstinence Association had been formed in Dublin by Fr. James Cullen, S.J. in 1898. The primary aim of the Association is to honour the Sacred Heart of Jesus by the promotion of total abstinence through prayer and self-denial. As well as undertaking to abstain from alcoholic drink, a member of the Association

FRANK DUFF

must say a particular short prayer daily and wear the Pioneer badge which depicts the image of the Sacred Heart.

Frank had a great devotion to the Sacred Heart of Jesus. Nevertheless, it was the idea of publicly wearing this emblem that deterred him from joining the Pioneer Association. And now here was Gabbett, his great hero, wearing this badge. It made him think more deeply. Then one day he came across the words of Christ in the Gospel: "If anyone declares himself for me in the presence of men, I will declare myself for him in the presence of my Father in heaven. But the one who disowns me in the presence of men, I will disown in the presence of my Father in heaven" (Matt 10:32-33). Well, if it was like that, then there would be "no two ways about it." He wasn't going to be accused of timidity or moral cowardice on Judgment Day. He went along to enroll at the Pioneer Centre.

There he was told that he must serve a probationary period of two years. This meant that he would be compelled to wear the probationer's badge for a period of fifteen months; it had been nine months since his last "drink." He was indignant, got up and walked out. However, he soon realized that he had allowed pride to take over and that this disappointment was another little cross from the Lord. One week later he returned and was enrolled as a probationer. He was an ardent promoter of the Pioneer Association for the rest of his life, so highly did he value its aims and ideals.

Giving up drink was not very difficult for him, although he admitted that he had liked his occasional drink of cider or lager. As for the badge, he suffered torture at the very thought of having to wear it publicly. But wear it he did.

This little badge of such light weight was a heavy cross for Frank but he knew that by displaying it publicly he was crushing the spirit of human respect within him and, thereby, winning grace for those who were drinking from a well other than that of Christ which would quench their thirst forever. Henceforth, as a loyal soldier of Christ, he would regard it as an honour and a privilege to wear publicly that little emblem of the Sacred Heart. Of such significance was it for him, that he arranged, that very year—it was 1914—to have a special gold-rimmed pioneer badge made

Enter Joe Gabbett

for himself. He wore it with pride until the day of his death.

● ● ● ● ●

Displayed in a prominent place in Gabbett's Breakfast Centre in Cheater's Lane was a large framed picture of the Sacred Heart of Jesus. This picture had an extraordinary fascination for Frank. Very many times over the next sixty five years he would gaze lovingly on that picture.[3] His devotion to the Sacred Heart was intense, and the accounts of Our Divine Lord's revelations to Saint Margaret Mary Alocoque in the year 1675 moved him deeply.

As St. Margaret Mary was kneeling before the Blessed Sacrament, she beheld, with the eyes of her soul, the Sacred Heart of Jesus Christ encircled by a crown of thorns and a cross above it. She described, in her own words, what happened: "My Divine Master revealed to me the marvels of His tenderness and the secrets of His heart. 'My heart,' he said 'is so inflamed with love for men that it is no longer able to keep within itself the flames of its burning love. It must make itself known unto men in order to enrich them with the treasures it contains.' " On another occasion, Jesus again appeared to her and showed her His Sacred Heart, saying: "Behold this heart which has loved men so much and yet is so little loved in return."

The message was not lost on Frank and, day after day, he was happy to kneel in prayer before the Divine Master in the tabernacle, "returning love for love." Perhaps he lamented that for the first twenty years or so of his life he had been indifferent enough in the service of Our Lord, fulfilling his basic duties alright but looking on religion more or less as a routine affair that must, somehow or other, be "fitted in." In 1916, he wrote some prayers that probably reflect how he felt:

> "O, my God, my heart has been set upon the things that pass. But henceforth I will give myself entirely to you. Give me the time, and faithfully do I promise now to serve you. Give me back the years that the worm and the locusts have devoured, that I may one day restore them to you full of achievement. O Jesus, I desire to become a saint—not that I may be great, but that you may be greatly loved."[4]

FRANK DUFF

He read more, studied more, prayed more. Especially did his reading the Lives of the Saints goad him on and provide him with wonderful and attractive examples of dedication and zeal. "Saints," he wrote, "are the doctrines and practices of holiness made visible. If we frequent their company, we will soon imitate their qualities."[5]

As Frank's love for the Sacred Heart of Jesus intensified, so did his zeal to promote this devotion. In his very first pamphlet, "Can we be Saints," he aimed at drawing others to appreciate the treasures that are to be found within the loving heart of Christ. "We must," he wrote, "attentively consider the Divine Model. His slender form and serene, lovely face, His words, His actions—take them one by one, and, as best we can, reflect upon them with affection. What an incomparable beauty beams forth in all. Such mildness, wisdom, purity, patience, tenderness; and a love which is true to us in all our waywardness and disloyalty. Look and admire, and seek to draw a breath of their loveliness into ourselves. . . . The treasury of perfection in Him is not like the treasures of the world, behind bars or in museums—to be admired but not possessed. Each perfection shining in Jesus is there solely to be communicated to us. With all His heart, He desires to give them to us. So look on them, and long to have them, and they will become yours. . . . Our Lord and His qualities are not only holy but sanctifying: that is, the mere looking upon them with good intentions will imprint them on our hearts and make them part of us. And let our gaze be as Mary's must have been. Ask her help in this contemplation. It was her employment from the night she first looked upon her newborn babe's face."[6]

Frank was, naturally, enthralled by the truly marvelous promises made by Our Lord to St. Margaret Mary. The ninth promise held particular interest for him, "I will bless every home in which a picture or a statue of my Sacred Heart shall be displayed and honored." He zealously promoted the Enthronement of the Sacred Heart in homes. Referring to the apostolate to lapsed families, he said: "Get the Sacred Heart enthroned in that home and you have already won the day."[7] Later when he founded the Legion of Mary, he told his legionaries that they would see for them-

Enter Joe Gabbett

selves what a powerful weapon they had when they approached even the "hopeless" cases: "The Enthronement visitation forms the most fruitful of all introductions. As it is the mission of Mary to bring about the reign of Jesus, so there is a special appropriateness (which should attract the special graces of the Holy Spirit) in the Legion of Mary propagating the Enthronement."[8]

Frank claimed that the tenth promise, "I will give to priests the grace to touch the most hardened hearts," . . . "belongs in a measure to those who go as the priest's representatives."[9] And, indeed, the wonderful fruitfulness of his own individual apostolate to many "wayward" families in Dublin surely substantiated his claim. Frank was speaking from experience.

While Frank appreciated that devotion to the Sacred Heart of Jesus ensured a greater effectiveness in his mission to souls—as, indeed, had been promised by Our Lord—he looked on the devotion primarily as an efficacious means of loving and honoring his Divine Master. His love of the Sacred Heart was refreshingly pure and unselfish. "Our hearts," he wrote, "were made to hold the biggest and purest of loves. For nothing less than this did God intend them. It is dishonoring such vessels to keep in them a love based only on motives of reward or punishment, wholesome though these are. So let us try to send our love for the Good Shepherd to summits far above such thoughts of self,

> and love Him
> not that in heaven we may reign
> nor to escape eternal pain
> nor in the hope of any gain
> but for Himself,
> and that we may satisfy with something clean
> that great love of His which craves for our love.
> And as this pure love strengthens in our hearts,
> it will soon, like the eagle,
> grow impatient even of the mountain peaks,
> and hunger after heights of heights,
> till—with the Little Flower—we cry out in longing:
> Jesus, Jesus, I would so wish to love you,
> love you as you never yet have been loved."[10]

35

FRANK DUFF
NOTES

[1] "Can we be Saints" by Frank Duff, Page 1.
[2] "Can we be Saints" by Frank Duff, Page 3.
[3] *Note:* When the Breakfast Centre ceased to operate in 1916, Frank "rescued" this picture and brought it to Myra House (S.V.P. headquarters), and there it remained until 1922 when Frank brought it to the Sancta Maria Hostel. On the "opening night" of the hostel, it was used in the ceremony for the Enthronement of the Sacred Heart. When the hostel was closed in 1974, the picture was brought to the Legion Headquarters in North Brunswick Street. Frank commented: "that picture has looked down on a lot of Legion history."
[4] "Can we be Saints?" pp. 4, 16.
[5] ibid., p. 18.
[6] "Can we be Saints," pp. 19, 20.
[7] Legion of Mary Handbook, p. 242.
[8] Legion of Mary Handbook, p. 202.
[9] Legion of Mary Handbook, p. 202.
[10] "Can we be Saints" pp. 31, 32.

6 The Easter Rebellion 1916 — and Troubled Times for Ireland

On Monday, April 24th, 1916, Frank's father came home to lunch. He was in a serious mood. "There are," he said, "rumours floating about that a rebellion has broken out in the city." In fact, the Easter Rebellion had broken out that morning.

Frank came from a family that was deeply patriotic. They were, according to a strong family tradition, direct descendents of Lord Hugh Maguire who was hanged for his part in the 1641 Rebellion. When Frank was a young boy his mother went occasionally to visit her brother. She took Frank with her. The conversation was often about the great Daniel O'Connell for whose cause of Catholic Emancipation Frank's grandfather had worked. The Liberator was, naturally, a hero in that household.

But as yet, political freedom seemed a distant prospect. Some, by this time, had grown apathetic and were resigned to living under foreign domination. Others were angry, determined, watching for an opportunity to finally overthrow the "foreign foe." Mr. Hegarty, a fellow member of the S.V.P., was a staunch nationalist. Frequently he walked home with Frank after the S.V.P. meetings and tried to recruit him into the Sinn Féin movement. Frank refused. In the first place he simply hadn't time; he was very involved in various religious works. And, secondly, he would have

FRANK DUFF

nothing to do with violence, no matter how just the cause.

For quite some time before Easter, there had been rumours of a planned rebellion, but very few people took these rumours seriously. The rebel forces would be totally outnumbered and could have no real hope of success.

But now, on this Easter Monday morning, the Rebellion had actually broken out. Frank was terribly saddened at the very thought of bloodshed. Later that evening, he heard the gunfire. His mind was filled with agony and misery. It was no great surprise to him that the superior British forces were able to quell the rebellion within a very short time. He wondered about the fate of the leaders and about his friend Mr. Hegarty who was arrested and taken to a London prison.

The following Wednesday, Frank was on his way to attend his S.V.P. meeting. As he was walking up Dame Street, he saw the newspaper boys running down the street and calling out the headlines—the leaders of the Rising had just been executed. He was horrified. He felt it so keenly that—to use his own description—a terrible black passion flamed up in his heart. It was some little consolation to him that Mr. Hegarty was not executed and was released shortly afterwards.

The summary executions of the fifteen leaders of the Rebellion transformed the Irish nation from an apathetic people into a vigorous, fighting force, determined to end the British regime in Ireland. The War of Independence went on from 1917 to 1921.

Michael Collins, famed for his daring and for his scarlet-pimpernel tactics, became the Chief of Intelligence of the Military wing of Sinn Féin. He was a ruthlessly efficient organizer of the (military) resistance and made things extremely difficult for the vastly superior British forces. Public opinion in America and in Britain itself demanded a truce.

The British Government faced the inevitable—they would have to grant at least some measure of independence to the Irish people.

The leaders of Sinn Féin were invited to send representatives to London to discuss terms for a possible Treaty. The invitation was readily accepted.

It is a measure of the high regard in which Frank Duff

The Easter Rebellion 1916

was held by the Sinn Féin leadership that, even though he had taken no part in the movement, he was chosen to accompany the delegation as manager and also to ensure, as far as possible, the safety of the men on a journey which was fraught with danger. He also helped in the preparation of their briefs. This he did with the consummate skill of a top civil servant.

A few days later the Irish delegates, accompanied by Frank, departed by boat for London. Because of the dangers involved, each man was issued a revolver. Frank declined to accept one for himself.

The receptionist at the desk in a London hotel could hardly have guessed that the young man who signed himself on the register as F.S. Mitchel was, in fact, Frank Duff. Frank felt that, for security reasons, it was wise to conceal the true identity of the delegates whom he was checking in to that hotel. He himself, of course, was not involved in the political aspects of the Treaty or the actual negotiations. But, thorough in all things, he was taking no chances in regard to the safety of the men. He ensured, therefore, that each member of the delegation was given an alias when signing the hotel register. The alias he chose for himself was F.S. Mitchel.

The Anglo-Irish Treaty was signed on December 6, 1921.

Under the new regime, serving Civil Servants were given options of early retirement with generous pension terms. Frank chose to stay at his post and, no doubt, this was greatly appreciated by the Minister, as a State servant of his calibre was invaluable at that crucial time.

Frank was also given another assignment which links him up in history with the most famous name in the struggle for independence. His superiors sent for him.

"Mr. Duff," they said, "Michael Collins is, as you know, the Commander-in-Chief of our National Army. We are assigning you as his private secretary. We would like you to go, for the time being, to Portobello Military Barracks to look after him."

The meeting between these two men must have presented a contrast; Michael Collins of commanding appearance, powerful, efficient; Frank Duff of lesser size, gentle, equally efficient in a different way. Michael Collins must have

FRANK DUFF

been very pleased to have such an efficient and amiable person as Frank looking after his official business.

On the morning of the 22nd of August, 1922, Frank Duff came into Collins' office as usual.

"Frank, I'm travelling to Cork today, give me a hand so that I can get moving smartly." Frank did so, then saw him off and waved good-bye. It was the last time he saw Collins alive. The great Commander-in-Chief of the Irish Army was shot dead that very day on his way to Cork.

● ● ● ● ●

There was a knock on Frank Duff's door in Drumcondra. Mrs. Connolly, the widow of James Connolly, who had been executed a short time previously by the British Crown forces for his leading part in the 1916 Rebellion, wanted to see him. She had a strange tale to tell and she sought his advice.

A Mr. Murphy, who was not a very staunch Catholic, had handed over his three young sons to a proselytizing agency. Subsequently he had a change of mind but the proselytizing agencies did not easily surrender their prey. Hence, Mr. Murphy, who had later become hospitalized because of an affliction of paralysis, was unable to take any effective steps to have his sons transferred to a Catholic institution. In desperation he wrote a document appointing Mrs. Connolly and Mrs. Pearse as guardians of the three children.

Mrs. Connolly was a convert to Catholicism and was a very devout adherent of the faith. She dearly wanted to recover the children from the so-called "Bird's Nest." But how?

Frank advised her that she had a legal right to remove the children from the "Bird's Nest" because of the signed document Mr. Murphy had given her; but that, in fact, it would be an extremely difficult and expensive business to institute proceedings in the law courts.

"Mrs. Connolly," he said, "will you authorize me to look after the matter for you in my own way?"

"I will be very grateful to you, Mr. Duff."

● ● ● ● ●

The taxi came to a halt at a discreet distance from the

The Easter Rebellion 1916

entrance to the hospital. Frank Duff sat quietly and unobtrusively in the passenger seat and awaited his opportunity. He explained his plans to the taxi-man because he was going to need his help.

When he saw three young boys approaching and entering the hospital, he noted that they fitted the description he had been given.

After Mrs. Connolly's first visit to Frank, he called to see Mr. Murphy in the hospital and developed a very friendly relationship with him. He told Mr. Murphy what he proposed to do and got him to write a letter to the manageress of the "Bird's Nest," saying he would like to have a visit from his children in the near future. Mr. Murphy received a reply telling him his children would come to visit him at a specified time on a certain day.

When the three children left the hospital after visiting their father, Frank grabbed them and bundled them into the taxi. The taxi-man drove straight to Artane where the Christian Brothers looked after them and eventually transferred them to the "Catholic Boys Home," in Glasnevin. There they settled down and were very happy. All three grew up as good Catholics.

• • • • •

The years passed. Once again there was a knock on Frank's door. This time it was Mr. Murphy, Jr., one of the three young lads who had been "kidnapped" by Frank many years before.

"Mr. Duff, I came back to thank you for what you did for my brothers and myself. You remember, I suppose?"

"Indeed I do," said Frank. "And what's more," he added with a smile, "I remember that the three of you screamed your heads off in the back of the taxi as we made our getaway." And the adventures of that momentous day were re-enacted as they both strolled down memory lane for a very pleasant hour.

As for Mrs. Connolly, she surely deserved a reward for her noble part, and indeed the Lord did reward her abundantly — Frank subsequently took her with him on the famous Lough Derg pilgrimage — even twice!

41

7 "Pure Communication with God"

When he was about 24 years old, Frank Duff had an experience that was to shake him to the depths of his being; he "lost" his faith. It happened like this: On a Saturday afternoon he went to Confession in the Carmelite Church in Whitefriars Street. After his Confession, he went immediately to kneel in front of the high altar to say his penance. Then it happened. His faith was suddenly gone! It wasn't merely a question of doubts; his belief simply "disappeared." At that moment God just did not exist for him. And, if God did not exist, then nothing else in the whole world really mattered. Life had no meaning any more.

Frank was shattered by this terrifying experience, this hell on earth. He couldn't afterwards calculate how long that state of "unbelief" lasted. Perhaps not more than a few minutes, but it seemed like an eternity to him.

Then, as quickly as his faith had disappeared, it was restored to him. It was as if God had allowed him to experience the total darkness of unbelief. He was glad, subsequently, of the experience because it made him realize, more than ever before, that faith is essentially a gift of God and that no intellect can attain it by human reasoning alone. Perhaps, too, this experience was permitted by God in order to strengthen him for the trials ahead by showing him that he must depend completely on God and never on himself.

If Frank developed in his life a faith that was truly ex-

"Pure Communication with God"

traordinary, it was simply because, by the grace of God, he worked hard for it. And that hard work included study, crosses, courageous action and prayer. But prayer, solid authentic prayer, was the "king-pin" of all these.

St. Teresa of Avila, a great saint and a very practical woman, declared that it was by no means easy to find an enlightened and competent spiritual director for the guidance of one's soul but that one should seek diligently for such a priest. Frank Duff was fortunate in this regard. He appreciated the value of having a regular spiritual director. And he found one who was to be a tremendous help to him in his pursuit of holiness.

Father Michael Brown, a Jesuit priest in St. Francis Xavier's Church, Dublin, was renowned for his great sanctity. It was most likely on this account that Frank Duff went to him for Confession and spiritual direction. And from early 1915 until 1922 Frank ordinarily went to no other priest. He also went to see him from time to time outside the confessional for advice.

According to Frank's own account, "Father Brown's idea of life was to get as much as possible out of the human machinery in the way of work, prayer and penance, without causing injury to one's health." Then Frank added: "Sometimes I found it very hard to agree with his judgment, but I did obey him fully during all the time I had him as my spiritual director, and I have never regretted it. Subsequent events proved him to have been right on those occasions. Anyone who came into contact with Father Brown noticed at once his deep devotion to the Blessed Virgin. This was a great help to me who was trying to probe my way in that direction."

Undoubtedly Father Brown's greatest contribution towards Frank Duff's spiritual development was that he gave him a proper appreciation of prayer and especially an appreciation of the Divine Office, the prayer "par excellence."

In 1915, Frank had decided to say some form of Office daily. He joined the Third Order of the Carmelites and took on the recitation of the Little Office of Our Blessed Lady. He continued to say that Office until 1917. He then felt a remarkable attraction towards the fuller Office, generally known as the Divine Office. Father Brown taught

FRANK DUFF

him how to say it. The psalms and the readings from the holy Bible took on a new significance for Frank and he began to appreciate that the essential element of prayer is, not the asserting of oneself, but rather the acknowledgement of one's own nothingness and unworthiness and the praising of God's infinite beauty and goodness.

> "Not to us, Lord, not to us,
> but to your name give the glory."
>
> (Psalm 113)

"I have looked on the Divine Office as pure communication with God" was Frank's way of summarizing it.

Frank "tackled" the full divine Office for the first time on the feast of St. Nicholas in 1917. It took him about three hours to recite it. He found it tiring and abandoned it. But he took it up again after some days. This time he persevered and recited it faithfully every day to the end of his long life. As soon as he had become familiar with the books of the Divine Office, he was able to recite it devoutly, and without haste, in about one and a half hours.

Frank never travelled any place without his breviary. On one occasion, when Frank and a group of legionaries went mountain-climbing, his breviary was rather conspicuous in his pocket. He explained that he would never risk being separated from his breviary. He felt that, if he should be injured in an accident and taken to hospital, he would like to be quite sure his breviary went with him. Determination!

Late in his life, Frank was able to say "Since I first started saying the Office in 1917, I have never missed a line of it."

In 1914 (he was just 25 years old at the time), Frank decided he would go to Mass every morning for the forty days of Lent. But, not surprisingly, by the end of Lent he just couldn't content himself by saying: "Well, that's my duty done." So, from that time forward, he became a daily Mass-goer for the rest of his life.

Frank began to take his religion really seriously. In spite of being involved in many apostolic activities, as well as conscientiously carrying out his duties in the Civil Service, he began to spend more and more time in prayer, and

"Pure Communication with God"

especially in prayer before the tabernacle. There he could pour out his heart to the Divine Master. The amount of time he spent in prayer during the years from 1914 to 1922 was truly astonishing. Rarely was it less than four hours per day. And at least three out of those four hours were spent in various churches.

His normal "prayer timetable" was as follows: Every morning he attended Mass, sometimes at 7:00 a.m., in the Redemptoristine Convent which was situated at the end of his road (at that time he lived at 55 St. Patrick's Road, Drumcondra) and sometimes at 7:15 a.m., in St. Francis Xavier's church, which was also fairly near. After this Mass, he would remain to assist at other Masses. He would spend one hour in the church. At lunch time, he had a quick lunch in his office and then went to do a "Holy Hour," in Marie Reparatrice Convent, which was a convent of Perpetual Adoration of the Blessed Sacrament. Then after his day's work in the office he would spend another hour in church, usually either in Whitefriars Street or Clarendon Street. In addition to all this, he spent at least another hour in prayer in his home.

A friend of Frank's one day asked him if it was the important nature of his apostolic work that made him pray so much, since a fruitful apostolate must have its roots in prayer and the spiritual life. Frank's answer was "no." His prayer life, he said, was independent of all his works. He had already read a great number of solid spiritual books, especially the "Lives of the Saints." In the lives of the saints, the absolute necessity of prayer was manifest. Therefore, he had come to appreciate the intrinsic value of prayer apart from the necessity of prayer for a fruitful apostolate. The position of work in relation to prayer in his case was, he said, that the work was only a "filler in." It wasn't feasible for him to spend all his time in prayer, so he went out and "filled in" his time by doing apostolic work.

• • • • •

The Easter Rebellion of 1916 had an extraordinary effect on Joe Gabbett. He was so upset by it, that he closed

FRANK DUFF

down the Cheater's Lane Breakfast Centre and rejoined the British Army. A number of the poor people who had partaken of the breakfasts now drifted back to the proselytizing Centre in Whitefriars Street.

Frank was dismayed, but he could and did continue the good work among the soldiers in Portobello Barracks. He took over the Sunday morning Services and preached a regular weekly sermon. Sargeant Major Baxter, the commanding Officer and a convert to the Catholic Church, looked on with full approval and encouragement, and allowed Frank to march into the barracks at any time to "harangue" the men.

In the beginning of 1918, the soldiers in the Barracks' hospital were transferred to the military barracks on Spike Island, Co. Cork. In the preceding weeks, Frank was particularly active. On the Sunday before the transfer, every Catholic in that hospital went to the Sacraments.

Now that they were gone, Frank had to find another "filler in."

8 The Price of a Breakfast

The Ladies Sodality meeting had just ended in the Carmelite Church. Outside the church doors, the priest was bidding farewell to the women and girls. Then, pointing to a lone figure down the street, he said: "That is our local madman." The lone figure was Frank Duff. Rosary beads in hand, he was picketing the Proselytizing Centre at 6 ½ Whitefriars Street.

Emma Colgan, one of the Sodality members, was fascinated. She commented: "Oh, Father, that's where you're wrong. There's method in his madness; he will succeed in closing down that place yet." Later, the same Emma Colgan became one of the first recruits enlisted in the Legion of Mary.

It hadn't taken Frank long to find his "filler in." He saw that proselytizing was still going on and, as very few were doing anything about it, he started picketing again. His method was: he would take his rosary beads in his hand and approach every man and woman entering the Centre, begging them not to do so. He'd give them a little sermon about betraying their religion for a meal and a Protestant Service.

It required extraordinary moral courage for him to do this work. There was a tendency in those days to think that the "good or practising Catholic" is one who looks after his own soul and takes no active interest in the salvation of others; he does the minimum to stay out of hell; he attends Mass every Sunday, avoids mortal sin and, generally speaking, he is neither hot nor cold.

Fifty years later, the Second Vatican Council would clearly outline the obligations of every Christian. "The Christian vocation, by its very nature, is also a vocation to the apostolate" (Vat. 2. Laity: 2). "The laity are assigned to

FRANK DUFF

the apostolate by the Lord Himself" (Vat. 2. Laity: 3). "On all Christians is laid the splendid burden of working to make the divine message of salvation known and accepted by all men throughout the world" (Vat. 2. Laity: 3).

But back in 1918, the average catholic layman was definitely not "his brother's keeper." Emphatically, Frank Duff was "odd man out." Today it can be seen that he was "a man born before his time."

In Whitefriars Street, the passers-by looked on with indifference, some with hostility. But Frank was having a fair amount of success with the poor "customers" at the Centre. Some of them, having been spoken to by him, decided not to go in. Others, weak in religion and hungry in body, were more difficult to dissuade.

Frank vividly described an early experience. "The very first time I went picketing," he said, "was nearly being my last. 'Business' was more or less over. All had gone in and I was taking things easy, waiting for them to come out. You often get people on the 'rebound.' But up came a drunken soldier. He was very drunk, because he wasn't able to walk straight. When he came up, I stood there and I said to him: 'If you are a Catholic you should not be going into that place, because you will have to take part in a Protestant Service.' The next thing I knew was that there was a knife in his hand and he lunged at me with the knife with all his force. I was so taken by surprise, I didn't make a move. And only that he was so drunk and that he missed his aim, he would have driven that knife into me. I recovered my balance then and Joe Louis himself couldn't have done any better! The blow I gave him was a terrific one, and it landed him flat on his back. The knife fell out of his hand. I stooped down and I took possession of the knife and then I stood over him waiting for him to get up. I was going to give him a dreadful beating if he got up. Next thing was, there was a terrible scuffle. I was shoved out of the way and a woman, who had been viewing the whole incident from a drawing-room window opposite, when she saw the attack coming came down and hurled herself on him. She kicked him, she beat him, she pulled his hair, she scraped his face. I never saw anything so destructive . . . Well, that was my first experience."

The Price of a Breakfast

In spite of all the difficulties attached to such an apostolate, Frank persevered. However, after a very short time, he realized that it was very difficult to say to people "You shouldn't go in there," when you knew they were downright hungry. In those days there were no State benefits or pensions for poor people. But up in Meath Street, Father Alphonsus Ryan was organizing free breakfasts for the poor. To keep the scheme going, everyone had to pay the small sum of three pence. So Frank out of his pocket would give his "customers" the price of the breakfast (using a ticket system in order to prevent abuse), and send them up to Father Ryan.

After a while, however, he had so many clients that it was too much even for his generous purse. He summoned a special meeting of the S.V.P., explained his project and asked if they would help to finance the breakfasts. They were most willing, they said, to finance such a worthy project. As a result, the poor people were catered for in a Catholic Centre.

The picketing of the Proselytizing Centre continued for six and a half years. By that time, the number of its clients had fallen to sixteen persons, so it was closed down. The sixteen remaining clients were transferred to another Proselytizing Centre, called the Metropolitan Hall, where this same deceptive practice was carried on in a big way and attracted twelve hundred people.

When Frank had summoned that emergency S.V.P. meeting to lay his plans before them, it was mainly financial help that he sought. But when the meeting had ended, Tom Fallon, one of the members, approached him and offered to accompany him in the actual work of picketing. Tom Fallon was a great worker for the Church and a man of great organizing ability. His offer was a great boon to Frank who had been picketing by himself for the previous twelve months.

Gradually, others volunteered to help in this work, so Frank decided to organize a picket at the Metropolitan Hall. This time the picketing continued for sixteen years, and was so successful that at the end of that time, the Metropolitan Hall Proselytizing Centre was forced to close down because of "lack of customers."

9 Mother

In the meantime back in the Duff home in Drumcondra, because of the retirement due to ill health of his father, Frank had taken on all the responsibilities of providing for the family. The oldest girl, Isabel, was afflicted with poor health and was unable to undertake any higher studies. John, Frank's only brother, was brilliant at school and Frank put him through University. John was very soon in an excellent post in the Civil Service and was eventually to rise to the post of Secretary of the Department of Justice. It used to worry Frank a lot that John was careless about his religion.

Sara and Ailis were teenagers now and Frank was also able to finance their way through University. Ailis, the youngest of the family, was Frank's favourite sister. When she was born, he was the first to take her in his arms. He had also been the one who had taken her tiny hands in his and had trained her to walk. She was only fifteen years old when her father died. So Frank became a father to her as well as a loving brother. Sara and Ailis were brilliant students at University College, Dublin, and both became doctors.

There had always been a marvelous bond of unity between all members of the family. The foundations for such a bond were undoubtedly built by Mrs. Duff who was so patient and calm and loving. She was, indeed, a good wife and a good mother.

Since Eva's death, Mrs. Duff had become very anxious when any of the family became sick. She remembered also, only too well, how Frank, at the early age of nine had almost been snatched from her by typhoid fever. She began to worry more now about her husband's decline in health. Conscientiously she looked after him with care and affection. Then came the day she had been dreading. Her fe-

Mother

male intuition told her he was more sickly than usual.

"John," she said, "you really must go to the doctor."

At first he was reluctant to go; finally he yielded to her gentle persuasion. When he returned, Frank was in the kitchen, but it was the mother who took her husband aside into another room to hear what the doctors had diagnosed. Then she broke the news to Frank.

"Frank," she said, "your father has cancer!"

"Is it certain?"

"Yes, his doctor called in two consultants for further examination. I'm afraid it is only too certain. In fact, they told your father he has only about six months to live."

It was like a thunderbolt to Frank. He had got so much from his father—a good home, a healthy wholesome upbringing, a love of sport and outdoor life, an introduction to literature and the arts. But just now there wasn't really much room in Frank's mind for reminiscing. Just one thought predominated—eternity. Frank's father was a practising Catholic but he wasn't what you would call "over religious." And now the doctors had "pronounced the sentence of death!"

The father took the doctor's verdict calmly enough. He suffered pain, of course, but bore it bravely. One day he and Frank were alone. Such was his regard for his son's maturity and wisdom, that, as far back as Frank's early teenage years, he had often consulted Frank on even serious affairs. Now again he turned to him. He said simply:

"Frank, what priest would you advise me to go to?"

These were sweet words to Frank's heavy heart. All was arranged. The father went to the priest and made a marvelous preparation for his final days. His death was edifying and holy. He died on December 23rd, 1918, and was buried three days later.

• • • • •

A couple of years after his father's death, Frank purchased a house in Dartmouth Square. It was number 51. It was a large spacious house, beautifully situated. Frank was particularly glad for his mother's sake. He knew she would like it. He was glad of it, too, for Isabel's sake. Her health

FRANK DUFF

gave her a good deal of discomfort and his heart went out to her.

And, of course, it was ideally situated for Frank himself. He was now quite near his Government Office and he was close enough to the areas of his many-sided apostolic and spiritual activities. His mother used to say of him, "I don't know where Frank picked up all his religion!"

The bond between her and Frank was truly extraordinary. There was nothing she wouldn't do for him. There was nothing he wouldn't do for her.

Occasionally, when he was young, she used to call him "Old Reliability," because he was "always there." "My mother could never have imagined," he admitted later, "the extent to which her words sank in and gave my thoughts an inclination. I valued that commendation and tried to live up to it."

One of the big regrets he had in life was that he had to leave her so much on her own. His activities kept him away from his home until quite late at night. He also knew that, however late it might be, she would always be "waiting up" until he came home.

But whatever he could do for her, he did. When he was twenty-one years old, he was already earning a good salary and so he took her on a holiday to Paris. Practically ever year he took her to London. He had discovered a small private hotel there which was run by a very nice family. It was very comfortable and quite close to the park. Together they would explore London and go to the theatre and the shows. And she simply loved going around the shops. Never did he go on a holiday without her.

And, of course, in Dublin at that time there were five theatres and a big choice of good plays with great actors. Every Saturday night Frank took his mother to the theatre. Later on, when his hearing began to fail, they switched over to the cinema.

Frank loved to reminisce, in his later years, on his mother and he insisted that it wasn't just out of a sense of duty that he took her with him whenever and wherever he could. No, it was for him sheer delight. She was his closest and best friend on this earth. And one of his great human

Mother

consolations in life was that, come what may, his mother would stand by him. He could always rely on her. She could always rely on him.

Certain it is that through this marvelous relationship between mother and son, this mutual faithfulness and dependence, Frank acquired wonderful and enriching insights into the meaning and beauty of true motherhood.

10 The "True Devotion"

Frank Duff in his youth was a very ordinary, rather casual Catholic. He kept the commandments of God, he was regular at Sunday Mass, he had what would be called a sentimental devotion to Our Lady. But that was all. He did not have any proper understanding of the basis of devotion to Our Lady nor did he have any real appreciation of Her role in God's plan of salvation.

Then in 1918, something happened that Frank subsequently regarded as a great grace from God; he came into possession of a small book called "True Devotion to the Blessed Virgin," written by St. Louis Marie de Montfort.

Frank was tidying up the room one evening after his S.V.P. meeting. The other members were standing around in a group and were discussing something very intensely. In the centre of the group was Vincent Kelly who had in his hand a copy of "True Devotion to the Blessed Virgin" by De Montfort, and he was explaining the subject of that book. By the time Frank had finished the tidying up and joined the group, the discussion had more or less ended. However, he did get the impression that Vincent Kelly thought very highly of the book.

A few days later Frank saw a copy of that book for sale in a second-hand book shop down by the River Liffey. He bought it for fourpence.

When he read the book, he was not at all impressed. It seemed to be claiming too much for Our Lady. He put it away with the intention of never opening it again.

Providence had other designs. In retrospect, we can now see how this man was being prepared for a great mission.

The "True Devotion"

If Our Lady had a plan and needed someone to implement that plan, she knew that here was a man of great promise whose faith had already been tested and not found wanting, whose life was one of prayer, a man of dauntless courage and conviction, a man, the like of whom had not, perhaps, been seen for generations.

Tom Fallon, who had by this time joined Frank in the work of picketing the Proselytizing Centre at 6 ½ Whitefriars Street, said to him one day "Frank, have you read de Montfort's book on True Devotion to the Blessed Virgin?"

"Yes, I have read it."

"And what did you think of it?"

"Well, it's beautifully written but I'd regard it as wildly extravagant."

"Oh, not at all. You just can't have read it properly. Go back and read it again; you must get to the bottom of that book."

And he practically compelled Frank to read that book repeatedly. The sequel is best told in Frank's own words:

"I was engaged on a final forced reading, when a sort of phenomenon occurred. Without any process of thought leading up to it, something, which I could only regard as a divine favour, was granted to me. As a sort of light, the sudden realization came to me that the book was true, a complete conviction that what I had been regarding as exaggerated and unreal was fully justified. The excesses which I thought I found in the book were really deficiencies in myself, wide gaps of knowledge and comprehension. That moment has remained in my mind with an absolute clarity."

Of course, Frank already had a great love for Our Lady. There was no doubt about it. And he prayed regularly to her. In July 1964 he was able to say in a letter to Pope Paul VI: "I have said five decades of the Rosary daily, without ever omitting it, since the year 1914." But in spite of all that, the fact was that back in 1918 there were these gaps in his knowledge. His faith was strong but he realized now that he had a duty to support it by studying the theology of Our Lady. In fact, the suspicion was growing on him that his devotion to Our Lady might actually fall embarrassingly short of what she was entitled to. But where

FRANK DUFF

could he get the theology, the background knowledge, that he so desperately required? Somehow, somewhere, he must get hold of that knowledge that De Montfort was presuming.

It was fitting that the Trappist monks of Mount Melleray Abbey should come to his rescue.

• • • • •

Mount Melleray Abbey is the largest and best known Cistercian Monastery in Ireland. It is situated on the scenic slopes of the Knockmealdown mountains between Tipperary and Waterford. The extensive farm and woodland of the monastery was originally part of the mountain itself and was donated by Sir Richard Keane to the first monks who came there in February 1832.

The new foundation gradually began to take shape. The monks worked hard to reclaim the poor, mossy soil. Slowly but surely the crops came. There was, at that time, great poverty in the countryside around Melleray and many a peasant was forced to come to the monastery doors to seek food for himself and his family. The monks willingly shared what they had with those who had not. For them every poor man was Christ in disguise.

The monks' daily life is a life of prayer, work and penance. Their vocation is to praise and glorify the infinite goodness and love of God. The holy rule of the monastery prescribes many hours of silence daily in order to lessen distractions and create an atmosphere conducive to prayer.

Into this atmosphere, on a cool October evening, in 1919, stepped two unlikely figures, Frank Duff and Joe Gabbett.

Gabbett had just been demobilized from the British army. Frank went to visit him and was dismayed to find that he had broken his pioneer pledge and was drinking heavily. Anxious to help him, he discussed the matter with two of his S.V.P. friends, Mr. Sweeney and Mr. Lalor. They said: "Frank, bring him down to Melleray." It was well known that the monks had helped many an alcoholic to overcome his "weakness."

Frank was already very well informed about the Cistercian Order. He had a great devotion to St. Bernard, the

The "True Devotion"

founder of the Cistercians. He had read everything available concerning the life of the monks and they fascinated him. He regarded the monks as hardly human at all. The idea of actually spending some days in their monastery on that mountainside was for him far more adventurous than an exploration into a jungle.

The two men set out from Dublin by train, then travelled the last stage of their journey by the old-fashioned side-car, at that time such a regular feature of Irish country life.

It was evening when they arrived. The light was fading. Nevertheless, as they approached, they could see the pointed spire of the monastery and the outline of the buildings. Ever after, Frank could vividly recall the emotion he felt at the time.

They were welcomed by the guestmaster and given a simple supper, "monastic style." Frank immediately felt "at home."

Next day, he was up early and found his way down to the chapel. The monks made an extraordinary impression on him; they really didn't seem to belong to this world. He watched them as they came in single file into the chapel. They walked rather leisurely and unhurried, each distinctly an individual in regard to size, shape or expression and yet all having that monastic ascetic look. Frank knew it was hardly possible that they were all saints. But they looked so holy, so wrapped up in prayer, so near to God. He surely envied them and their contemplative way of life, but he knew deep down that he would never be able to join them. He had, even before this time, made up his mind that he would never marry, but he also knew his vocation was not to the priesthood or to the monastic life. His was a different mission. He was quite sure about that, even if he wasn't quite sure yet what precise form that mission would take.

In the mornings, after breakfast, some of the monks took good care of Gabbett. He responded well and made marvelous headway.

Meanwhile, Frank had the opportunity to explore some of the monastery grounds—the paths by the pond, the woods, the gardens, the hills. It was as if nature itself was providing a lovely reflection of God's beauty, almost like a sacred garden in which a dedicated soul could blossom into holiness.

Father Brendan was a wonderful guestmaster. He walked

FRANK DUFF

through the garden with Frank, and they talked about spiritual things. Father Brendan asked: "Mr. Duff, would you like to have a book to read?" The monastery library was well stocked with spiritual books. Frank answered: "Oh yes, I'd like to have a book about the Blessed Virgin, a book that wouldn't be too deep for me to understand but which would, nevertheless, be a theological book that would explain the full position of Our Lady."

The priest went off and returned with a book called "The Knowledge of Mary" by Father de Consilio. The book gave Our Lady a prominent place in the Mystical Body. Frank, hungering for something like this, began reading it. He tells what happened:

"I took it up immediately to read and I became wildly excited because I found it was what I wanted. It was the missing foundation for De Montfort's book. It gave me what De Montfort's book had taken for granted. Here was a theology of Our Lady. Oh! I was quite overwhelmed. I knew that a new world had been opened for me."

Since his entry into the Society of the S.V.P., his appreciation of the Mystical Body had developed greatly, but now it began to dawn on him that his appreciation of that doctrine was still quite inadequate. Upon reading this newly discovered book, he saw that the reality was absolutely stunning and that in some incredible way Our Lady was the key. She is, of course, as nothing compared to Jesus. Jesus is the great Mediator or Accomplisher of Salvation. But His design has included her as His helpmate. He has incorporated her in His redemptive mission from beginning to end. In His inscrutable wisdom, He decreed that His whole scheme should depend on her extraordinary love and fidelity. On the degree to which we adapt ourselves to that arrangement of God, will largely depend our life's work.

From the day that Frank returned home from Melleray, he read every book on Our Lady, whether in English or in French, that he could lay his hands on. He absorbed and digested every idea in those books. He plumbed the depths of their message. And he dedicated himself to spend the rest of his life spreading a proper appreciation of Our Lady, and training people to express their appreciation by serving her.

11 Matt Talbot — and Others

There was joy and excitement; there were speeches. Young Charlie Andrews had just got married and the wedding reception was in Frank Duff's home. Mrs. Duff was accustomed to catering for Frank's wide assortment of friends and among these friends were the poorest of the poor, such as Charlie and his bride. It was many a wedding reception that was held in the Duff home. And Mrs. Duff's catering was second to none.

Charlie Andrews was deeply appreciative of what Frank did for him and he had a great regard for him. One day, when he was speaking to Frank, he asked:

"Mr. Duff, do you know my uncle, Mr. Talbot?"

Frank replied that he didn't know him.

"Well," said Charlie, "my uncle's name is Mr. Matt Talbot and he has a reputation for great holiness, and he has visions." Frank did not pay too much attention to that, but that same day, at the top of Grafton Street, he happened to meet his great friend, Ralph O'Callaghan. The subject of Matt Talbot, Charlie's uncle, came into the conversation and Frank discovered that Ralph knew Matt very well.

"Oh yes," said Ralph, "Matt and I are great friends. In fact, I often visit him and he comes to visit me. You see, Matt lodges in my aunt's house."

And thus on the sidewalk of Grafton Street, Frank learned the remarkable story of Matt Talbot.

Matt Talbot was born into a poor family in Dublin on May 2nd, 1856. When he was twelve years old, he got a job in a wine shop. Unfortunately, many of the men there gave him free drinks and he became an alcoholic at a very early age. Later, he worked as a laborer and spent most of his wages on drink.

Nevertheless, Matt always remained pure and was never guilty of using indecent or obscene language. He always said his morning prayers and never missed his Sunday Mass. He had reverence for Our Lady. However, he was far from religious. He ceased going to the Sacraments. When he had taken drink, he was quarrelsome and used to curse and swear.

Then came his conversion. One day he took the Pioneer pledge for a probationary period of three months. The following morning, he went to Mass and Holy Communion.

It was a slow, uphill struggle but he persevered with the help of his daily Mass, his rosary and his penance.

Then he had the good fortune to meet his landlady's nephew, Ralph O'Callaghan. Ralph, an exemplary member of S.V.P., took a great interest in Matt and even more so when his aunt told him that Matt's mother had shown her the plank bed on which he slept during the few hours he allowed himself for repose every night.

Matt came occasionally to Ralph's house for spiritual discussions. Among the spiritual books Ralph lent him, was de Montfort's "True Devotion to the Blessed Virgin." This book had a profound effect on Matt. It intensified his love for Our Lady; it deepened his union with her. He read in that book: "It is glorious and worthy of high praise, if those who have thus consecrated themselves as slaves of Jesus, in Mary, wear — as a sign of their loving bondage — some little chains that have been given a special blessing" (part 2, ch. 3).

Matt adopted the practice of wearing those chains. They were for him a reminder that he had become a loving servant of Our Blessed Lady. He later told John Gunning, a friend of his, that the wearing of a chain "lifted him from earth to heaven."

Was it any wonder that Frank Duff should be fascinated as he listened to Ralph's account of this wonderful person?

As time progressed, so did Matt's holiness. His prayer life, his penances, his heroic virtues, his degree of union with God were truly remarkable.

His health deteriorated as he got older. His loyal friend, Ralph, visited him in hospital and again, later, when he returned to his poor lodgings.

Matt Talbot — and Others

Matt Talbot died as he was walking to Mass on the 7th of June, 1925.

When Frank heard of Matt's death, he thought it would be regrettable if the life story of this man of heroic virtue were allowed to disappear into oblivion. So he brought Ralph O'Callaghan to meet Sir Joseph Glynn and introduced him. Sir Joseph was very impressed by Ralph's account and agreed to undertake the study of Matt's life with a view to writing a biography.

Frank then took Sir Joseph to meet Matt Talbot's sister, Mrs. Andrews, and she was most willing to supply detailed information. Apart from being justifiably proud of the virtues of her brother, Matt, it was natural that she would have been very pleased to oblige Frank in return for all he had done for her son, Charlie.

Sir Joseph Glynn published his "Life of Matt Talbot," in 1928, and brought the remarkable story of this holy man to the notice of the world.

• • • • •

Mrs. Duff was worried. Her brother, who lived in Dublin, had lapsed from the practice of his religion and now he was ill. She spoke to his wife.

"I'm very concerned about my brother," she said, "he hasn't been to the Sacraments."

"Indeed, I can well understand your concern, Susan, but rest assured that if he gets any weaker, I'll 'land' the priest in on him whether he likes it or not."

"Oh, thank you so much, that will make my mind easier."

Frank, being a nephew of the sick man was, naturally, very concerned. He wished to do something about it, but he realized it would be extremely difficult to talk to so close a relative about eternal salvation.

Providence stepped in. The uncle made a partial recovery, then suddenly got very ill and was taken to a nursing home. He was so ill that he was in intensive care with "round the clock" nursing attention.

"Ah, the Lord has delivered him into my hands" was the clear conviction of Frank. He explained all the facts to his great friend, Fr. Robinson, and asked him to visit his uncle.

"Father," said Frank, "perhaps you'll have no success but I'll be so grateful if you'll try. You can tell him I asked you to call."

Fr. Robinson assured him he would do all he could.

The following day, Fr. Robinson phoned Frank. Undoubtedly, Frank had prayed fervently during the night, yet he hardly dared to ask how the priest had fared.

"Frank, I have very good news for you; I have given your uncle the Sacraments."

Oh! the sheer relief and joy. Afterwards Frank said: "Of all the moments of joy in my life perhaps this was the greatest."

The following morning he went to the nursing home to visit his uncle. His uncle was very pleased to see him.

"Frank," he said, "your friend Fr. Robinson was here with me. He is a very kind man. He gave me the Sacraments. I can tell you, a very great burden has been taken off my mind."

Until that moment, Frank had not realized how concerned his uncle had been all along about not practising his religion.

The uncle died about a week later. But in the meantime, he received Holy Communion every day. And each evening, the three nurses who were attending him came to his room to join him in the recitation of the Rosary.

● ● ● ● ●

Mrs. Duff had another brother in London and whenever Frank and his mother went there for a holiday they would always spend a few days at this uncle's house. They were saddened to note that he, too, had given up the practice of his religion completely.

Then word came that he was seriously ill. Frank decided that, difficult as it may be, he must make some effort to get him back to the Sacraments. The remark his uncle in Dublin had made remained clear in his mind—"a great burden has been removed from me."

Frank, therefore, took up his pen and wrote to his uncle.

Matt Talbot—and Others

In a serious but gentle strain, he said he hoped he wasn't giving offence by presuming to touch on the question of religion. "Mother and I," he said, "would be terribly upset if you were to die without the Sacraments." He posted the letter immediately. It was Good Friday.

A month passed without a reply. Because of the seriousness of the matter and because of Frank's solicitude, the delay was a great strain. Then a letter arrived thanking Frank for his concern and assuring him that no offence was taken.

"Why should you," the letter ran, "have any fears that I would take offence at your writing to me about this serious matter? Indeed, I am pleased that you were concerned and that you took an interest in my welfare. However, about your concern, I can assure you that, like St. Paul, I have kept the faith."

Frank, however, was not fully reassured. There was no mention in his uncle's letter of the Sacraments. Thorough in all things, and especially in things religious, Frank wrote to Fr. Ripley in England and asked him to do what he could about the case. Fr. Ripley had difficulty in locating the uncle's house but enlisted the help of a Passionist priest who succeeded in visiting the sick man and administered the Sacraments to him. Thus fortified, Frank's uncle entered into eternal life shortly afterwards.

12 The Legion is Born

Elizabeth Kirwin was deep in prayer as she knelt before the altar. It was her daily custom to visit the Marie Reparatrice Convent chapel during her lunch-break; there was perpetual adoration of the Blessed Sacrament there. The convent was just around the corner from where she worked. She never bothered to take off her work-apron when she came into the little chapel; she knew the Lord would understand.

Just now she had a problem on her mind; she knew of someone who needed help but it was a difficult case and she really did not know how to tackle it. She realized fully how near she herself had been to going off "the straight and narrow path." She must surely have thought: "how strange are the ways of the Lord."

Elizabeth O'Loughlin was born of Catholic parents in Dunedin, New Zealand. Her father was a lawyer. When Elizabeth was nine years old, the family moved to Melbourne, Australia. She came to London some years later and trained as a nurse. In London she became very casual about her religion and in due time lost all interest in it. But God had a special place for her in His plans. She came to Dublin and married John Kirwin, a devout Catholic. By trade John Kirwin was a lamplighter.

The streets of Dublin were gaslit in those days. The gas-lamp standards were very ornate and beautiful works of art, especially in the fashionable streets of the city centre. At eventide, as the daylight waned and night was spreading her mantle over the city, the lamplighter could be seen moving, mysterious and ghost-like, on his bicycle, holding a long, light pole in his right hand. He stopped at each

The Legion is Born

lamp and, raising his right arm, he touched with his pole the vital spot that set the gas mantle aglow. On he went through the gathering gloom, leaving a chain of incandescent lights in his wake. Then, in the pale light of daybreak, when the stars were flickering out, the figure of the trusty lamplighter could again be seen, in silhouette, as he moved silently along the streets of the sleeping city and methodically quenched the lamps as God blessed the capital with the glorious light of a new day. The older citizens of today look back nostalgically at the romantic era of the gaslit streets and the old lamplighters.

But Frank Duff used to say, later: "The most important light that John Kirwin ever lit was the one he enkindled, from the embers of dying faith, in his wife's soul." And indeed he did succeed in blowing a fire aflame from the spark of faith still left in her.

When John Kirwin died, his wife Elizabeth was in rather straitened circumstances and was glad to get a small job of office-cleaning which was in proximity to her home and was also fairly near the convent chapel.

As she knelt in prayer on this particular day and pondered over her "problem case," she felt that a solution might not be far away. She glanced again at the refined, well-dressed young man who was kneeling in devout prayer near by. She had noticed that he spent his whole lunch-hour every day in this chapel. She had learned also that his name was Mr. Duff, that he held a responsible position in the Civil Service and that he was a member of the S.V.P. Society.

She rose from her prie-dieu, genuflected and left the chapel. Then she waited in the small chapel porch. As Mr. Duff left, she approached him and introduced herself. She also explained her "case."

"Mr. Duff," she said, "I have knowledge of someone who needs help and guidance. I'm not able to manage the case myself; it's too difficult for me. Would you be so kind as to look after it for me?"

Frank was quite surprised. He wondered how she could possibly have known his name but he soon discovered she was the sister of Fr. O'Loughlin, the chaplain of Portobello Military Barracks with whom Frank himself and Joseph

FRANK DUFF

Gabbett had been so closely associated. He was pleased that Mrs. Kirwin had approached him. He guessed she was about sixty-five years old. She seemed a reserved but competent sort of person. He readily agreed to look after the case she had entrusted to him and after some days he was very pleased to visit her in her little home and report that he had dealt successfully with the case.

• • • • •

By 1917, the number of dedicated members of the S.V.P. Conference of St. Nicholas of Myra had grown so large that it was decided to divide it into two Conferences. The new one was called, St. Patrick's Conference, and Frank Duff was appointed as president.

That very year, the S.V.P. moved into "Myra House" which had been donated as a gift to Frank Sweeney by a charitable lady, named Mrs. Keogh. This spacious building gave ample scope for diversifying the works of the Society. Frank Duff's Conference, St. Patrick's, straightway introduced many new works, as various needs came to be recognized. They set up catechism classes to teach religion to spiritually neglected children. They started a Pioneer Total Abstinence Centre and undertook to recruit members for it. They recruited also for the League of daily Mass. They arranged for the Enthronement of the Sacred Heart in homes and also for enrollments in the Brown Scapular. Not surprisingly, Frank was the inspiration and the driving force behind these initiatives.

The marvelous thing was that a big step had been taken by lay people into various spiritual apostolates covering a wide spectrum.

Some of these works were geared towards women and children and the nature of the works necessitated the help of women. Thus, for the first time, females were called in to assist the Society. Frank, however, was the guiding light in all the ventures through his inspiration and his organizational ability. Among the volunteers were a number of the girls who had already helped Joe Gabbett and Frank Duff in the Cheaters' Lane Breakfast apostolate.

It was decided to set up a governing body that would

The Legion is Born

meet once a month to co-ordinate and supervise the various activities. Frank had been "looking around" for someone capable of taking charge and of running the monthly meetings. He remembered Mrs. Kirwin and decided to pay her a visit.

"Mrs. Kirwin," he said, "we have been engaging in a number of apostolic activities in Myra House, such as catechism classes, youth works and so on. Do you think you could come along and help us?"

"Indeed, I will be pleased to help in any way I can, Mr. Duff."

● ● ● ● ●

Month after month for the next four years, these meetings were held in Myra house. Fr. Toher, the local curate, also attended. The prayers that were recited were much the same as the prayers of any S.V.P. Conference meeting except that the Rosary was recited in lieu of the one "Hail Mary" usually said.

It was inevitable that De Montfort's book on "True Devotion to the Blessed Virgin" should be mentioned. Frank Duff's discovery of this book had produced such an indelible impression on him that he just had to talk about it. The others got interested and asked many questions concerning the book. It was eventually proposed at one of the monthly meetings that a special meeting should be held to discuss the book and the teaching of De Montfort. A date was fixed; Frank gave a talk on the subject and a discussion followed.

Later Frank Duff was to write: "It is impossible to believe that the connection between the 'True Devotion' meeting and the immediate emergence of the Legion from the next monthly meeting was a mere coincidence. There was too much supernatural design and too little human contriving. Nearly four years had gone by without incident until the 'True Devotion' meeting was held. The moment it established in minds the true stature of Our Lady in the Christian system, things were ready for the Legion."

Within seventeen days of the 'True Devotion' meeting, the Legion of Mary was born. It happened like this: When

FRANK DUFF

Matt Murray gave his usual report at the next meeting of the governing body, he gave a very impressive account of his visit to the Dublin Union Hospital. At that time, such an apostolate to hospitals was done by men only. Matt's report had a moving effect on everyone present. Immediately after the meeting, while some of the ladies were preparing the traditional "cup of tea," two other ladies approached Fr. Toher and Frank Duff and asked: "Would it not be possible for the ladies to do that same kind of work?"

"Yes, of course." Frank answered: "Can you interest some more of the ladies in this work?"

The two ladies went around to "chat-up" the other ladies who were present. Within a few minutes they were back with the news: "We have six already."

It was agreed that a first meeting would be held on the following Wednesday evening at 8:00 p.m. It was only later that somebody drew attention to the fact that the evening decided upon was the Vigil of the Feast of the Nativity of Our Lady.

So, at the appointed hour on the 7th of September, 1921, fifteen persons assembled—Fr. Toher, Frank Duff and thirteen ladies. Most of the ladies were quite young. It was the first meeting of the Legion of Mary.

When Frank Duff arrived into the room, he was delighted to see on the table the statue of Our Lady of the Immaculate Conception, with flowers and candles around it, exactly as can be seen at any Legion meeting today. The vexillum, of course, was designed and added later. Remarkably, the design of the Legion altar and statue had not been discussed beforehand. It was simply arranged by one of the early comers, Alice Keogh, on her own initiative.

Furthermore, the statue on that first Legion altar was the very same one that had been purchased by Joe Gabbett and placed in a prominent position overlooking the Breakfast Centre of Cheaters' Lane.

The first sight of that statue on the Legion altar that evening made such an impression on Frank that he retained a vivid memory of that glorious moment for the rest of his life. Like a thunderbolt it struck him: it wasn't that the new members had come together and then invited Our

The Legion is Born

Lady to join them; not at all. Rather the truth was that She was there before them, waiting to receive them and accept their enrollment in her service. They were not simply going to form a society; they were going to love and serve a person. That statue would always remind them that their Mother, Mary, was present in their midst.

In the beginning, the new society was called the "Association of Our Lady of Mercy." Later, it was renamed the Legion of Mary.

From the start, the members undertook an apostolate of a pastoral nature which meant the breaking of entirely new ground for the laity, as there had been no precedent for it at that time. They would try to incorporate into their lives what they had learned from De Montfort's True Devotion to Mary. And the emphasis would be on practical service, that is, serving Our Lady not just in words but also in deeds. They would serve her by serving her Son Jesus in every man, woman and child they would meet. They would see Christ suffering in the poor patients in hospital; they would console the lonely Christ in the people who lived alone; they would encounter the Child Jesus in every young boy and girl they met; they would seek out Christ crucified in every sinner.

Moreover, every time they looked at the statue on their Legion altar, they would try to remember that it was the Mother of Jesus who was herself sending them forth on their privileged mission. They would depend on her and strive to live a life of holy union with her. In a word, their clarion call would be: "At your service, Mary, for the glory of God."

The person chosen to be their first president was the oldest, as well as the poorest, person in the room; yes it was Elizabeth Kirwin.

13 "Shall He Not Leave the Ninety-Nine?"

The first apostolic work undertaken by the legionaries was the visitation of the patients in the South Dublin Union Hospital, known as St. Kevin's, and under the care of the Mercy nuns. But from the very beginning it was envisaged that all kinds of apostolic works would eventually be undertaken.

High on the agenda was the big problem of the streetgirls of Dublin. Prostitution existed on a fairly large scale in Dublin city at that time. A number of factors contributed to the problem—grinding poverty, appalling slum conditions and the fact that Dublin was a port city and had, in common with all port cities, its share of undesirable visitors.

Surprisingly enough, the problem of prostitution had never before been tackled seriously, either in Dublin or elsewhere. It was regarded as an incurable social problem. Whatever efforts had been made to deal with the problem had been directed towards confining it to a particular area. The sort of faith that can move mountains was conspicuous by its absence whenever the subject was mentioned, and all sorts of excuses were thought up, even by clergymen, to evade the real issue. "It's impossible to solve a problem of that kind." "That problem is as old as mankind, it has never been solved up to now, do you think *you* can solve it?" "It's a tragedy but the fact is the girls are driven to prostitution by their poverty, we can only tackle it when social and material conditions have improved." "If

"Shall He Not Leave the Ninety-Nine?"

you close down the houses of prostitution, you will not solve the problem, in fact you will only scatter it and it will then spread all over the city," etc., etc.

As Frank Duff saw things, the reality of the matter was that often when we say: "It is not yet the opportune time to approach these poor people," or "the conditions aren't right just yet," the truth often is that it is we who are not ready to talk to them, or perhaps we haven't the courage to face up to a difficult task, or maybe our faith is of a poor quality.

Well, even if it meant dying in the attempt, Frank Duff was determined that he—and the legionaries—would tackle the problem. He would be called "imprudent," "reckless," "indiscreet." But that, he reckoned, would be but a small price to pay for even one soul. He had trained himself never to begin his examination of a problem by considering either the difficulties of the undertaking or the inevitable criticism by other people. To begin thus would be to court failure. The mind would only be distracted and frightened by all sorts of apparent impossibilities. For Frank there was only one honest approach to a problem, namely: "Does God want this work done? If so, then it must be done." Once that is clear, then—and only then—may we consider how to tackle the difficulties one by one as they occur, and we will, of course, act as discreetly as possible. The further consideration that made Frank decide to help the prostitutes was that he knew that if the Legion didn't tackle this work, nobody else would either.

It was obvious that a second branch of the Legion needed to be set up. This branch was called the praesidium of "Our Lady of the Sacred Heart." Later, the name was changed to "Sancta Maria."

Thirty-one street-girls, practically all of them young, were living in a house of ill-repute in Low Street. Perhaps an enclosed Retreat could be organized for them? The very idea seemed preposterous. But Fr. Devane, a Jesuit priest, was keen on the idea; so was Frank. Could they get a convent that would accommodate street-girls for a Retreat? Some Sisters shuddered nervously at the very thought of it. Besides, very few convents had facilities for such a Retreat as that proposed. Eventually, the Convent of the Sisters of

FRANK DUFF

Charity in Baldoyle came to the rescue. The Superior of the convent, Mother Angela Walsh, said: "I must be crazy, but I cannot turn you down." On her part it was a heroic act of faith and charity.

Frank and five sister legionaries went to the house of ill-repute. There were six young girls in the first room they entered. After half an hour of explaining, coaxing, pleading by the legionaries, the six girls promised to come to the Retreat. Then on to the next room occupied by another four girls. There followed more explaining, more appeals. Then the six in the first room got "cold feet" and changed their minds. The legionaries had to start all over again. But at last, after five agonizing hours, the legionaries had obtained promises from practically every girl in that house. There were still many anxious moments before the Retreat actually got under way, a day later, in Baldoyle Convent. One has to read Frank Duff's own complete account in his book, "Miracles on Tap," to realize the dreadful fears and worries that accompanied practically every minute of the enterprise.

But faith triumphed, the sort of faith that can move mountains. The Retreat was an amazing success. Father Philip, the Franciscan priest who conducted the Retreat, was marvelous. The girls listened with rapt attention to his talks. There was, of course, a noticeable tension at times, and the occasional spasm of uncertainty and restlessness. Nevertheless, the "impossible" became possible. The miracles of grace began to happen. One by one, the girls went to Confession. They had discovered during the Retreat that there was one thing which was even greater than their sins and that was the mercy of God. Satan's grip was loosened. Years of misery faded into oblivion. Refreshing and beautiful graces filled their souls, and the tense atmosphere was replaced by one of serenity and peace.

Sunday night approached, and a great calm descended on all. The legionary helpers went back to their homes. The girls—they were no longer street-girls—retired to their beds in the convent. Beds and mattresses had been hastily bought and transported to the convent for them.

Frank Duff who had also travelled to Baldoyle Convent to help out was kept extremely busy. By nighttime, he was

"Shall He Not Leave the Ninety-Nine?"

exhausted but happy. An extra bed was rigged up for him in the room where Fr. Philip was to sleep. But the excitement of those previous eventful days ruled out even the thought of sleep. And so Fr. Philip and Frank walked around the convent gardens for hour after hour discussing the marvelous events that were happening. Besides, they had to discuss plans for the future of those girls.

Earlier that very day Frank had come from the office of Mr. Cosgrave, the Minister for Local Government, with the assurance that large and suitable premises would be available for the housing of the girls when they left the Retreat house of Baldoyle. This had solved the painful problem of finding a suitable place for the girls when they finished their Retreat. It would be called Sancta Maria.

After their walk and chat, Fr. Philip and Frank entered the chapel by the outer door. It was about 3:00 a.m. They said their prayers and concluded with the Stations of the Cross. Then they retired to bed.

Morning broke. The convent bells signaled the time for rising. The nuns and the girls came down to the chapel for Mass. All the girls, with the exception of the two protestants, received Holy Communion. Frank knelt between two of them at the altar rails on that glorious Monday morning. He declared later that it was the most wonderful Mass at which he had ever assisted, and the Holy Communion "a moment of the most intense joy that can be imagined." With the eyes of faith he had seen wonderful graces being showered on these penitent girls, and he felt humble and small before the greatness of God's mercy which is above all His works.

14 The Sign-Language of Faith

The new organization, the Legion of Mary, spread slowly but surely. New praesidia were formed. In those early praesidia there were women and girls only. It was considered wise to delay the entry of men, in case the society would be considered as a sort of rival to the St. Vincent de Paul Society. But from the start it was clearly envisaged that membership would also be open to men. In the meantime, Frank himself remained a member of the praesidium, partly to maintain a sort of liaison with the St. Vincent de Paul Society, but also because he wished to ensure that at no stage could the Legion be looked upon as for women only.

In May 1927, Frank Duff received a letter from a nun in the Ursuline Convent, Waterford, expressing the interest of the Community; they would like to start a branch of the Legion. He went to Waterford without delay and set up a praesidium there. In November of the same year, Mrs. Don Mahoney of Blarney Mills, invited Frank to Cork to give a talk on the work of the Morning Star Hostel. This led to the setting up of the first praesidium in Cork, on the 21st of November of that same year. Belfast was soon on the list. Now it was time to move farther afield.

•••••

It was late March 1928. The Burns-Larne Steamboat looked sturdy and proud as it waited patiently at the dock-

The Sign-Language of Faith

side. The passengers were making their way up the gangway. The journey from Ireland to Scotland was scheduled to take 17 ½ hours. Seasoned travellers had a look of resignation on their faces. First-timers were keen and excited. Others who were emigrating to Glasgow in the hope of getting jobs looked lonesome and wistful.

Eventually, at 6:30 p.m., the boat moved away from the pier and the passengers settled down to make themselves as comfortable as possible for the long tiresome journey. Perhaps some of them cast a casual glance at one rather well-dressed young man who sat quietly in their midst. Had they but known, they were looking at a man who was in the process of making history. That well-dressed young man was none other than Frank Duff—a man with a mission. He was bringing the Legion overseas. His mind that evening was on Glasgow. And all because of a sign!

For many people, faith is simply believing that everything which Jesus taught is true and that likewise everything the Church teaches is true. And it ends there! Their understanding of what their faith should mean in their lives is very limited. For Frank Duff, it was different. He had learned the hard way, through prayer, through study, through experience. He had come to appreciate what he called, "the sign-language of faith," that is, that we should watch out for the hand of God in even the most insignificant—or apparently insignificant—happenings in everyday life. Every person is baptized to be "Christed," to be an apostle. But because of our natural tendency to be selfish and cowardly, we tend to be blind to the opportunities that arise to help other people spiritually. In fact, we will invent a million excuses to convince ourselves that it isn't our duty, or that the moment isn't opportune, or that such a course of action would be imprudent. So God has to intervene a little. He has to arrange strange "coincidences." He has to, so to speak, resort to a sort of sign-language to prompt us to take notice that here is an opportunity, even a divine invitation, to co-operate with Him so as to yield a spiritual profit. And so, when something a little out of the ordinary occurs, we should wonder if it may not have been arranged by the Holy Spirit for the purpose of enabling us to bring a soul to Jesus and Mary.

FRANK DUFF

Once, when Frank was asked, "how did you first learn to see signs," he replied simply, "from happenings." There had been, for instance, the "coincidence" of seeing the "True Devotion" book for sale in a second-hand book shop shortly after he had heard it mentioned by a St. Vincent de Paul brother. There had been the "accidental" meeting with Joe Gabbett at the very time when he, Frank, was planning to counteract the proselytizing movement. There was the "coincidence" of the first Legion meeting being held at the time of the First Vespers for the Feast of Our Lady's Nativity.

When Frank went down to North William Street to get Pioneer supplies he bumped into one of the nuns, Sister Josephine, who was very interested in the Legion.

"Sister, my sights are now on Glasgow," he said. Shortly afterwards Sister Josephine sent him a message saying that she had been told to make her Retreat in Glasgow, at the house of the Sisters of Charity, in Wilton Crescent. She added that she would do what she could to pave the way for the Legion there.

For Frank, that was the sign. Not that he needed a sign. He had already realized that the Legion was quite different from any other organization on this earth. He had noticed in the Legion a remarkable faith and fervour and endeavour, also a willingness to tackle anything, even the most difficult, for God and for souls. And then, also, there had been a marvelous intake of new recruits and the undertaking of new and daring works. In this, they were confronted by a world full of problems, of evil and neglect and sin.

Yes, Frank was quite sure that in the Legion he was dealing with something that was divinely inspired and planned. As he said himself: "I was deadly certain that in all these things I was being led, there was no room for a change in my mind about it." The signs were simply pointers, though undoubtedly they gave Frank valuable reassurance.

Sister Josephine made her Retreat and subsequently spoke to Sister Brendan, the Superioress at Wilton Crescent, concerning Frank's hopes for setting up the Legion in Glasgow.

Shortly afterwards, Sister Brendan told Frank, by letter,

The Sign-Language of Faith

that the Vicar General of the diocese had agreed to arrange an interview between him (Frank) and the Archbishop, in Glasgow.

Frank promptly decided to take one week of his vacation period and now he was on the boat, setting out on a journey which would later be followed by many journeys of heroic envoys to the ends of the earth where the rainbow rests — to all who needed the saving power of Christ's love, brought by His Mother.

To enable him to attend Mass, Frank disembarked at Greenock at noon on the next day. Then he took the first available train to Glasgow. Upon arrival he went straight to St. Andrew's Cathedral to meet the Vicar General. It was now 9:00 p.m. He had no meal that day, having neither the time nor the opportunity to eat. He was hungry and tired but glad to have reached his destination.

But what a disappointment was in store for him! The Vicar General was exceedingly nice. Imagine Frank's shock, though, when he said: "Wasn't it about architecture you wished to see the Archbishop?" Frank quickly replied that it wasn't exactly that kind of architecture he had in mind and then he proceeded to explain the Legion of Mary. The Vicar General was not impressed. "Oh, put it out of your mind," he said. "The Archbishop wouldn't even see you about that, as he believes that this diocese has too many organizations. What it needs is pruning, not additional societies." And then, as a sort of afterthought, he added, "And I have to say that I myself am of the same view as the Archbishop."

Oh! The agony of it. Frank was afflicted with a sense of hopelessness. He had taken a whole week of his holiday leave to concentrate on this project. Where was the Lord leading him? He was confused, puzzled. But he was not giving up. He continued to talk to the Vicar General. He found him becoming more receptive. It was one o'clock in the morning when the Vicar General said: "You have done something which I would have believed to be absolutely impossible; you have made me enthusiastic." Then he asked: "How long will you be in Glasgow?"

"One week."

"Well, then, if you can stay till Friday, I will secure an

FRANK DUFF

interview for you with the Archbishop at the Vicariate Office."

"Could I not see him at his own house?"

"Oh no. Impossible! The Archbishop is unapproachable in his house. Only the other day he turned away Father X, who had called to the house to meet him."

Frank knew the disadvantages of having the interview at the Vicariate. There would probably be a queue waiting to meet the Archbishop. Time would be very limited. However, at this stage, Frank had to be grateful for small favors.

Friday was still some days away and so he decided to make the best use of his time. He contacted the St. Vincent de Paul Society who gave him a great welcome and arranged that he should give a talk at their meeting the following Sunday. Also, he was invited to speak to the Catholic Evidence Guild on Saturday evening.

Friday came. Frank presented himself at the Vicariate Office to meet the Archbishop. The Vicar General was there and said to him:

"This is the most unhappy circumstance; the Archbishop has not turned up today."

"What am I to do then?" asked Frank, numbed once again by shock and frustration.

"There's nothing you can do except to come to Glasgow again some time."

Frank could still catch the Friday evening boat back to Ireland, but he had to honor his commitment to speak on Sunday at the St. Vincent de Paul meeting.

Meanwhile, there was one thing he could do, and that he did. He retired to his room in the convent and wrote a letter to the Archbishop. The only writing pad available was of very poor quality; the ink seeped through the paper. The envelopes were equally bad. He even made the mistake of putting inadequate stamping on the envelope, not realizing until later that the Scottish postal rates were higher than the Irish rates. He shuddered at the thought of the Archbishop having to pay the dues!

It took him hours to write that letter. It was a very long one in which he dealt with the precise problem raised by the Vicar General, namely, that the diocese was over-orga-

The Sign-Language of Faith

nized. The letter went to the kernel of the matter and proceeded to outline the real needs of the Church. It explained, too, how the Legion of Mary was geared to meet these needs and how, in fact, it was already dealing with urgent problems back in Dublin. Early the following morning, he posted the letter on his way to Mass.

Frank realized that he had, in fact, very little confidence in the outcome of that letter but he said to himself: "I have been brought over to this place. There is no doubt of this in my mind. It is the same as if an angel had led me. There is some divine purpose in it."

Then he thought: "Perhaps it isn't for Glasgow I have been brought over, perhaps it's for Edinburgh!" He knew there was the Sacred Heart Training College at Craiglochhart. And, not so long ago, he had met in Dublin one of the nuns from that convent. He now decided: "To Edinburgh I will go and I will meet that nun."

That same afternoon, he got the train to Edinburgh, proceeded to Craiglochhart Training College and asked if he could see the nun. The Mother Superior came to greet Frank Duff in the parlor.

"You're very welcome, Mr. Duff," she said. "Unfortunately, though, it won't be possible for you to see your friend; she is on Retreat." Undaunted, Frank began to talk about the Legion of Mary in his most gentle manner.

"Ah well, I can bring Sister out of Retreat for a little while," interjected Mother Superior.

After a few moments, the Sister joined Mother Superior and Frank in the parlor. Frank had little difficulty in enthusing both of them. If only the Archbishop of Edinburgh could be persuaded to give permission!

"Oh," said Mother Superior, "we can arrange that. We will get the permission for you. Our Archbishop has been ailing for some time but I'm sure Dr. Grey Graham, the Assistant Bishop, will give permission." This was wonderful news. Mother Superior went off to phone Dr. Graham. As she returned, Frank noted the blank look on her face.

"He's in Ireland," she said. Then, seeing his look of disappointment, she added: "but when he comes back, we'll see what we can do."

The nuns gave Frank a nice lunch. Then he rushed off to

FRANK DUFF

catch the train to Glasgow. He was due to speak to the Catholic Evidence Guild that evening. So tired and dispirited was he, that he fell asleep on the train. At Glasgow station, he was abruptly brought back to reality by the husky voice of a friendly porter. And off he went to speak, as promised, to the Catholic Evidence Guild.

Sunday morning came. Frank went out to Mass and then returned to the Convent in Wilton Crescent for breakfast. Sister Brendan, the Superioress, was the essence of kindness and hospitality. As was customary then for a nun, she refrained from dining in the presence of visitors, but she sat by the table and chatted as Frank ate.

The phone in the room rang. Sister Brendan went to answer it. Her voice betrayed her sense of awe. She placed her hand over the mouthpiece and, turning to Frank, she said in a hushed tone:

"Mr. Duff, it's the Archbishop; he wants to speak to you."

Frank took the phone. "Yes, your Grace, this is Mr. Duff," he said, trying not to betray the excitement that had risen up inside him.

"When could you come out to my house to see me, Mr. Duff?"

"Oh, as soon as a taxi will take me out, your Grace."

"I will be glad to see you when you arrive."

Sweet words that must have sounded as if heard in dreamland. And from Archbishop Donald McIntosh the formidable! The world had suddenly turned upside down and downside up again.

Almost immediately the phone rang again.

"Mr. Duff, it's for you again. It's Lady Mary Carr from Edinburgh on the phone."

Frank once again took the phone. "Oh, Mr. Duff, the Reverend Mother of the Convent here has been telling us about you. Could you possibly come to Edinburgh tonight or even on Monday? I think we will be able to help you in regard to your objectives."

Frank was stunned as he listened to Lady Mary Carr. The Carrs were one of the most important catholic families in all Scotland. Lady Mary's husband had at one time been Commander of the British forces in Ireland. Their son,

The Sign-Language of Faith

Viscount Lothian Carr, became British Ambassador to Washington during the war. Their two daughters, Lady Cecily Carr and Lady Margaret Carr, were both marvelous girls.

"I am most grateful to you indeed," said Frank into the phone's mouthpiece. "I will come by train on Monday."

As quickly as he could scramble through his breakfast, he did. Then off in a taxi to the Archbishop's house, in Glasgow.

● ● ● ● ●

Archbishop Donald McIntosh was an impressive figure. He was a Catholic Scot from the Islands, over six feet tall, of commanding presence, a Gaelic speaker. Before him stood Frank, rather slightly built, a very gentle figure, with an ever-present smile on his face.

The Archbishop was extremely kind and friendly. He had already read Frank's long letter and had been completely won over by it. Hence Frank did not have to indulge in any long explanations.

"A little while ago," the Archbishop confided, "I was asked by Rome to forward my suggestions in regard to Catholic Action. How unfortunate that I didn't have your letter and your ideas before me at the time; I could have done something worthwhile."

The interview lasted two hours. The Archbishop gave full permission for the founding of the Legion of Mary in his diocese. Furthermore, he promised he would encourage it by all means in his power and, in fact, supplied a list of the names of four parish priests whom he suggested Frank might approach. Then he brought Frank into his domestic chapel and together they prayed for the success of the Legion.

As the Archbishop opened the hallway door to let Frank out, who was standing on the doorstep but Canon McNealy whose name was one of the four on the list in Frank's pocket!

One can only guess at the inner feelings of Frank Duff as he left the Archbishop's house that day. Later that evening he fulfilled his engagement with the S.V.P. Society. It had been a memorable Sunday.

FRANK DUFF

On Monday morning he once again traveled to Edinburgh and had lunch with the Carr family. They promised to try to get the necessary permission and get the Legion started.

On Monday night a tired but happy Frank Duff embarked on the Burns-Larne Steamboat for the return journey to Dublin.

To finalize things, he returned to Glasgow on the 23rd of April and three days later, set up the first praesidium there. Father Conlon, the curate, canvassed for recruits. Twenty wonderful girls came along and there and then they held their first meeting under the presidency of Minnie McGarry. They titled it, "Our Lady of Lourdes praesidium." It was in the parish of St. Peter's, Partick. The parish priest was, of course, Canon McNealy, the very one who had greeted Frank on the Archbishop's doorstep.

From the moment of its foundation, that praesidium had marvelous successes, and the Legion of Mary began to spread rapidly in Glasgow.

Meanwhile, in Edinburgh, the Carrs were as good as their word. They secured Bishop Graham's permission and started a praesidium of the Legion themselves. By the time of Frank's next visit to Edinburgh, the Legion was flourishing there.

Now that the Legion was firmly established in Scotland, Frank decided to see what he could do about setting up the Legion in England before he returned home to Dublin. Besides he had an appointment with his great friend, Mr. Lalor, who was coming over to London to meet him.

15 Enter Mr. Lalor

Matthew Lalor was born in Castledermot, Ireland, and was brought up by an uncle who had a shop there. At an early age, he came to Dublin and was apprenticed to a large fashionable department store. Switching later to the tobacco business, he soon had his own tobacco shop, specializing in high-class cigars and tobacco. Within a few years, he had become a very wealthy man.

A deeply religious person, he joined the S.V.P. Society in Blackrock and, in time, became the president of the S.V.P. Council of Dublin. He gave away most of his money to charitable causes, being especially interested in financing the training of missionary priests.

It was Tom Fallon who brought Frank Duff out to Lalor's house in Blackrock for the first time. Mr. Lalor was tall and thin, rather ascetic looking, but very well dressed. He wore a well-trimmed beard which gave him a distinguished look. Although he was, at that time, over sixty years old, his mind was young, enterprising, forward looking. Frank, who always referred to him as *Mr.* Lalor because he was so much older, was soon impressed and, in spite of the big difference in their ages, the two men became very good friends, so much so in fact that, during the next twenty years, Frank went to Mr. Lalor's house in Blackrock every Sunday for lunch.

Frank was under tremendous strain for most of his long life. This was, to some extent, because of the very difficult nature of many of his apostolic works, but more so because he was a man "born before his time," and he encountered much misunderstanding and even opposition along

FRANK DUFF

the way. He was aware that at least some of the clergy wanted to have the Legion closed down. The very thought was a torture to him. Therefore, his Sunday afternoons in Blackrock were a great tonic for him. Immediately after his Morning Star Hostel meeting, he would set out on his bike for Mr. Lalor's house. Every Legion problem, every Legion crisis was discussed there. He could pour out his troubles and give vent to his feelings of frustration. Mr. Lalor, so much older than Frank and of a calmer disposition, always gave a sympathetic hearing and such helpful counselling as can come from someone who has advanced in age and wisdom and spirituality.

Sunday lunch at Lalor's house was a heart-warming event. Often there were other guests for lunch besides Frank. Tom Fallon was a regular visitor, also Mr. P. J. O'Hanlon, a middle-aged businessman whom Mr. Lalor had provided with a room in his own house. Mr. O'Hanlon undoubtedly regarded himself as a lucky man. Apart from the convenience, it was a privilege for anybody to be in close contact with such a wise and spiritual man. Fr. Toher and Fr. Creedon, Legion spiritual directors, also dropped in from time to time and, of course, Frank Sweeney, the S.V.P. president.

No doubt, nearly all the major spiritual enterprises of that time for which Irish lay persons were responsible were discussed in Mr. Lalor's house. Surely, the Holy Spirit hovered over that dwelling in Blackrock, on those Sundays, for under that roof were gathered saintly men who were busy with their Father's business.

After the Sunday lunch, they sat around the fire while coffee was served. The atmosphere was pleasant and jovial. Then, after coffee, Mr. Lalor and Frank went for a walk. Both had been great readers, especially of spiritual books, and now the conversation was mostly on religious topics. Frank was edified and encouraged when he found that Mr. Lalor also practised the True Devotion to the Blessed Virgin as preached by St. Louis Marie de Montfort.

After their walk, which was refreshing for soul and body, the two men returned to the house for tea. Then, shortly afterwards, Frank cycled back to his duties in the Morning Star Hostel. He knew that, inevitably, many prob-

Enter Mr. Lalor

lems awaited him but he felt he could tackle them with enthusiasm and energy. His "spiritual batteries" had, so to speak, been recharged.

• • • • •

From Glasgow Frank took the train south. He made a stop at Newcastle-on-Tyne in the north of England. There he met Nellie Gaughan, a young schoolteacher who had once come to visit him at his house in Dublin. She was, some time later, instrumental in establishing the Legion in that area. Then he went to London where he had a most fruitful interview with Cardinal Bourne. The Cardinal was most enthusiastic and sanctioned the introduction of the Legion in his diocese. The first English praesidium was actually started a year later, i.e. in 1929, with the co-operation of the Rev. Mother Woodlock, of the Sacred Heart Convent in Hammersmith.

After that interview with Cardinal Bourne, Frank had one more appointment in London; it was with Mr. Lalor, who, by this time, was over 70 years old. In Frank's eyes he was a venerable and saintly man and now he was coming to London to meet Frank. They had a plan that thrilled both of them. But first Mr. Lalor had to keep some appointments in London in connection with his tobacco business and Frank accompanied him on his rounds.

Business completed, the two men were now free to carry out their plan. And their plan was to make an enclosed three-day Retreat in the Carthusian Monastery of Parkminster. The quiet, prayerful atmosphere was an oasis in the desert to Frank. They were the only two outsiders in the monastery. Although they sat opposite each other at meals, they did not speak during the three days.

When they arrived at the monastery, Fr. Paschal Geoffries, the guestmaster, asked Frank: "Mr. Duff, is there any particular topic you would like me to preach about during your Retreat? What are your leanings?"

Undoubtedly, Frank would have loved to say: "Father, speak to us about Our Lady," but he didn't say that. He feared that Fr. Paschal might not take too kindly to that suggestion. Instead, Frank mentioned another subject

FRANK DUFF

which particularly interested him, namely, the Sacred Liturgy.

"Father," he said, "it would be wonderful if you could speak to us about the Sacred Liturgy."

Fr. Paschal was a bit taken aback.

"No, no," he said, "you must know Our Lady before anything else. Our Lady is at the foundation of all Christian understanding and spirit. If she is left out, you are bankrupt and you won't understand anything else."

An unbelievable stroke of divine Providence to have such a Retreat-Master, thought Frank.

All the 12 lectures of the Retreat were on the subject of Our Blessed Lady, exclusively. They were purely theological and Fr. Paschal gave the reasons why we must be truly devoted to the Virgin Mary. To Frank, they were an inspiration. The lectures filled in some gaps in his knowledge and gave him an even greater appreciation of the role of Our Lady in the sanctification of souls. He now had a burning desire to find out more and more about the humble Virgin "to whom alone God gave the keys of divine love and the ability to enter the most sublime and secret ways of perfection, and lead others along them."[1]

The weather was beautiful during those three days. Some of the lectures, therefore, were given in the lovely monastery garden and some were given in the greenhouse, but when the sun was high in the heavens and at its hottest, the lectures were given in the shady bowers.

Ever afterwards, Frank retained happy and holy memories of that Retreat. He looked on it as a landmark in his life.

It was a marvelous end to a memorable week, a week in which history was made. It was, too, a period in which the "cellars of divine love" were unlocked by Mary and graces were showered on her devoted servant. He would need all those graces to face the long and difficult road that lay ahead.

NOTE

[1] "True Devotion to the Blessed Virgin" by de Montfort, ch. 1, par. 45.

16 The Morning Star

During the whole Scottish enterprise, Frank never had any doubts about the direction in which he was going or about his undertakings. Nevertheless, such certitude did not in any way ensure that he would be free from worries and difficulties. In fact, in practically all his undertakings, both then and later, there were great obstacles and many tribulations to be faced. What, then, kept him going? What was it that made him persevere? How did he make such extraordinary conquests during his long life?

Frank himself attributed a great number of his "achievements" to the fact that he had some simple principles clear in his mind. The basic one could be summed up as follows: "Never embark on an enterprise by considering all the difficulties you may meet or the opposition you may encounter. If you do so, you will never get anywhere. Of course, you will have to face difficulties and opposition but those aren't the starting points. Instead, when a noble enterprise suggests itself to you, study it well, pray about it, but most of all ask yourself: 'does God want this?' If you decide, under the guidance of the Holy Spirit, that God wants it, then follow it through and know that nothing on this earth can stop you, not because it is you that is involved but because it is God's work. And remember God has to use whatever instrument is available to Him, even if that instrument is only you."

That manner of thinking was, for Frank, a vital ingredient of faith.

Frank was convinced that God wanted Dublin to have a hostel for "down-and-out" men, and that He was asking

FRANK DUFF

him, frail though he was, to undertake the gigantic task of providing a home for these, "the least of Christ's brethren." Most mortals would never have dared to even contemplate such a venture, because of the enormity of the undertaking and the inevitable difficulties that would accompany it. (See now the necessity of Frank's first principle!)

But for Frank, there could be no doubt about it. There was abject poverty in the city of Dublin. There were hostels already established there, but the maximum period for which homeless men were allowed to stay in them was two weeks. Something had to be done for the "down-and-outs" who were chronically and permanently homeless.

Another consideration was that the Protestant proselytizing Centres were "cashing in" on the pitiful plight of the poor people, offering them the bribe of a free meal if they would participate in a Protestant Prayer-Service.

But the most important factor of all, in Frank's mind, was that, seemingly a great number of these "down-and-outs" were nobody's responsibility because they had no fixed abode, and therefore they were spiritually neglected.

Frank proposed his idea of a hostel at a meeting of the S.V.P. Naturally, such a scheme gained their immediate interest. They set up a sub-committee to discuss it. Then the difficulties began to emerge. Some thought the idea was one of sheer fantasy, an impossible venture. Others were enthusiastic. Eventually a document, outlining the scheme, was drawn up to be presented to the S.V.P. for formal approval. It was an honest document which made reference also to the difficulties which they envisaged.

As it was such a highly important matter, it was arranged to call a special meeting for further discussion and to have the Mass of the Holy Spirit offered in the Pro-Cathedral, Marlborough Street, prior to the meeting. Frank was optimistic regarding the outcome.

The day of decision arrived. Then came the shock. Before the meeting began, Mr. Lalor handed a letter to Frank. He opened the letter and then stared incredulously at its contents. It was from Monsignor Wall, the Vicar General, vetoing the proposed scheme. The S.V.P. Society were told not to proceed with the matter.

"I nearly died," was Frank's comment to a friend later.

The Morning Star

However, Frank had his principles clear in his mind. God wanted the hostel. Therefore, some other way must be tried. Whatever the cost, the matter must not be dropped. Out of obedience to the Monsignor, he knew he must not try to persuade the S.V.P. to pursue the matter further. But there was nothing to prevent his setting up a small committee himself. This he did and, week after week, this new committee met to discuss the proposed "Morning Star Hostel" scheme.

It was providential that Mr. P. C. McCarron, Secretary of the Department of Local Government, set up a Commission of Enquiry to examine the problems of homeless and destitute men in Dublin. Frank Duff, who had been a high ranking civil servant of outstanding ability during the British regime and had given sterling service to the Free State Government during the birth and infancy of the State, was also well known for his interest in this problem. He was one of the people consulted by the Commission and asked to submit, in writing, his views on the matter. So impressive were his ideas, that he was asked to attend a meeting of the Commission. After further questioning on points of detail, Mr. O'Connor, the chairman, asked Frank to leave the room while they deliberated further. He left and, while waiting patiently outside for a recall, he chatted with the secretary. When he was summoned back later, he was told that there was unanimous agreement that the case he had made for the homeless was a sound one and that it would be incorporated into the recommendations they were submitting to the Minister.

Subsequently, the Minister for Local Government sent for Mr. Duff.

"Mr. Duff," he said, "I understand that Monsignor Wall is not in favour of the S.V.P. Society opening a hostel for homeless and destitute men, as he fears the financial burden of it could land them in heavy debts."

"That's right."

"What if we took the matter outside the S.V.P., how about that? I am sure they would still be willing to help you and it would dispel any apprehensions of the Monsignor concerning the use of the S.V.P. funds. Would you still be prepared to do business with us?"

FRANK DUFF

"Yes, I would."

"And may I presume the same interest on your part under the new scheme?"

"Yes."

"Can you guarantee the support of your friends?"

"Yes."

Mr. McCarron was very pleased, even relieved. The Government was only too well aware of the magnitude of the problem of the homeless. To provide premises and staff it, would cost millions of pounds. And money was not plentiful then. Besides, where would the Government find staff with the "know-how," or the competence to deal with such an unpredictable and perhaps difficult category of inmates with whom they may be dealing.

Yes, Mr. McCarron was pleased. Here standing before him was a man of proven organizing ability. Moreover, the extraordinary achievements of Mr. Duff in the rescue and rehabilitation of street-girls were recognized and appreciated by the Government.

"Mr. Duff, I can tell you now that the Government completely approves of your plans and your ideas on this matter. Furthermore, we are deeply grateful for the service you are rendering to your city and your country. You can take it, as from this moment, that we are entrusting to your care the large premises of the North Dublin Union Buildings for the purpose of your proposed hostel."

Frank breathed a sigh of relief, and probably, too, a silent prayer of gratitude to God.

"Of course," continued Mr. McCarron, "while the buildings are, I think, suitable, it will be necessary to make some interior alterations. But I am authorized to tell you that the Government will finance the cost of those alterations. They will also look after whatever repairs need to be done, from time to time. And, needless to say, it will be rent free."

Frank Duff and Mr. Lalor were appointed as trustees of the hostel by the Government. One gnawing doubt remained; would Dr. Byrne, the Archbishop of Dublin, have any objections? It was no secret that he had been hitherto less than enthusiastic about some of Mr. Duff's "new-fangled" ideas. Mr. Lalor was "dispatched" to see the Arch-

The Morning Star

bishop. Mr. Lalor was President of the Council of Ireland of the Society of St. Vincent de Paul. Frank waited anxiously. Back came Mr. Lalor, elated.

"You will be glad to know," he told Frank, "that the Archbishop is pleased and, in fact, promised to say Mass for the success of the venture. He expressed a wish that we keep him informed about how it goes."

Frank lost no time in contacting his fellow helpers. They came to inspect the premises. Excitedly, they walked through every room, along every corridor. Plans for alterations were made. There was great rejoicing. The Morning Star Hostel was scheduled to open its doors on the 25th of March, 1927.

17 The Unexpected Guest

The 23rd of March was a day of great activity, with much coming and going, in Morning Star Avenue. Frank sold his house in Dartmouth Square, and now he and the other members of his family were taking up residence in a large Victorian house just a few doors away from the Morning Star Hostel, formerly the North Dublin Union.

Frank's mother, now aged sixty-three, was still hale and hearty. It was a bit of an upset for her to be uprooted once more but she was a calm, gentle person who took everything "in her stride." Had she been a proud person, undoubtedly she would have regretted leaving the rather "posh" area of Dartmouth Square. After all, her new neighbors, the "down-and-outs" of the Morning Star Hostel, would be speaking quite a different language to that which she was accustomed to hearing. She couldn't really have liked the move but she was a practical, matter-of-fact sort of person. By this time she had geared her life-style to accommodate Frank and his work, so when Frank judged that this move was necessary, she resignedly fell in with his plans.

Cupboards, tables, chairs, beds, etc., were being transported up the avenue, and, of course, cases and cases of books.

That night of March 23rd, 1927, was one that remained vivid in Frank's memory for the rest of his life. He was very, very tired. Not only was there the physically tiring work of lifting the furniture and trying to arrange it in the different rooms, but there was also the tedium and mental strain caused by the opposition to his project and by the

The Unexpected Guest

uncertainties concerning the official "go ahead" for the proposed hostel.

No more could be done that night anyhow. The rest of the family retired to bed. It was after midnight but Frank still had to say his entire Office, and that prayer, which would normally take about one and a half hours would take very much longer on this occasion because of his great tiredness. He was exhausted. Nevertheless, he opened his breviary and began to pray.

And it was then he heard it! A terrible howling. In spite of his impaired hearing, he was quite sure about it. A spine-chilling howling as of a dog but with a weird, uncanny element in it. Frank was too exhausted to investigate. He felt sure that if he looked out through the window, he wouldn't be able to endure what he might see. He just went on saying his prayers.

The following morning when he came down, he found a large dog lying on the porch outside the front door. The dog was absolutely without hair. It was a horrible sight. Could it be, thought Frank, that the devil had possessed the dead body of a dog in order to frighten him off the course he had chosen? The very thought was terrifying but even if that interpretation was the correct one, could it not also mean that the hostel was destined to give the devil something to howl about; might it not be an indication of great graces to come through the hostel? At any rate, Frank was going straight ahead with his plans.

Two days later, on the 25th of March, the great feast of the Annunciation, the hostel for homeless men opened its doors. The hostel was staffed by a committee of men, many of whom were S.V.P. members. The committee met regularly, held their meetings and ran the hostel more or less along Legion of Mary lines. Within a short time, in fact, they set up a Legion praesidium to take charge of the hostel. This was the first men's praesidium to be set up in Dublin.

There was no shortage of "customers" for the hostel. The "down-and-outs," the alcoholics, the outcasts and the friendless, all came in big numbers and found a ready welcome and a permanent home. In order to restore to the residents at least some little dignity and self-respect, each

FRANK DUFF

resident was obliged to pay the very small fee of eight pence per day, and this was a strict rule. Problems, of course, there were in abundance. In many cases, the residents were responsible citizens who, perhaps through no fault of their own, were downright poor and destitute; but the legionaries had also to contend with refractory characters who swore and fought and thieved and were often drunk. The hostel was able to accommodate two hundred men and it was regularly full.

The fighting sometimes was terrible and the legionaries were often attacked. It wasn't normally possible, or feasible, to send for the gardai (police). Especially in the hostel's early days, Frank often wondered, when he was going into the hostel in the evening, if he would be in a fit condition physically to walk out at the end of the day. Each day he ran the risk of having his legs broken. But his prowess at athletics stood him in good stead. He was very fit, and unusually strong for a man of his slender build. Soon, the men learned to have a healthy respect for him. Many of them had literally been floored by him in a fight. No one ever got the better of him. And in all his years in the hostel, the most he ever suffered were a few broken ribs.

But there is something else that casts a light on his strength. He had put himself into the hands of God and God did certainly protect him from all harm. Furthermore, Frank was quite sure that God at that time gave him a special strength, because in those days strength was an absolute necessity for the running of the hostel.

Years previously, when Frank had joined the S.V.P. Society, the thing that had captivated him most was the great emphasis that was placed on the message of Christ in the gospels: "As long as you did it to one of these my least brethren, you did it to me." It was the realization of the stark truth of that teaching that had, by God's grace, transformed Frank Duff from a very average Catholic into one of the greatest apostles of the twentieth century. But in the meantime, his life of prayer and faith had grown prodigiously, and he had reached an extraordinary degree of understanding and appreciation of that teaching. Every destitute man that stood before Frank was, indeed, Christ in

The Unexpected Guest

disguise. And Frank realized that it was not just a duty but an extraordinary privilege for him and for other legionaries to serve Christ in these poor people.

Because of this realization, Frank refused to regard the inmates of the hostel as "down-and-outs." "Down," yes, but "out," no. These people, in spite of their sad condition, had a unique dignity as members of Christ's Mystical Body that poverty or destitution could not efface. Henceforth, the so-called "down-and-outs" would be called "residents" of the hostel.

And so in the midst of these often noisy, troublesome residents, Frank was not only the man with the iron fist but he was also a man of extraordinary gentleness and kindness and patience. His gentle appeals, his gracious smile, his unassuming manner and his constant good humor won the respect and even the affection of the toughest of tough men. The numbers he raised up from the depths of degradation are beyond reckoning; the numbers he reclaimed from the mire of sin and vice are known only to God.

And, to-day, in the hostel chapel, the lovely poetry of the psalms can be heard rising in a great crescendo of prayer to God, as the indoor legionary brothers recite the Divine Office in common. The setting is not that of a Cistercian monastery but surely the angels join in the great paean of thanksgiving to God. And what a joy it is to our heavenly Mother, the Morning Star!

• • • • •

In the nearby house which had now become the Duff home, things began to fall into shape. Mrs. Duff was busy putting the house in order. Isabel was still in poor health but she was able to give her mother a little help around the house. The other two girls, Sara Geraldine and Ailis, had now qualified as doctors. John was often absent from home because of the demands of his job and also his social commitments.

Mrs. Duff loved flowers and within a rather short time she had brought harmony and beauty into the garden plot at the back of the house, from which she provided flowers

FRANK DUFF

for the Legion altar at the praesidia meetings. She never actually joined the praesidium, as she preferred to be in the background. But she was a tremendous support for Frank in all his enterprises. Her life and her interests were intertwined with his. When he, in consultation with the priests and other officers, was writing the Legion Handbook, he brought it to her, chapter by chapter, to be corrected by her. If there was a word or a phrase that wasn't entirely appropriate in its context, she told him so. Her mind had lost none of its brilliance.

It was a marvelous blessing for Frank that whenever he had visitors or callers—and they were many—he could always invite them to share a family meal. He knew it meant extra work for his mother but he also knew that she was glad to do it. In fact, she expected him to rely on her absolutely for her cooperation in this as in so many other matters.

One night Frank had a rather strange experience. It was very late, 1:00 a.m. There was a knock at the door. Frank had not yet gone to bed. He went downstairs and opened the door. Standing there in the cold was a young boy, about twelve years old. The boy wanted shelter for the night. He was a dirty enough little urchin, with unkempt hair and dishevelled appearance. Frank took him in and arranged a bed for him. When he awoke in the morning, he found, to his surprise, that the boy had already gone. The servant girl said to Frank:

"Oh, Mr. Duff, the most beautiful boy I ever saw passed down this morning and went out."

Neither Frank nor any of the household ever saw the boy again. That was the end of the story, but many years later when Frank related it to a friend, the friend asked:

"Mr. Duff, wasn't that a rather extraordinary matter. Have you a theory about it?"

"Well, I have," he replied. "I must begin, of course, by telling you that I have no way of knowing for certain who that beautiful boy was. But I have often wondered 'is it possible the Boy Jesus came to my home?' In the Gospel, we read that the Boy Jesus was lost for some days in Jerusalem. Nobody has ever known where Jesus spent those nights. Could it be that he deigned to come and spend one

The Unexpected Guest

night in my house? You know that time poses no problem for God. A thousand years are as one day for him. At any rate, of one thing I am sure and that is, that whether it was the Boy Jesus in person or not is not the important thing. The important thing is that it was surely designed by God to be a lesson to me to keep in mind that in every man, woman and child who knocks at my door, Christ is really present and appealing for help and compassion."

And so it was that day after day, year after year, Frank was the humble servant of the poor men in the Morning Star Hostel, receiving them at the reception desk, cutting bread for them, pouring for them mugs of strong hot tea, preparing the beds, and listening patiently to their tales of woe.

And this was only one of three hostels he would run. The Sancta Maria was already going strong. And soon he would open another women's hostel, the Regina Coeli. In addition to this, he carried out a many-sided apostolate to souls privately.

● ● ● ● ●

Many years later, on a cold December morning, Frank Duff was walking with a priest friend along Morning Star Avenue. Standing nearby, was a resident of the hostel, a strong, powerfully built man.

"Good morning, Father, and good morning, Mr. Duff," said the man.

"And good morning to you, too."

When Frank and the priest had passed out of earshot of the man, Frank related an incident that had happened a short time before. It could be summed up as follows:

Frank was walking along when a man — let's call him John X — approached him and suddenly, by way of a joke, pinned Frank's hands to his side and put his own hands in his "victim's" pockets. "Now, Mr. Duff," said John X, "I've got you where I want you and I could rob you if I wished; I've got you helpless." True enough, Frank was helpless with his hands pinned to his sides by this powerful man who had once been a commando in the British army.

Frank knew, of course, that John X wouldn't rob him.

FRANK DUFF

The man, in fact, had a great respect for Frank. But Frank did, nevertheless, get rather a shock as well as getting quite annoyed, because he had some precious things in his pockets. He had with him at the time a relic of the True Cross and also rosary beads which had a special sentimental value for him. He managed to worm his way out of the grip of John X and then the roles were quickly reversed. John X was caught in Frank's vice-like grip and felt himself sinking to the ground. Then Frank relaxed his grip and allowed John X to go free.

Embarrassed and humiliated at being overpowered by an elderly man — Frank was eighty-six years old at the time — John X said:

"Of course you took advantage of me, Mr. Duff. Now let's try it out on level terms," and he stretched out his right hand in a challenge.

"Well," thought Frank, "if a man needs a lesson, he must be given a lesson." And he took the challenge, stretching out his right hand to take John X's right hand. The two opposing hands closed upon one another. Both men squeezed and squeezed. Then, in stupefaction, John X found himself slowly bending backwards. His mighty strength was once again reduced to nil. Mr. Duff was the stronger man.

The man had been taught his lesson. Frank released his powerful grip on his opponent's hand and helped him to his feet. Then in a gentle, though reprimanding way he said: "John, you know you shouldn't do things like that."

When Frank had told the priest his story, the priest said:

"Mr. Duff, you once told me that in the early days of the Morning Star Hostel a special help had been given to you 'from above' because it was necessary for you in the running of the hostel."

"That's correct, Father."

"Do you mean now, when you tell me this story about you and John X, that you were once again given back that strength for the occasion?"

"No, that's not exactly what I am saying. What I am telling you is that that strength has never been taken away from me."

18 First Visit to Rome

Father John Hays was a curate in the Archdiocese of Cashel and Emly, in the south of Ireland. He was a priest and preacher of rare quality. His eloquent sermons could set even the coldest hearts on fire with the love of God and man, and his compassion for the less fortunate was proverbial. He won his place in Irish history as the founder of "Muinntir na Tíre," an organization set up to foster community progress through brotherly charity, co-operation and enterprise, particularly among the rural community.

In 1930, the Pallottine Fathers invited Fr. Hayes to preach the Advent course of sermons in San Silvestro in Capite, in Rome. In his sermons, he spoke in vivid and dramatic terms of the work the Legion of Mary was doing in Dublin. The Vicar of Rome, Cardinal Marchetti-Selvaggiani, approached him afterwards and expressed great interest in the Legion work. He suggested to Fr. Hayes that he should ask Mr. Duff to come to Rome to speak in more detail on the organization.

The message was duly delivered. For Mr. Duff it was more than a thrill, it was a sign. He said to himself: "Well now, this will be my introduction to Rome, it can be most advantageous to meet such a person as Cardinal Marchetti." Then he began to think of the possibility of an audience with the Pope himself, Pius XI. Having reflected on the idea, he decided that he really must see the Pope. Pope Pius XI had been making urgent appeals to lay people to become involved in Catholic Action. The Legion of Mary must be brought to his notice, thought Frank.

But there were problems. Letters of introduction would

FRANK DUFF

be necessary. Frank knew he could not approach the Archbishop of Dublin for a letter of introduction, because the Legion of Mary was not as yet officially sanctioned in the diocese of Dublin. The Archbishop was, of course, kept informed of all Legion activities in his diocese and he had promised to consider giving his official approval, but as yet it had not been granted.

In fact, one of Frank's great crosses in those days was that a number of the clergy seemed to resent the coming into existence of this organization for lay apostles, some even going so far as to allege that Frank Duff was anti-clerical, that he was taking over the functions of the priest, that the legionaries were "busy-bodies," and so on. In time, of course, they would come to appreciate that the Legion placed itself utterly at the service of the priest and was absolutely loyal and obedient in every possible way to Church authorities, and that, in fact, the Legion was offering itself to the priest as extra arms, extra limbs by means of which he could reach out effectively to many more souls. But most of all, priests would in time learn the Legion system whereby very ordinary people could be given a solid understanding of the great truths of our religion, could become marvelous apostles, and could be guided into paths of great, even heroic sanctity.

But that appreciation did not come overnight. And Frank Duff had sufficient spiritual insight to realize that in the Cross lies the best sign of hope and that, furthermore where there is sufficient faith all obstacles can be overcome.

However, just at that moment, Frank had to face reality. Without a letter from his Archbishop, it seemed impossible to secure a private audience with the Pope. But for Frank, the word "impossible" just didn't exist. He would take some step, in faith, and "force" God's hand. ("Symbolic action" it is called in the Legion Handbook.)

There was one such step that Frank could and did take. His great friend, Mr. William Cosgrave, who in 1922 had authorized the transfer to the Legion of the premises that became the Sancta Maria Hostel, had since become Taoiseach (Prime Minister) of the Irish Free State. Mr. Cosgrave was very well informed about the whole history of

First Visit to Rome

the Legion. He was also a very devout catholic. In 1925 the Pope conferred on him the Order of the Grand Cross. Frank now went to him and explained what he needed, and Mr. Cosgrave, appreciating the delicacy of the situation, gave him a personal letter of introduction to the Pope. This letter opened the doors of the Vatican to Frank.

Monsignor O'Brien of Liverpool accompanied him to Rome. Frank was very excited about Rome. His profound knowledge of Roman history, both remote and recent, enabled him to appreciate so many sacred places. The Colosseum, soaked long ago with the blood of the martyrs, the catacombs, the great basilicas, the old churches, the Vatican, all thrilled him to the depths of his being. But his excitement was moderated, somewhat, by the awesome prospect of talking to the Pope! He knew, of course, that the Pope would by this time have been "briefed" about the Legion. Frank had already presented his "case" in elaborate detail to some cardinals and other officials of the Roman curia, whose duty it then was to assess the organization, present a summary form of the discussions to the Pope and make their recommendations.

In due time, Frank and Monsignor O'Brien were ushered into the presence of His Holiness, Pope Pius XI. The audience lasted twenty minutes. That meeting of the Pope with the founder was a landmark in the history of the Legion of Mary.

Pope Pius XI was known as the Pope of Catholic Action, repeatedly appealing that the role of the laity in the Church's mission be recognized. The bishops of dioceses around the world were most anxious to implement the Pope's wishes, but they kept asking him: "What exactly are we to do?" It was with great interest, therefore, that the Pope now listened to Frank Duff. Frank noted that his Holiness was quite serious and didn't even smile. He asked Frank many questions about the Legion. Then came the big moment!

"What is it you wish me to do for you?" the Pope asked.

This was the very question Frank was hoping to hear and he had tentatively drafted a carefully worded reply. He answered:

"If we could say that it was the personal desire of Your

FRANK DUFF

Holiness that the Legion of Mary would spread over the whole world, this would be a great mode of propaganda for spreading the Legion."

Every word of that sentence had been thoughtfully prepared.

There was a pause. The Pope then said:

"With all my heart I express that desire."

Frank's joy knew no bounds. He knew that from that moment the Legion was safe. He could hardly wait to get back to Dublin to plan for world conquest. It was 1931.

●●●●●

The Legion was safe. Yes, but only to a certain extent. If Frank thought that the encouragement he got from the Pope would speed up official sanction for the Legion in his home diocese of Dublin, he was very much mistaken. The prejudices against the Legion were too deep to be easily dissolved. The ideas of the lay apostolate that the Legion was propounding seemed, at that time, to go far too far. A number of the senior clergy were genuinely alarmed. "My goodness, it will be impossible to control these people," "meddling in the affairs of the priest," "they will want to run the parish soon," "why go upsetting things?" These were the fears in the minds of some of the priests, and some senior priests were putting pressure on the Archbishop to suppress the Legion.

Frank's intense study of the doctrine of the Mystical Body, no doubt aided and inspired by his life of prayer and faith, led him to a clear and comprehensive understanding of the role of every baptized person in the Church. The precise problem was that the clergy of his time — with exceptions, of course — were either unable or unwilling to accept his ideas. To quote Dr. Michael O'Carroll, "The established clerical order did not favour initiative from the laity."[1]

It was not surprising, therefore, that for many years Frank was "in the wars" with the ecclesiastical authorities in Dublin, but his skilful diplomacy secured at least a measure of toleration for the infant organization. Still, the threat of closure that hung over the Legion caused him in-

First Visit to Rome

tense agony. He never doubted the great work that the priests were doing for souls—he always had the greatest respect for priests—but he saw that much more could be done with the help of the Legion. To see what he considered to be God's designs thwarted, or at least hampered, was a torment to his sensitive soul.

The Legion continued however to develop and expand, though not without many trials and disappointments. Sometimes, the prospects looked so hopeless that Frank's only ground for persevering was sheer faith. "I saw clearly," he said, "that God wanted the Legion." Therefore, he would persevere whatever the cost to himself, and he realized he would have to pay a price. "I tell you, most solemnly, unless a wheat grain falls on the ground and dies, it remains only a single grain; but if it dies, it yields a rich harvest" (John 12:24). There would have to be a long, slow process of dying to self. To become more Christ-like, he would have to have more sacrifice, more prayer, more patience, more humility. Yes, especially humility, as "all other virtues derive their value from it; only when humility exists will God bestow His favours."[2] Besides, if he hoped to be formed into the likeness of Christ, he could hardly expect to be spared the humiliations and frustrations that Christ had to suffer.

Many more years were to pass before the Legion Handbook was eventually given the "imprimatur" in the diocese of Dublin. In the meantime, Frank was learning many valuable lessons about holiness, and he was learning the hard way. But his determination remained undiminished.

NOTES

[1] cf. Maria Legionis, no. 1 of 1981.
[2] Legion of Mary Handbook, p. 107.

19 Regina Coeli

Mr. William T. Cosgrave was the Irish Prime Minister, or President of the Executive Council of the Irish Free State, during the first decade of Independence. It was he, in consultation with his Cabinet, who had given some of the semi-derelict buildings of the Old North Dublin Union, in trust, to Frank Duff and the Legion of Mary for the purpose of setting up the hostel for destitute men, known as the Morning Star. Having seen the successful outcome of this project, President Cosgrave and his Cabinet allocated another large area of the North Dublin Union complex to Mr. Duff for the purpose of setting up a hostel for destitute women and unmarried mothers. Thus, when the necessary repairs and renovations were completed, the Regina Coeli Hostel threw open its doors of welcome and hospitality to these distressed women.

Whereas the Morning Star operated on the basis of bed, supper and breakfast, the Regina Coeli gave full-time accommodation to the women and their children. But, again, Frank was insistent that any women taken into the hostel—they would be called "residents"—must make some contribution towards their upkeep, albeit a nominal one. This was intended to help restore their self-respect. Those who had no money and no employment were provided with the opportunity to earn the required minimum by working in the special timber yard operated by the Morning Star Hostel.

It was necessary, of course, to find legionary sisters who would give their services full-time to the hostel. These legionaries were called "Indoor Sisters." Their daily programs included Mass and Holy Communion, the recitation of the Divine Office as well as the Rosary and the Legion prayers. For the most part, however, theirs was an active apostolate

Regina Coeli

par excellence—catering for two hundred women and children; washing, cleaning, cooking and a "hundred other things" as well as taking an active interest in the spiritual welfare of the women, many of whom had got very careless about the practice of their religion.

"It's a woman's world in there!" someone said. But, in fact, Frank Duff was very much part of the scene. He was gifted with his hands and became the "handyman" around the place, mending doors, windows, crockery, pots and pans and "every blessed thing." He was the one who bought the furniture, who arbitrated in quarrels, who protected the women. A rough, strong man once came and attempted to beat up a woman against whom he had some grudge. He hadn't reckoned on meeting Frank who suddenly appeared on the scene, gave the man a good beating and then threw him out.

The successful running of such a hostel naturally involved many difficulties. Frank used to say that the shadow of the Cross always hung over the Regina Coeli, so many were the problems that were encountered. It was truly run on faith. And yet, not only did it survive but it prospered. Indeed, it was a remarkably happy place. Admittedly, some of the residents were very difficult characters but the majority were really good, respectable people who had "come down" in the world due perhaps to a drink problem or to the "slings and arrows of outrageous fortune." They were very content in the hostel. It had the atmosphere of a true home; there was security and kindness: they knew somebody cared.

A "discreet" marriage bureau was also in operation there. Sometimes, a respectable but poor lad would knock at the front door and ask the legionary sister if it was possible to arrange an introduction to some resident who might be a willing and suitable life-partner for him. Usually he got his request. Introductions were arranged and if, after some time, the couple had a mutual attraction, a marriage was arranged.

The residents were very faithful to their Sunday Mass and, indeed, a number of them became daily Mass-goers. Their sons were trained as altar servers.

The children of Regina Coeli were sent regularly to

FRANK DUFF

school. The regular contact that Frank and the sister legionaries had with these children bore great fruit, and when professional social workers from at home and abroad expressed amazement that the hostel, with its very limited resources, could produce such first-class citizens—delinquency is practically unknown among those who "graduate" from the Regina Coeli—Frank would smile and ask: "And do you wish to know the secret of our success?" After much conjecture on their part, he would supply the answer: "Real reverence for the child; each is a member of Christ's Mystical Body and must be treated and trained accordingly, with the very necessary help of Mary, the Mother of that Body."

Over four thousand children have been brought up and nurtured in this atmosphere of the Regina Coeli, a credit to their faith and fatherland.

Frank knew all the children by name. He was very fond of them and loved chatting with them and even, sometimes, teasing them.

One sunny day, Frank was in the front room of Regina Coeli looking out the window—no doubt with affection and pride—on a group of the Regina children who were playing in front of the building. One boy, named Frankie, aged about eleven years, seemed to be the self-appointed leader of the group. He was making a lot of noise. Frank Duff couldn't resist having his bit of fun and also taking the youngster "down a peg." He went into the kitchen of the Regina Coeli, picked up a mug from the draining board and filled it with water. He "eyed" the open window. Then, realizing he needed more "runway" to ensure that the water would be "on target" he opened the door of the adjoining room and backed into it with his mug. This enabled him to "let fly" through the window and poor Frankie got a dowsing. The roars, it was said later, were "something awful." Frank, holding the tell-tale mug behind his back, chuckled heartily to himself as little Frankie came to try to identify the perpetrator of the awful deed, saw Frank at the window and shouted out: "It was Miss Daly done it, Mr. Duff; it was Miss Daly, I saw her." The said Miss Daly was, of course, far from the scene of the "crime" at the time!

So engrossed was Frank in his bit of fun, that when he

Regina Coeli

backed into the adjoining room, he did not see anybody there. Now, suddenly, he got an uncomfortable feeling that he wasn't quite alone in the room. He turned around and faced the stupefied stares of a group of legionary ladies who were in the middle of their praesidium meeting. Mumbling an awkward word of apology, he made an undignified and speedy exit from the room

Fr. Brian Byrne, the Spiritual Director of the praesidium, was the most stunned of all. When he found his power of speech again, he said: "Is that the man we saw with the sanctimonious face at the Concilium on Sunday last?!"

For years afterward, Frank would roar with laughter as he recounted the incident, giving special emphasis to Fr. Byrne's remark about him.

Frank's love of children was so great that one day he surprised Mary Rowe, one of the legionaries in Regina Coeli, by saying to her: "Do you know, Mary, I think if I ever got married I would lose my religion?"

She looked at him in astonishment and said: "Mr. Duff, how can you say such a thing?"

"Well," he explained, "I would be so intensely wrapped up in my children that I'm sure I'd forget everything else."

A rather strange remark, but it does at least indicate the intensity of his love for children.

On one occasion, one of the residents got very ill; it was considered advisable to send her to hospital.

"Please don't send me to hospital," she said. "I am not going to get better, I know I'm dying. Please let me die at home." The legionaries' tears of sorrow for the woman were mingled with tears of joy that she had called the Regina Coeli her home. And, indeed, they did not send her to the hospital. They cared for her tenderly until the end. She had a happy and holy death with the legionaries and the residents at her bedside.

The pattern was repeated countless times after that. They died with dignity in an atmosphere of holiness and affection, and souls that otherwise might have gone astray were guided safely home.

20 Poor Old Lizzie

One of the most difficult cases ever encountered by Frank Duff was that of Lizzie McDermott. Lizzie was once a street-girl and she had reached terrible depths of depravity.

Frank saw her for the first time when he was picketing outside 6 ½ Whitefriars Street. He watched her approaching the proselytizing Centre and she looked wretched and miserable. She was clothed in rags and had a filthy appearance. As she walked past him, he handed her the "Messenger of the Sacred Heart," a small catholic booklet. She took it, glanced at it and then, realizing it was a religious magazine, threw it back in his face.

Lizzie came regularly to that place. Frank got to know her name. He spoke to her gently.

"Lizzie," he said, "you know you shouldn't betray your religion by going into that place."

She never answered him. Every time she came, he approached her in the same gentle manner, appealing to her with a few kind words. She came week after week, month after month, year after year. Not once in all that time did she answer him or speak to him. She simply ignored him.

He always had his rosary beads in his hands when picketing, saying a few "ave's" when he had some free moments, but he made sure that the beads were well out of Lizzie's reach when she was passing him, as she would snatch them, if possible, and spit on the crucifix.

The years went by. Then one Sunday morning, Lizzie came as usual to the Centre for her breakfast. Once again, she ignored Frank and entered the building. To his surprise, however, she reappeared after a few moments and

Poor Old Lizzie

walked directly towards him. He thought she was going to attack him physically but she didn't. Instead, she stood in front of him and said:

"Mr. Duff, do you know what day today is?"

"Yes, Lizzie, I do indeed."

"It's Passion Sunday, isn't it, Mr. Duff?"

"That's right, Lizzie, it's Passion Sunday."

"Well, Mr. Duff, when I was in there just now, I thought of that and I'm never going to go in there again."

"Oh! Lizzie, you're a great girl. May God grant that you'll keep your resolution, but I'm afraid you won't unless you settle yourself up."

"Do you mean I should go to Confession?"

"Yes, that's what I mean."

"Very well then, I'll go to Confession."

Frank, grateful for the merciful ways of the Lord, decided to bring Lizzie over to Father Creedon who was a curate in St. Nicholas of Myra, Francis Street. They presented a strange contrast as they walked along the city streets, Frank looking neat and clean, Lizzie, an ugly picture of unkempt wretchedness.

"Lizzie," Frank said before they reached the church, "you have lost your breakfast this morning and I haven't had mine yet. We'll drop in to "The Cozy" and have breakfast together." "The Cozy" was a little cafe in Francis Street.

Fr. Creedon was a big man and looked even bigger in his Mass vestments. He was just about to enter the church to celebrate Mass when Frank and Lizzie met him in the sacristy. After some brief introductions, Fr. Creedon turned to Lizzie and said: "If you will be so kind as to remain here until the Mass is finished, I will give you my full attention. Frank waited with her in case she might be tempted to depart. When Mass was finished, Lizzie went to Confession and made her peace with God. She was persuaded also to enter the Sancta Maria Hostel and make a new start.

It would have been too much to expect that Lizzie would be changed from a "wolf to a lamb" overnight. Her past behaviour had left its mark on her character. Frank felt that she would always be a problem case. And indeed she was. She did not stay very long in the Sancta Maria; her

FRANK DUFF

nature was too restless, her spirit too violent. She moved from place to place and eventually Fr. Creedon persuaded her to enter the Regina Coeli Hostel.

"That," said Frank, "was at once a joyful and a sorrowful day for the Regina Coeli;" joyful because the Regina Coeli was especially established by the Legion to serve the most destitute type of women, and who was more destitute than poor Lizzie? Besides, who else would take her? It was at the same time a "sorry" day for Regina Coeli, because Lizzie was an inveterate trouble-maker and could make life extremely difficult for others. The deciding factor in taking her was that she had an immortal soul which must be saved, whatever the cost.

Lizzie loved glass windows and mirrors. They were very breakable! She vented her rage on these objects and the devastating sound of crashing glass seemed to please her very much. Her first "victim" was a very large mirror that Frank had bought at an auction. He had got it cheaply, because that kind of mirror was not fashionable at that time. It was affixed to the wall in the women's large recreation room. Frank's policy was to let the women see themselves, particularly the most dishevelled, as others saw them. "The first step in rehabilitating a woman," he said, "is to stimulate in her an interest in her personal appearance."

One day, Lizzie was walking towards that large mirror; she had her tea-mug in her hand. Then came the action. To quote her own words: "I saw a terrible looking woman coming towards me with a tea-mug in her hand. I had to get in my blow first." And indeed she did, shattering the mirror into a thousand pieces. It was, of course, herself she had seen in the mirror. This was only one of the many violent incidents that occurred as a result of her irascible temper. But the legionaries knew they must continue to love her, despite her depravity. Our Lady had assigned them to serve her Son in that poor creature.

The years passed, but, in spite of her terrible ways, Lizzie was never evicted. The Regina Coeli had become her home, the only real home she had ever known. Yet never once in all those years did she say "thanks," or show the slightest sign of gratitude. But she did receive the Sacraments from time to time.

Poor Old Lizzie

As she got older, she got weaker. Then one morning, she was found in an unconscious state in bed and was taken to the South Dublin Union Hospital in James Street. She never recovered sufficiently to be able to leave the hospital, but she was content there and was always pleased when her friends came to visit her; her friends were, of course, the legionaries from the Regina Coeli.

Then one day Lizzie got a great grace; it was the grace to say "thank you." Probably she would have liked to say it long before that but her stubborn boldness and proud nature prevented her from doing so.

Mary Rowe and May Mortell, two of the legionaries, came to see her. She "put her pride in her pocket" and thanked them for everything and especially for putting up with her for so long. Legionaries had been helping her for thirty long years.

"I'm so happy now," she said, "and I have been receiving the Sacraments regularly. God has been patient with me. I am very ill, but I don't mind dying now." She paused and then said humbly, "Will you do me a favour?"

"Yes, of course," they replied.

"Then tell Mr. Duff that poor Lizzie McDermott wants him to know that only for him, she would never have been able to save her soul. I'm so grateful to him, though maybe he doesn't know that, because I've cursed him so often in the past."

"Well, we'll tell him, Lizzie."

"Do you think Mr. Duff would come to visit me? Just to have him at my bedside would make me die happy. And in case he can't come, will you tell him that even if he never saved another single soul, 'twas worth founding the Legion of Mary just to save Lizzie McDermott."

When the two ladies reported back to Frank and told him about Lizzie's request, he asked:

"Is it very urgent?"

"No, Mr. Duff, it's not very urgent; she's not in any immediate danger of death."

"Oh, that's good, because I'm engaged on something very important at the moment; it would be impossible for me to break off just now; it will take at least another week. And then I will go to visit her."

FRANK DUFF

To Frank's own surprise, the work he was engaged in "petered out" unexpectedly, the very next afternoon, and later he reflected on that amazing fact. Mindful of Lizzie's request, he at once got up on his bicycle and cycled over to the hospital. He located the ward where Lizzie was and was surprised to see a nun kneeling at the bedside reciting the prayers for the dying. A number of the healthier patients in the ward were also around the bedside. Yes, Lizzie was dying; Frank knelt down and joined the prayers and in his mind was the absolute and clear conviction "I was brought up here to be present at her death." And while he was there Lizzie McDermott died.

All the insults and sufferings that Frank had endured over the years because of that pitiful creature now seemed as sweet joys in the light of the wonderful mercy of God.

21 Encircling the Globe

Frank Duff was quite excited when a letter arrived from the pastor of St. Patrick's Parish, Raton, New Mexico, asking him for information about the Legion of Mary. This was the first such inquiry to come from the U.S.A. The pastor had read a news item about the Legion in the "Denver Review," written by Father Joseph Donovan, who had seen the Legion in operation when he was visiting Dublin in the summer of 1931. The result was that the first Legion praesidium in the U.S.A. was set up in Raton, on the 27th of November of that year.

The following year, bishops and priests from all over the world came to Dublin to attend the International Eucharistic Congress. Many of them were introduced to the Legion during their stay and when they returned, started it in their own dioceses. Thus the Legion was set up in Los Angeles and St. Louis. Celia Shaw, a Dublin legionary, paid a brief visit to the States to help with the formation of praesidia. Then a wealthy San Francisco businessman, Mr. Bartley Oliver, requested that an envoy be sent to extend the Legion all over the U.S.A. and he offered to pay all expenses.

Mary Duffy, the legionary chosen to go as the first envoy, had nine years' Legion experience behind her. A little apprehensive but yet enthusiastic, she was confident that her mission would be successful. The Legion system is basically simple, and priests who desire to have it in their parishes could learn the fundamentals in a very short time. Likewise, they would find it easy enough to train the members. She had vivid recollections of the first meeting she herself attended in Dublin and of the beautiful Legion altar

FRANK DUFF

with the statue of the Immaculate Conception as the centre-piece. She had so often heard Frank Duff stress that a praesidium of the Legion could be imagined as a kind of local presence of Our Lady. Through the praesidium She, the spiritual Mother of all men, would bestow her unique gifts. Hence the importance of the statue as a reminder of that "presence." She remembered, too, the strict discipline at that meeting. Her president had been trained by Mrs. Kirwin, the very first president of the Legion. In a way, the strict discipline surprised her and yet she liked it. After all, it was an army, a spiritual army it is true, but nevertheless an army and one dealing with very important matters, such as grace and souls and evil. If the rules had been introduced merely for the sake of efficiency, they would have been justified. But they had, in fact, a higher value. Just as monks and religious have their own rule of life to help them along the path of holiness, so, in another way, the Legion rules help the members to make solid progress in the virtues, such as humility, obedience, charity, sacrifice and so on.

Mary set sail on the 3rd of June, 1934. As Frank stood on the quayside waving good-bye, he was filled with emotion. He knew the possibilities were immense.

Within a few years, two more Irish legionaries, John Murray and Una O'Byrne, were assigned to join Mary as Legion envoys to the U.S.A. And soon the great push was on all over the New World. They trekked from coast to coast and up into Canada, visiting the bishops to secure the necessary permissions, addressing groups and explaining the essentials, organizing praesidia, training officers, moving further on, then returning to review and to consolidate.

In some places, priests were slow to realize or admit the value of the Legion. The idea of lay people being involved in a spiritual apostolate seemed risky and revolutionary to them. This was thirty years before the Second Vatican Council. That Council would declare: "The Church has not been truly established, and is not yet fully alive, nor is it a perfect sign of Christ among men, unless there exists a laity worthy of the name working along with the hierarchy" (Vat. Co. Missions—21). And again: "Wherever possible, the laity should be prepared, in more immediate coopera-

Encircling the Globe

tion with the hierarchy, to fulfill a special mission of proclaiming the gospel and communicating Christian teachings" (Vat. Co. Missions—21). But back in 1934, the Legion envoys did not have such strong backing as that. However, there were many other priests who welcomed them with open arms and invited them to set up praesidia of the Legion. Bishop Charles Helmsing, spiritual director of the first Senatus in the U.S.A., said: "I cannot recommend the Legion too highly to our priests, religious and laity. I beg no one to despise it because of its simplicity and humility. Please try it."

Through the legionaries, the priest could now multiply himself, as it were, and reach out to very many more souls. There were, for example, many parishioners who belonged to no Church, or practised no religion, and to whom the Gospel must be preached. Then, in every parish there were some catholics who were lapsed. The Lord, the Good Shepherd, must surely need helpers who would "round up" these stray sheep and bring them back to the fold by gentle persuasion. Probably, too, there were elderly, or lonely, or sick people who would appreciate a visit and a helping hand, and this would provide wonderful work for the Junior legionaries.

And Father Roger Mary Charest of the De Montfort Fathers, Long Is., New York, through his bi-monthly magazine, "Queen," constantly emphasized the most valuable treasure of all in the Legion of Mary which is the sanctification of its members, with special emphasis on True Devotion to Mary.

The growth of the Legion in the U.S.A. was phenomenal and it was destined to bring forth great fruit. One priest, Father Edward Kotter, started a praesidium in his parish of St. Louis, in Cincinnati, in 1938 and, during his fourteen years there, received 500 people into the Church. A Legion Comitium in Rockville Centre, New York Senatus, reported that in one year their legionaries had brought 257 lapsed catholics back to the Church. A praesidium of Blacks in Pennsylvania was responsible for 23 people being received into the Church in one year.

And these are only a few of the hundreds of such reports that are received from all parts of the U.S.A.

FRANK DUFF

Monsignor Donnelly of Los Angeles, expressed it beautifully: "The Legion consists of cohorts of disciplined Christians by the thousands, young and old, married and single, with one goal in mind: to share Christ with others." Up in Canada, Archbishop Gordan, O.M.I., addressing the legionaries, said: "I attribute the phenomenal growth of the Legion throughout the world to three basic conditions: personal holiness of the members, a spirit of dedication, a lively devotion to the Mother of God. The Legion must succeed under these conditions."

As the pilgrim Church is by its very nature missionary, it was not unexpected when, after some time, a number of legionaries from the U.S.A. volunteered to help the Legion in its mission work outside their own dioceses and even overseas. Mary Peffley was greatly responsible for establishing the Legion throughout all Pennsylvania. Others went to Central and South America. Fr. Willie Ryan led a small band of legionaries from the Los Angeles Senatus on a peregrinatio to Russia. When Frances Conley from Minnesota wrote to Frank Duff, volunteering to work wherever she was needed, he replied: "Why not Iceland?" And so Frances and another American legionary, Ivy Tominec from Cleveland, Ohio, were among the first volunteers to go as *incolae Mariae* to Iceland.

The idea of envoyship had worked out so well in the U.S.A., that the Concilium, the supreme governing body of the Legion, based in Dublin, decided that, if sufficient funds could be raised, Legion envoys would be sent to other far-away countries. Legionaries in the U.S.A. showed their gratitude for what had been done for them by supplying a large proportion of these funds for the Concilium. It was quite certain now that the Legion was going to encircle the globe.

• • • • •

The Legion in England was growing. It was arranged that a curia would be set up in London. This would supervise the praesidia, train officers, promote new and challenging works and ensure extension. Frank Duff was invited to London for the curia's first meeting. It was a great

Encircling the Globe

joy for him to meet Philippa Szczepanovska, president of the first praesidium, which had been established in the Sacred Heart Convent, Hammersmith.

After the curia meeting, a young lady, Mrs. McKenzie-Smith, was introduced to Frank as a legionary. In the course of conversation, she told him she was shortly leaving for India; her husband had just been appointed sheriff in Madras. Frank saw this as a providential happening and asked her to establish the Legion there. "I will do my very best, Mr. Duff." And then she said: "I have one big sorrow, my husband is not a Catholic."

"Have you ever talked to him about becoming a catholic?"

"No, Mr. Duff, my husband is a very good man, but when it comes to religion, it's like as if there's a stone wall around him and I find it very difficult to discuss the subject with him."

"Well, then, let me tell you something; when you have established the Legion in India your husband will become a Catholic."

To Mrs. McKenzie-Smith these were remarkable and thrilling words.

"Of course," continued Frank, "I have no authority from myself to give you such a guarantee. But because you are going to do something wonderful for Our Lady, I take it on myself to guarantee to you on her behalf that what I say will come to pass. Our Lady will not be outdone in generosity."

Not very long afterwards, Mrs. McKenzie-Smith succeeded in establishing the first praesidium in India under the spiritual direction of Fr. Laurence Murphy, S.J. of Loyola College, Madras. It was 1931.

Encouraged by Mr. Duff's words, she persuaded her husband to take instructions on the Catholic Church. He began his instructions and then, to her intense disappointment, discontinued.

Some months elapsed. Then came the surprise. Mr. McKenzie-Smith came down to breakfast one morning and smilingly told his wife that he had, unknown to her, resumed his instructions and he had fixed a date with the priest for his reception into the Catholic Church.

FRANK DUFF

She was stunned. The date her husband had chosen was —without his realizing it—the first anniversary of the first Legion meeting in India. The gentle touch of Our Lady's hand!

• • • • •

A year later Mrs. McKenzie-Smith had an unexpected caller, Louise Gavan Duffy, who was returning to Australia, via India (she had a brother a priest in India), after a visit to Dublin. Louise's father, Charles Gavan Duffy, had been the friend of Thomas Davis. He had also been editor of the "Nation," the famous weekly newspaper founded by the Young Ireland Party to assist Daniel O'Connell in his repeal campaign in Ireland. Later, Charles Gavan Duffy emigrated to Australia and eventually became Prime Minister there.

Louise had substantial Legion experience, having joined a praesidium in Dublin in 1923. But, on her recent visit to Dublin, she had renewed her acquaintance with Frank Duff. Naturally, he stimulated her enthusiasm even more, particularly when he heard she was returning to Australia. Now Louise's sojourn in India gave her an opportunity to observe how the Legion could work in a mission country where conditions were quite different from those in Ireland.

Eventually, when she arrived in Australia, she was delighted to discover that Archbishop Mannix had already granted permission to Father Bakker, a Melbourne priest, to start a praesidium in Ascot Vale parish. He too had been met by Frank Duff when he visited Dublin to attend the Eucharistic Congress. Louise succeeded in starting a second praesidium in Frankston and later became president of the first curia. Slowly but surely, the Legion would spread to the neighbouring dioceses. And it is to the credit of the Australian legionaries that the growth and extension of the Legion in the whole of Australia was carried out without the aid of an envoy from Dublin, and, in fact, the Australian legionaries have sent out their own extension-workers to found the Legion in New Guinea and in many of the islands of the Pacific.

22 Africa's First Legionary

Fr. James Moynagh, an Irish priest of St. Patrick's Missionary Society, was based at Ifuho, Calabar, Nigeria. His parish was large but only a small proportion of the people were Catholic. The priests and nuns faced a herculean task. Nigeria's population was thirty million people, most of whom were pagans.

In this situation, Fr. Moynagh realized that he must try to mobilize the catholics as lay apostles. He must endeavour to make them active participants in the Church's mission of bringing all men to the fulness of truth which is to be found only in the Church founded by Christ. Then into his hands came a copy of the Handbook of the Legion of Mary! The Legion had not as yet been started in Africa. There followed some correspondence with the Concilium in Dublin and soon Fr. Moynagh decided to make a start. He needed a president and he did know someone who, he thought, would be the right man for the job—Michael Ekeng.

Ekeng was born in a tiny village in the district of Aro-Chuku in Western Nigeria. When he was only six years old, he and his brother, Kalu, were kidnapped by slave traders who held them in a "hide-out" until nightfall and then, under cover of darkness, brought them as far as the river Cross where a canoe and sturdy oarsmen awaited them. The wailing of the two boys was hardly heard above the noise of the swirling waters as the canoe sped on its hazardous journey downstream towards the coast. Nature and primitive conditions had sharpened the skills of the oarsmen. Currents, rapids and crocodiles were all expertly outmaneuvered, and the following morning, as the sun was rising high in the sky, the canoe with its precious burden reached the busy trading town of Calabar.

Ekeng was sold in the market. His master, a Protestant, was a kindly man who treated his slave well. When he found that Ekeng was a pagan, he sent him to bible classes and had him baptized. The boy was also given the opportunity to go to school where he proved to be both intelligent and hard-working. When he passed his examinations in the elementary school, he was encouraged to continue his studies and become a teacher. He was still a slave.

One day Ekeng was passing by a small Catholic church. Slowing his pace, as if in indecision, he cast a furtive glance around him, then quickly stepped inside. The feeling of peace and happiness that he experienced there affected him deeply. Soon, he was asking questions about the Catholic Church. An Irish priest instructed him and, the following year, Ekeng became a Catholic, taking "Michael" as his new name.

When Michael Ekeng qualified as a teacher of elementary grade pupils, he received a regular salary. He had no great interest in money as such, but he did have one great ambition—to buy back his freedom! As soon as he had enough money saved, he approached his master and handed over his "price." Michael Ekeng was now a "free man of God." St. Paul has told us: "the weak things of the world God has chosen, that He may confound the strong" (1 Cor. 1:27). Michael Ekeng, former slave-boy, was chosen by Divine Providence to be the first legionary in Africa. The date of the foundation of the first praesidium there was September 7th, 1933.

Fr. Moynagh and Ekeng worked hard to build up and extend the Legion. Bishop McGetterick, of Ogoja, wrote about Ekeng: "Michael Ekeng's capacity for work is amazing. I have known him to start from Calabar at 1:00 a.m., travel by canoe to Oron, a distance of eighteen miles, go from there to a Legion meeting fifty-five miles away, and, after the meeting, cycle another twelve miles to the nearest mission to receive Holy Communion. He fasted during the whole journey."

Within a comparatively short time, there were more than fifty praesidia flourishing in that area. And the legionaries

Africa's First Legionary

were having marvelous successes, instructing the little ones in the faith, searching for the strays and bringing them back to the fold as well as teaching catechumens. The priests in surrounding parishes began to realize the immense possibilities there were, through the Legion, of reaching out to vast multitudes of people. Most especially, they saw the wonderful spiritual effect the Legion was having on the legionaries themselves.

Back in Dublin, of course, Frank Duff was extremely pleased with this progress. He knew, though, that this was only the proverbial "drop in the ocean." Africa was so immense. Frank visited the seminaries in Ireland that were sending missionaries to Africa and to other missionary countries. He visited also communities of Religious Sisters who were destined for foreign mission fields. To all, he spoke about the Legion as a powerhouse from which the missionary could draw great spiritual energy, which would be a godsend where the missionary laborers were so few and the harvest so great.

Very soon the legion was springing up in the south end and in other parts of Africa. In Nairobi, East Africa, Bishop Hefferman had heard reports of the Legion's effectiveness in distant missions. He wrote a letter to Legion headquarters, Dublin, and asked them to send a Legion envoy to extend the Legion in East Africa. He never regretted sending that letter.

● ● ● ● ●

One of the persons whom Frank Duff often met at Mr. Lalor's house in Blackrock was Mr. P.J. O'Hanlon. They became good friends. Mr. O'Hanlon was now planning to set up his own business and was on the "look-out" for suitable premises and for a good secretary. Again, Mr. Lalor, who had already given him a room in his own house, was his benefactor, offering him the top-floor rooms above his tobacconist shop, in Nassau Street.

Then it happened. It was the gentle knock of a young lady. She had found her way to the top floor office. It was Monday morning. When Mr. O'Hanlon opened the door, there stood before him a beautiful girl, eighteen and a half

FRANK DUFF

years old. She was petite with golden hair and a lovely face and large blue eyes. Her charming smile betrayed a slight trace of shyness. Bashfully, she told Mr. O'Hanlon that she had just completed a commercial course at Rosses' College, and had heard that he was looking for a secretary.

Mr. O'Hanlon was very impressed, recognizing at once her sense of modesty and respect. Besides, her bearing and manners gave indication of competence and reliability. She offered to go home and bring along her certificates and testimonials. But Mr. O'Hanlon needed no written reference. He knew for certain that the ideal secretary had just presented herself before him.

"My only problem," he said to her, "is that I am only starting up my business and I cannot afford to give you the salary I would wish."

"O, Mr. O'Hanlon, don't worry about that. I will be happy with whatever salary you decide upon. This is my first job."

The weeks and months that followed proved Mr. O'Hanlon's first impressions to be justified. His new secretary was a real find. Her name was Edel Quinn.

23 Edel Quinn

Edel Quinn, born in Kanturk, Co. Cork, on the 14th September, 1907, was the eldest of five children. Her mother went to Mass and Holy Communion daily, and, from an early age, Edel acquired the same habit. An exceptionally obedient girl, she was always full of consideration for the other members of her family.

Her gentleness and unselfishness endeared her to all her companions. They loved too her bubbling sense of humour. On the school playgrounds, she so excelled in games that she was the automatic choice for school captain; a born leader she was. Even on rainy days, she could be relied upon to entertain her companions with a selection of lively tunes on the piano. And she simply loved dancing.

At an early age, her devotion to Our Lady was so great that her school pals remarked upon it. When she was seventeen years old, she was put in charge of Our Lady's sodality in her final school year at Upton, England. One of Edel's pals there said later: "You could easily see how extraordinary was Edel's devotion to Our Lady. There was something very personal and touching about the way she even thought about Her. For example, if one of us even referred to Our Blessed Lady in Edel's presence, Edel would blush to the roots of her hair."

Not long after leaving school, Edel was recruited into the Legion of Mary by a friend of hers, Mona Tierney. Edel's family had moved to Dublin by this time. Her first Legion work was the visitation of elderly people who lived alone. She and her co-visitor also called on families for the purpose of inducing them to have the Sacred Heart enthroned in their homes. Edel never spared herself.

Within a comparatively short time, Frank Duff came to hear of this young legionary who seemed to manifest a truly great Legion spirit. At that time, he was the president of

FRANK DUFF

Actually the biggest difficulties arose before she went. Opposition to the plan mounted, even among legionaries. "Crazy, foolish, imprudent," they said, "to send such a delicate girl out to Africa." One legionary lady, a great friend of Edel's, met Frank Duff one day. Frank offered his hand in greeting. The lady put her hands resolutely behind her back and said angrily:

"Mr. Duff, I won't shake hands with you because your hands are dripping with blood."

Frank was deeply hurt by that remark, not because it was painful to himself, but rather because he lamented the lack of faith, the lack of vision, even in some legionaries, causing them to see things merely from a purely human point of view. Had his own faith been one whit less, perhaps he would have yielded. But no, he was quite sure what God wanted and he would continue to press for it. He saw deeper than others. He recognized in Edel an extraordinary spirit of faith and daring, an apostle led by the Holy Spirit.

"You can't keep a wild bird like that in a cage," he said. "She must be given her chance. Edel is going to make history, if she is let."

Years later, Frank was asked if he himself had had any qualms about taking such a risk. After all, Edel might have died soon after landing in Africa.

"No," he replied, "I had no qualms. Of course she might die. Let her die. Let her die. If I had known that she was going to die quickly I would still have pressed for her going out, because she was going to die on a higher plane; she was going to die as an envoy to Africa, which is what she wished with all her heart."

Such was the faith of the man. And such faith was rewarded. Opposition faded away. Formal sanction was granted by Concilium, the Legion governing body. And Edel Quinn set sail for Africa.

That kind of faith, the kind that moves mountains, is a rarity even among good people. But to a receptive soul like Edel it was a tonic, an energizer. It was to be an inspiration for her in the years to come, driving her on to great undertakings for Jesus and Mary. In a letter to Frank she wrote:

Edel Quinn

"I could not say 'thanks,' as I was afraid of breaking down, perhaps; but it is good to feel one is trusted and it will be a help to me in the days to come.

"I would like you to remember always, whatever happens, that I am glad you gave me the opportunity of going. I realize it is a privilege and also that if you had not persisted, I would never have been sent. I only hope I do not fail the Legion when the work comes to be done. I am counting on all the prayers to counteract that danger. Whatever the consequence may be, rejoice that you had the faith and courage to emulate Our Lord, in His choice of weak things. Any sorrow caused to others was worth it, remember; I know that you felt pretty badly about the suffering caused to others."

Edel's mission work in Africa, until her death eight years later, was as thrilling an adventure as any of the great exploits of history. In spite of her very poor health and the terrible traveling conditions, she traveled many thousands of miles throughout the high plateaus of Kenya, throughout the sun-scorched arid lands of Uganda, down through the jungle territory of Southern Africa, even far out to the Island of Mauritius in the Indian Ocean. Her mission—to talk to people about God and about the Blessed Virgin Mary being the spiritual Mother of all men; to train people to be apostles; to set up praesidia of the Legion of Mary. She established praesidia in the villages, in the schools, among the illiterates. She set up a praesidium for lepers on the shores of Lake Victoria.

New life and vigor came into the parishes. Even the simplest and most ordinary people were brought into the apostolate and involved in the Church's mission to all men. The Legion became, as it were, the extension of the priest, enabling him to reach out effectively to the most remote corners of his vast parish. There were many conversions among the pagans. Many lapsed or careless Catholics were brought back to the practice of their religion. Especially noticeable was a wonderful growth in prayer and holiness in the lives of the legionaries themselves. One priest remarked: "Truly the Blessed Virgin has done wonders through the Legion in the short space of six months since we started here."

FRANK DUFF

Edel was constantly receiving invitations to travel and start new branches. Wherever she went, she was full of mirth and good humour, "like a sunbeam, shining on everyone who met her." Her health, though, was rapidly deteriorating. Nevertheless, she struggled to keep going. She realized the value of souls. And she knew her time was limited. Whenever anyone said to her: "Edel, you'll never survive the journey," or "Edel, the dangers of traveling through the jungle are great," she simply smiled and replied: "The Blessed Virgin will look after me." And in fact, it can be said that the whole secret of Edel Quinn's extraordinary success was that she had consecrated herself to Our Lady and did her best, day after day, to unite herself with Our Lady and thus serve Jesus.

• • • • •

The years went by. Frank Duff kept in touch with her by letter. Then one Spring morning Frank opened a letter which was postmarked East Africa. It was from Edel. He read it again and again, as in a daze. Her letter told him, "Mr. Duff, I was very tired out after the Kisumu trip, so am resting at present." That same day, a telegram arrived from Nairobi telling him Edel was dead. A beautiful flower, delicate and fragile, had been given into his keeping. He had done his best to care for that flower, during its growth, with prayer and encouragement and stimulation. The flower had remained delicate and fragile but had grown even more beautiful. Now the beautiful flower had been plucked by God, to be His for all eternity.

24 A Man Set Apart

A young legionary was praying quietly in St. Teresa's Church, Clarendon Street. It was on a Saturday morning, in October, 1934. She saw Frank Duff kneeling before the high altar. She had noticed that he often came to this particular church on the way home from his office on Saturdays. This particular Saturday, Frank rose from his knees and was on his way out from the church, when he saw her. He came over to her.

"Mary," he said in a low voice, "I have thrown in the guns." By that she knew he meant he had retired from his post in the Civil Service. Later that day, she was about to tell the news to her friend, Celia Shaw, but Celia forestalled her: "Yes, I know; one of the officials of the Department said to me: 'Miss Shaw, grace has left the Department of Finance; Frank Duff has retired.'" It was a sincere and beautiful compliment to a man who had brought to both Departments (to which he was attached) a spirit of dedication to duty and a tremendous sense of responsibility; and whose irrepressible good humour and laughter had more than once lifted the spirits of those who needed it and showed them the lighter side of life.

For some time, he had been finding it increasingly difficult to cope with his many apostolic projects. He felt that his mission henceforth was to give himself fully and unremittingly to the Legion of Mary and all that it involved.

He broke the news to his mother. She took it, as she took everything else, in a calm, practical sort of way. But then philosophically she said: "Isn't it hard to be going back to the old times." She was referring to the fact that when her husband had to retire from his job because of ill health, there had been hard times for the family due to the shortage of money. Then Frank's rapid promotion in the Civil Service had given them an increase in their standard of living which was now one of comparative luxury. Frank had always handed his full salary over to his mother. And now, because Frank's income would be much reduced, it would almost be "back to the hard old times."

Of course, in no way did Mrs. Duff mean her comment to be a complaint or a grumble. That would have been contrary to her whole character. Nevertheless, the comment, innocent as it was, went through Frank's heart like a sword. His decision to retire had been one of the most difficult decisions of his whole life because he knew it would mean that his mother and his sister Isabel whom he was also supporting, would have less than heretofore. His course of action had been a responsible one and he had taken it for the supernatural reason that he was convinced God wanted it. His conscience was at ease in that regard but it did not lessen his anguish of mind.

However, his busy work schedule soon diverted his mind from such thoughts. He set up his headquarters in some rooms in the *Regina Coeli Hostel* next door to his home, and for the remaining forty-five years of his life he directed the widely expanding organization from there. Every morning he rose early for Mass. In hail, rain or sunshine, he could be seen on his trusty bicycle, heading for the Capuchin church, on Church Street. His mother had his breakfast ready when he came home. His sister, Isabel, to whom he was very attached, was mostly at home also; her poor health prevented her from going out very much.

After breakfast, there was a vast amount of correspondence to be dealt with. There were letters to be written to individual legionaries at home and abroad. There were letters also in connection with a multitude of private cases he was helping in one form or another. There were letters to Legion councils around the globe. To the Legion in one area alone, Australia, Frank wrote more than four hundred letters between 1932 and 1956, and few of these letters were less than five or six closely typed pages. What his total output of letters was during his lifetime is incalculable.

Excluding Sundays, Frank spent most of his evenings in

A Man Set Apart

the Concilium offices where the major Legion business is transacted. His fellow officers, therefore, had much contact with him and were, together with the indoor staff of the hostels, his closest friends. To a great extent, their lives revolved around him. Somehow, they felt he was a man apart; there was something indefinable about him which marked him out as a man of God. It was that very "apartness" which drew them to him. One felt good in his presence.

But he had his human weaknesses too which, of course, was good for his humility. For, as St. Paul says when referring to himself as one who preaches the 'Good News of the glory of Christ,' "we are only the earthenware jars that hold this treasure" (2 Cor. 7). Like St. Paul, Frank too could say: "It is when I am weak that I am strong" (2 Cor 12:10).

For example, he was impatient by nature and sometimes lost his temper. The Lord alone knows what efforts he must have made to keep that temper in check. He never, in fact, fully conquered it. Perhaps it was for him, like the "sting in the flesh" that had afflicted St. Paul. "I was given an angel of Satan to beat me and stop me from getting too proud," Paul said. "I have pleaded with the Lord three times for it to leave me, but He has said, 'My grace is enough for you: my power is at its best in weakness.' So I shall be very happy to make my weakness my special boast so that the power of Christ may stay over me" (2 Cor. 12:7-10).

Even late in life, Frank admitted that, were it not for Our Lady, his hasty temper might have had serious consequences. He instanced the case where he pursued with a big stick, some intruders who had broken into his home. Before he caught up with them, he slipped on a mat and fell heavily to the floor. Afterwards he shuddered at the thought of what he might have done with that stick if he had caught up with the intruders. He attributed his falling to the saving intervention of Our Lady.

Those who worked with Frank felt that he was oversensitive sometimes. If a fellow officer differed with him on some particular policy or method of approach, Frank could feel hurt and even display a certain amount of annoyance

FRANK DUFF

or resentment. He could be quite stubborn when his mind was set on a certain course of action.

Was it, perhaps, simply that his stubbornness was a "blind spot" with him? To some it seemed incongruous that a man so obviously saintly and kind could occasionally be hurtful and obstinate.

It is possible that the long years of misunderstanding and opposition which he encountered during the infancy of the Legion had rendered him fearful of being diverted from the direct and clear path of duty, as he saw it, and on which he had resolutely set himself to travel.

Notwithstanding the occasional lapses, there could be no doubting the extraordinary patience of the man. Despite his heavy schedule of work, he could spend hours listening to and counselling some afflicted soul; he so lavished his love on that person, really seeing and serving Christ in him, that time was forgotten. Likewise, in the hostels, when dealing with the less fortunate members of society, he was extraordinarily gentle and patient.

From time to time, reports reached the Concilium officers concerning some praesidia or councils that were defective. Frank would always counsel great patience in dealing with these, advising that every possible course of action be tried before contemplating any drastic action. If, however, he encountered any case of disloyalty, then it could cause him real agony. He could never, even remotely, countenance disloyalty.

One December evening, in 1936, the Dublin legionaries were holding their Annual Reunion. It was in the Gresham Hotel. Frank Duff's address was the highlight of the function. He spoke for one and a half hours on the subject of the Legion altar, emphasizing in particular the statue of Our Lady which is the centerpoint of that altar and which is symbolic of Our Lady's presence at each praesidium meeting.

On the fringe of that gathering was a young Legion recruit, named Sam Hughes, who was seeing Frank for the first time. Sam, destined to be a future president of the Concilium, was impressed and enthused by what he saw and heard. Soon he had become a praesidium president and within a short time was to discover, at first hand, what a great counsellor Frank was.

A Man Set Apart

"I went to see Frank," Sam recalled, "to get his advice on how to deal with some Legion problems. He gave me a long interview but when I came away I realized he hadn't really given me any direct answers to the problems I propounded. My puzzlement changed to admiration as the reason gradually "dawned" on me. I began to realize that he didn't believe in "spoonfeeding" any officer. Instead of answering my questions, or proposing solutions, he had talked at length on the importance of having clear, well-defined principles and on the place of faith and the supernatural in our Legion affairs, and, of course, he talked on Our Lady. Everything he said was spoken with such earnestness and conviction that I was very happy simply to accept it. I saw that I was being made to stand on my own two feet; that big responsibilities were being placed on my shoulders; that I was being trusted. All this was a great tonic to me, as I was a very shy young man at that time. I came away without exactly having got what I had expected but really feeling good and I resolved, by the grace of God, to try to live up to the trust he had placed in me."

On many a Sunday, there would be a Legion Congress in one or other of the provincial towns of Ireland. Frank would set out by car the day before, taking a few experienced legionaries with him. He himself never drove since the time he had, as a young man, tried to drive his brother's car. On that occasion the car had exploded and Frank and his brother were fortunate to escape serious injury.

The journey to the Congress would usually take a few hours and it was a wonderful opportunity for Frank's fellow or sister traveling companions to imbibe some of Frank's wisdom and knowledge. During the journey, he would talk, for example, about De La Taille's teaching on the Mass and in such a way that the Mass came to life for his listeners. Another time, he might talk about Our Lady's union with the Holy Spirit and the implications of this for us. Sometimes he would speak on speculative theology, discussing such questions as, "Was Our Lady present at the Last Supper?"

His understanding of the great doctrines of the Church was so profound and his enthusiasm about them so infectious, that one legionary remarked later: "I thought I knew

FRANK DUFF

a lot about my religion until I started traveling with Mr. Duff; but I soon realized that my grasp of many of the Church's teachings had been very superficial and vague. I can truly say that Mr. Duff instilled in me a proper appreciation of the marvelous treasures of the Catholic faith."

Of course, not all the conversation was on spiritual topics. There were stories, anecdotes, songs. Frank looked on these journeys as pleasant excursions which were salutary for soul and body. He enjoyed them immensely, and he loved the companionship of legionaries. It made no difference whether they were old or young, experienced or "raw" recruits. The newer recruits used to marvel that a man of Frank's vast knowledge and great mind could be so natural and at ease with "ordinary" mortals like themselves. One said: "I love Mr. Duff's laughing eyes. When he looks at you with that utterly gentle tenderness, it makes you feel so good. You are immediately at ease with him. You instinctively know he is your true friend."

When the carload of legionaries would arrive at the town of destination on that Saturday afternoon, the local officers would greet them, provide a nice meal and then have a preliminary discussion with Frank and his team. Frank loved meeting the local officers and especially their Spiritual Director. Practically everything, he said, depended on these officers and on their dedicated and spirited leadership. They, on their part, felt honoured to meet Frank.

On the Sunday morning after Mass, the Congress would begin and even Frank himself would often marvel at how the most "ordinary" legionaries had, because of the Legion system, become quite competent at discussing such doctrines as the Mystical Body, and the Motherhood of Mary, and relating them to everyday life.

Frank was always saddened if he heard of priests who refused to show any interest in the Legion. He thought it remarkable that some very good priests preferred to give their time and attention to purely secular or humanitarian societies rather than to the Legion of Mary which was a spiritual society through and through. He was keenly aware of the extraordinarily deep faith of the majority of the Irish people, and regretted the fact that many of them were never stimulated to rise above the common run of average

A Man Set Apart

Catholics, in the matter of progress in the spiritual life, or in enterprises that would raise the spiritual standards of the local community. He instanced the pathetically small attendance at daily Mass in many of the rural villages.

In his concluding address to the Congress, Frank would always compliment the legionaries on their efforts and then he would go on to suggest that they might set their sights still higher and embark on even greater enterprises for Jesus and Mary and for their parish.

* * * * *

The *Concilium*, based in Dublin, is the supreme governing body of the Legion. The meeting is held on the third Sunday of every month. Frank Duff became president of the Concilium when Mrs. Kirwin, the very first president, resigned and he held that office at various periods during his lifetime.

Overseas visitors who came to Dublin to attend Concilium were always impressed by the large number of countries which sent representatives; other countries were represented by local Irish correspondents appointed by Concilium. As well as visiting legionaries from the European countries, there were legionaries from places as far away as Africa, or India, or the Philippine Islands on some occasions.

There would be reports from all over the globe: letters from Legion envoys still in the mission fields; up-to-date accounts from *Incolae Mariae* who had returned to Ireland in the recent past; stories of new developments; and there would be animated discussion on all the happenings.

It was always a moving moment when some new envoy was being appointed to go forth to some faraway land as Our Lady's representative.

Frank, naturally, figured prominently in the discussions. He had strong views on many things and could press his viewpoint vigorously. It was of interest to the overseas legionaries who were present, that he did not always get his own way in the debates. When this happened, he simply accepted the decision of the Concilium. More often than not, however, when Frank made a proposal, it was adopted. Officers were ready and pleased to give due recognition

FRANK DUFF

to his vast experience. He had, also, a truly fantastic knowledge of history and of the geographical and social factors affecting each country in which the Legion operated, or in which it wished to operate. Moreover, his facility for grasping the various complexities of a difficult problem, and for finding a viable solution, convinced experienced legionaries that the Holy Spirit endowed Frank with the gift of wisdom to an eminent degree.

Frank's ready wit was proverbial. A legionary, a student in St. Patrick's Seminary, Thurles, told of an incident he witnessed when he visited Concilium. A rather heavyset lady, who was a legionary correspondent, stood up—all two hundred and forty pounds of her—to make some proposals about a certain legionary council. She said: "I have some proposals for Brother Duff." The Dublin legionaries, always with a taste for the funnier side of things, chose to read a little more into that statement than the lady intended, and there were roars of laughter at Frank's expense. He, enjoying it immensely, looked at the stout lady and said sweetly: "Sister, 'tis a pity you couldn't get some 'proposals' for yourself." The meeting exploded with laughter and the good lady enjoyed it as much as everyone else.

The same student told how once, after Mr. Duff had given a talk on the wonders and the vocation of marriage, he impishly asked Mr. Duff why he had not, in that case, got married himself. With a twinkle in his eye, Frank replied: "Why should I marry and make one woman miserable when by staying single I can keep dozens happy with hope!"

So, even though the Concilium must deal with serious matters, Frank aimed at keeping the legionaries from getting too serious. "God," he said "is the author of humour, for humour is definitely one of the admirable human characteristics." Then he would say, quoting G. K. Chesterton: "It is the test of a good religion if you can make a joke about it."

When the Concilium meeting ended, the visitors usually approached Frank Duff and grasped his hand. For many of them, a handshake with him was something they would remember for the rest of their lives. They just knew he was someone special.

25 Messenger for Our Lady of Knock

Pope Pius XI died on February 10th, 1939. Three weeks later, Cardinal Pacelli was elected as his successor, taking the name, Pius XII. Prior to his election, he had been Secretary of State to Pius XI and it was in that capacity that he first met Frank Duff, in Rome, in 1931. The new Pope was well acquainted with the Legion of Mary.

Just at that time, Frank received an invitation to Rome from Cardinal Pizzardo, the cardinal responsible for Catholic Action in Italy. This would provide Frank with an opportunity to pay his respects to the Pope and enlist further support for the Legion. He was assured that all doors would be open to him in Rome at that time. It was obvious at that stage that the reports which various Papal Nuncios and bishops around the world were sending to the Vatican concerning the Legion of Mary were very favorable.

There was one problem; a world war was imminent and everybody knew it. It was an extremely risky time for traveling. However, Frank did not hesitate; Jack Nagle would accompany him.

Shortly before his departure, he received a telephone message from the Papal Nuncio in Dublin, requesting him to call at the Nunciature. To his surprise, he met there Dr. Gilmartin, Archbishop of Tuam, a diocese in the west of Ireland. After exchanging courtesies, the Archbishop came to the point.

"Mr. Duff," he said, "The Nuncio has told me you are

FRANK DUFF

going to Rome. We will be most grateful if you can do us a very special favor."

"Indeed, I will be glad to be of service in any way I can," said Frank, casting a curious glance at the strong timber box the Archbishop had before him on the table.

"It's about the Apparition of Our Lady at Knock, in the west of Ireland," continued the Archbishop. "As you probably know, six weeks after the Apparition, in 1879, the then Archbishop of Tuam, Dr. MacHale, set up a Commission to examine the evidence of the witnesses of the Apparition, and that Commission reported that their evidence was 'trustworthy and satisfactory.' However, you realize how cautious the Church is in these matters, so it was decided to set up another Commission three years ago to seek further confirmation of the facts. Three of the witnesses of the Apparition were still alive. Now, the findings of this Commission are complete and are, I may add, most satisfactory; but we must forward our findings to Rome for the Church's official approval."

Then, pointing to the timber box, the Archbishop said: "All the documents of the case are in this sealed box. Because of the rumours of war, we can't risk mailing them in the normal way. If you are willing, we would like to entrust these documents to your care so that you can bring them personally to Rome."

Frank was somewhat overawed by this added responsibility, but he could hardly refuse the Archbishop's request, more especially as it concerned the cause of Our Lady at Knock.

"Your Grace," he replied, "I shall be honoured to be the bearer of your precious box."

• • • • •

Knock has a unique place in the history of modern Ireland.

The eighteen-seventies was a period of great poverty, suffering and hardship in Ireland, particularly in rural Ireland. There was agrarian strife, and Michael Davitt, a smallholder and a founder of the Land League, and the great patriot, Charles Stewart Parnell, both fought vigorously to end

Messenger for Our Lady of Knock

the tyranny of landlordism. The agents of the landlords, many of whom were absentees residing in England, could and did with impunity evict many hundreds of families of smallholders who were too poor to pay the rackrents imposed on them. Their little one-storey homes were razed to the ground and their only option was to take the emigrant boat.

It was against this background that Our Blessed Lady appeared at Knock, Co. Mayo, a very deprived area of the west.

Fifteen people of varying ages, from six to seventy-five years, saw the Apparition at the gable end of the small parish church on a windswept, rainy evening at about eight o'clock on August 21st, 1879. On either side of Our Lady stood St. Joseph and St. John the Evangelist and, on their left, an altar bearing a sacrificial lamb was seen. The apparition lasted for about two hours.

Knock has become a place of pilgrimage and many thousands visit it every year to pray and to seek healing of soul and body.

• • • • •

Frank Duff and Jack Nagle set out on the first stage of their journey by boat to Holyhead and then proceeded to Paris, where they stayed overnight. They left Paris by plane the following morning and arrived in Rome at exactly 3:55 p.m.

It was as it had been told to Frank beforehand — every door was open to them. Frank had interviews with many of the cardinals, including Cardinal Maglione, the Cardinal Secretary of State. All showed a great interest in the Legion and many of them were already well informed about it.

"We had no difficulty," said Frank later, "in meeting everybody we wanted to meet, and that is as significant as it is joyful."

However, Frank was momentarily stunned when, on his arrival in Rome, he was told at the 'Appointments Office' that there was no possibility of his getting a private audience with the Pope, as there were ninety distinguished personages at that moment in Rome awaiting such an audi-

FRANK DUFF

ence. A little disconcerted, he checked with some people in authority to ascertain his position. The reassuring message came back "The Holy Father will see Mr. Duff before anyone else in Rome!" The private audience was fixed for the 28th of April, a few days later. "Remarkable," said Frank, "that's the Feast day of St. Louis Marie de Montfort!"

At the appointed time, they were ushered into the Pope's study. The two chairs which had been placed in front of the large desk were facing the Pope's chair. Frank, aware of his own defective hearing, feared that he would be too far away from His Holiness to hear clearly what he had to say. His own explanation of how he coped with this difficulty is revealing.

"We knelt down on both knees and kissed the Pope's ring. He gave us his blessing and then beckoned us to the two chairs. His desk was very large and my chair was quite a distance away from his. I was extremely worried about my capacity to hear him. The Pope and I surveyed each other. His expression was unearthly; he had a celestial appearance, as if a light were shining from his face. I felt encouraged and, with a little word of apology to him, I took my chair, marched around the large desk with it and placed it beside his. There I sat and we had a most wonderful audience. We were absolutely at home with him.

And indeed, during his long reign of nearly twenty years, Pope Pius XII gave his ardent support and encouragement to the Legion of Mary.

Before returning to Ireland, Frank wished to fulfill a promise he had made eight years previously. Cardinal Marchetti, who had arranged Frank's first visit to Rome, had asked for all available literature on the Legion of Mary. Only now was it possible to satisfy that request. The Dominican nuns in Rome had completed the printing of the Italian translation of the Legion Handbook, just in time to enable Frank to present a copy to His Holiness during the Private Audience.

Cardinal Marchetti had been ill for some time but he invited Frank and Brother Nagle to visit him in his home in the country, where he received them most graciously.

"Your Eminence," said Frank, "we have not forgotten what you have done for us; we want to thank you again.

Messenger for Our Lady of Knock

You remember, no doubt, that when we were with you in 1931, we promised that, as soon as we could, we would supply you with complete information on the Legion. It is my pleasure now to present you with a copy of the Italian edition of the Legion Handbook which has just been published."

Frank pointed to the publication date printed on the book. They both smiled. The date was the 28th of April!

• • • • •

As for the timber box with the precious documents, Frank delivered it, safe and sound, when he arrived in Rome. In the years to come, it must have been a great joy to Frank to see the Knock Shrine recognized as one of the major Marian Shrines in the world as well as the chief centre of pilgrimage for the Irish people. How thrilled Frank must have been—as indeed were all his fellow-countrymen—when, forty years after he took that precious box to Rome, the Holy Father himself, Pope John Paul II, came as a pilgrim to the Shrine at Knock and declared in his sermon "Today I come here because I want all of you to know that my devotion to Mary unites me, in a very special way, with the people of Ireland. . . . Standing on this hallowed ground, we look up to the Mother of God and say . . . 'Queen of Ireland, Máthair Dé, keep Ireland true to her spiritual tradition and her christian heritage. Help her to respond to her heroic mission of bringing the light of Christ to the nations, and so making the glory of God be the honor of Ireland."

• • • • •

In early June, 1949, Frank accompanied a group of legionaries to Melleray. He returned to Dublin on the 10th of that month, anxious to be in time for his Regina Coeli praesidium meeting that night. When he arrived home, his mother greeted him:

"Frank Isabel hasn't been so well since you went away. In fact, she's been ill nearly all this week."

Immediately, Frank went upstairs to the bedroom. Isabel

FRANK DUFF

was very pleased to see him but she was very pale and weak. He spent some time with her and later went down to his praesidium meeting. Sometime during the meeting, his mother came down and tapped on the window to attract Frank's attention.

"Frank," she whispered, "she has got a turn, in fact I think she's dying."

Grief stricken, Frank hurried up the staircase. Isabel was, indeed, dying. He knelt beside the bed in prayer. He put his arms around his beloved sister and she passed away peacefully in his embrace.

John, Frank's only brother, was taken to hospital shortly afterwards. Scarlet fever was diagnosed and he was dead within two months. It was a great consolation to Frank that John, during his illness, had the good services of a priest and received the Sacraments before he died.

• • • • •

The deaths of Isabel and John were hard blows for poor Mrs. Duff. Even though she was eighty-six years old then, she had been hale and hearty up to that point in time, managing the house, reading her favorite authors and taking a keen interest in everything going on around her. Now, however, she was shattered. Her health began to fail and she passed to her eternal reward during the following winter.

On the night of his mother's funeral, Frank took Tom Doyle (a resident brother of the Morning Star Hostel), and Mary Rowe, aside for a quiet talk.

"You know," he said, "I'm not changing my life, I'm staying here."

"Well, Mr. Duff," Mary said, "at least Brother Doyle will stay with you tonight."

"Ah no, I'll just have to get used to it."

His sister, Mrs. Monaghan, suggested that he go to Navan and stay with her.

"I couldn't do that," he said. "I'd have tremendous comfort and all that, but it wouldn't be my life. I can't break it up."

"Well then," she said, "in that case I'll send up my

housekeeper to you. She's very good, as you know. She'll look after you."

"Thanks very much, Geraldine, but I can't let you do that. You know it wouldn't suit me to be tied down to fixed meal times and all that. I can arrange to have my meals in Regina Coeli. Thanks all the same."

And they knew it was useless to argue with him; he had a mind of his own plus a stubborn will.

It is probable that the three deaths hastened the death of Ailis, Frank's youngest sister. She had built up a big practice in England as a doctor. When she got ill, Frank went over to England to bring her home but she did not long outlive the others.

Frank himself was devastated by the rapid loss, one after the other, of the people most dear to him on this earth. There only remained now his sister, Mrs. Monaghan, who was at this time a widow in Navan, and himself. The death of his dear mother affected him the most deeply. They had shared so much together. She had been his chief support on this earth, his unfailing companion. He was so shattered by her death that he lost appetite and weight; he looked pitiful. He could hardly bear the thought of living without her. His only consolation was that it was but a temporary separation. Life on this earth was never meant to be a bed of roses or, if it was, then the thorns must be accepted as well as the roses. Only too well he realized that. As Solomon said:

> "All things have their seasons;
> and in their times all things pass under heaven.
> A time to be born and a time to die.
> A time to plant,
> and a time to pluck up that which is planted.
> A time to weep and a time to laugh.
> A time to mourn and a time to dance." (Eccl. 3:1-4)

Frank was still bowed down under his terrible weight of sorrow when news reached him from far-away China that his brother and sister legionaries there were being subjected to great pressures.

26 Melleray Revisited

When Frank said "good-bye" to the monks in Mount Melleray at the conclusion of his first visit in 1919, he knew he would be seeing them again. Melleray had captured his heart. He was back there for Holy Week of the following year, this time with two great friends of his, Tom Green and Tom Cowley. And he returned year after year, each time bringing a few more men with him so that the little group was growing apace. In later years, a number of women legionaries joined them.

Frank's annual visit to Melleray usually lasted one week. Every morning he rose at 3:00 a.m. and walked along the bare, whitewashed corridors to the monks' chapel for the singing of Matins. The chapel itself was simple and austere. The chanting of the monks, sometimes sonorous, sometimes soft and gentle, had an ethereal ring to it at that early hour when all things were in quiet silence. Frank saw more and more the beauty and the majesty of the divine Office as the prayer of Christ Himself, continued through the lips and hearts of His people. When the praetorian degree of membership was incorporated into the Legion system, the recitation of an Office was one of the requirements stipulated.

After Matins there was holy Mass. Frank often spoke of his indebtedness to Melleray for his knowledge and appreciation of the Holy Sacrifice of the Mass, which grew and developed into maturity over the years. He was indebted mainly to Father Brendan who walked through the gardens with him after breakfast and explained the true meaning and infinite value of the Mass in a way hitherto unheard by

Melleray Revisited

him. Furthermore, the very fact that the Mass is the great mystery of faith made him delve deeper into the mystery to increase his understanding of it. He read theological books on it, he discussed it with others, he wrote about it himself in a more popular form. He referred to assistance at Mass as a "thrilling adventure." "The Mass," he said, "is the divine expedient which obliterates the distance and the two thousand years which separates us from the event of the Crucifixion. It places Calvary in our midst or, if you like, transports us to the moment and spot of the actual Sacrifice of Our Lord. Through the Mass, we take part in the reality; we are present there along with His Mother, St. John and the others. . . . All Masses meet in Calvary just as the rays of the sun find their centre in the radiant sun; so that when Our Lord hung on the Cross, His eyes rested on all who would attend the Masses which would ever be said" (Woman of Genesis, p. 372).

So great was Frank's appreciation of the Mass, that it became the centre of his whole life. And he would take extraordinary steps, if necessary, to ensure that he never missed his daily Mass.

Frank did not leave the chapel when Mass had ended. He remained for a lengthy thanksgiving and only arose from his knees when it was time for breakfast at 8:00 a.m.

While the women legionaries stayed in a guesthouse outside the monastery, the men stayed in a special section within the monastery itself. The long timber tables in the dining room were made by the monks and were unadorned. The food was plain but wholesome. The monks baked their own bread and churned their own butter. They grew their own potatoes and vegetables. If Frank was an ascetic in his eating habits, he didn't betray it in Melleray. The fresh mountain air gave him an appetite that corresponded with the hearty meals which were set before him, and he ate and enjoyed them.

Only someone who has spent a few days in Mount Melleray can fully appreciate how good and refreshing it is for mind and soul and body. The rolling hillsides, the tall majestic pine trees, the fragrance of the purple heather, the luxuriant moss, tender and soft under tired feet, the humming of the bees, the singing of the birds, the lowing of

FRANK DUFF

cattle, all the scents and sounds of summer give an incomparable joy which makes one yearn for one's heavenly home where summer is eternal and winter is past forever.

For Frank it was a wonderful tonic to get away from Dublin city and from his endless labours. There were times when he was practically exhausted from stress and overwork. Melleray was the refuge, the haven where he could relax and have a little more time for prayer and enjoy some hours of laughter and companionship with fellow legionaries.

The holiday party grew in numbers over the years until eventually a whole busload was deposited each year at the monastery doors.

During the week's "holiday" there would be long walks through the woods. The Legion prayers were recited en route, often interrupted by such operations as crossing a river by "stepping stones," or the need at times to pay more attention to overhanging bramble bushes than to the words or thoughts of the prayers. But somehow they felt that Our Lady understood and that maybe she even shared the enjoyment of these temporary interruptions.

Then there was a restful interlude and maybe a picnic. Everybody sat as comfortably as a forest clearing or the ledge of a river bank would allow. There were songs and poetry recitations and comedy sketches—and lots of laughter. Frank himself was a very good storyteller. Sometimes he told stories of the early Legion days, sometimes he told hilariously funny tales. And his own merry laughter was the merriest of all. Everybody was glad to see him so happy, so relaxed. They were his big family; he loved them individually and they loved him.

At least once in the week they would climb Knocknafallia which is the highest peak in the Knockmealdown range of mountains. It was a full day's enterprise, so they brought their picnic lunches with them, borrowed heavy boots and raincoats from the monks, in case it should rain, and then set out. Frank, at the age of 79, was able to say that he had never missed that climb in 48 consecutive years since his first climb at the age of 31.

But one particular climb stands out as the most eventful of all. It was the year Annie Curran went to Melleray with the Legion party.

146

Melleray Revisited

Before Frank's youngest sister, Ailis, died, she was in the same hospital as Annie Curran, and, in fact, was operated on the same day as Annie and by the same surgeon. Ailis was Frank's favorite sister.

Because Annie Curran suffered from the same illness as his sister, Frank took a great interest in her progress. Annie made a reasonably good recovery but remained almost completely disabled. Ailis, however, never completely recovered and, when she eventually died, Frank was broken-hearted. So he took upon himself a sort of responsibility for Annie. Everything about her brought back the memory of his beloved Ailis. Annie joined the Legion and worked in her own limited way in Regina Coeli Hostel. Sometimes, when Frank came in and saw her, the tears streamed down his face.

When Annie was able to come to Melleray with the party, Frank was delighted. He was solicitous for her and, on the walks and outings, he insisted on helping her over the rivers and fences in his own gallant fashion. Jokingly the others referred to Frank and his "baggage," Annie being the "baggage."

Tuesday came and preparations were under way for Wednesday's mountain climb. A problem arose: Annie would have liked to go but that was out of the question because of poor health. On the other hand, it was against the legionaries' tradition to leave anyone behind. What did Frank think? They asked him privately.

"I'm afraid," he said, "she can't go. Only a lunatic would take her up that mountain."

Annie accepted that this was the only sensible solution, though naturally she was disappointed. Frank understood her feelings, so he agreed to defer his decision until the following morning. Next morning he declared: "I am going to pray for light about the matter."

He went into the chapel and prayed. Some of the legionaries waited outside. Most of them agreed it would, indeed, be lunacy to take Annie with them. When Frank came out, they asked:

"What will we do about Annie?"

"Well, we're taking her with us up the mountain," he said. "I have prayed about it and the answer I got from the Lord was: 'take the baggage with you.'"

FRANK DUFF

By the "baggage" they knew he meant Annie. And so that day Annie climbed to the peak of the mountain with the rest of the legionaries. There were, indeed, some anxious moments when it looked as if the decision had been indiscreet and foolhardy. But the fact was, that not alone did Annie survive that climb but seemingly her health even improved afterwards.

When later, in private conversation, a legionary pressed Frank a bit further on his "prayer and answer" in the chapel that morning, he admitted:

"I went in to have a chat with the Lord. I prayed. Then I felt a strange sensation, a sensation I have had on other occasions also: it was a sensation of sweetness. I am accustomed to interpret that sensation to mean "everything is all right." So I went out and told Annie that the Lord had said I could take the baggage."

And among themselves the legionaries agreed that only a man of great faith would have dared to do such a "lunatic" thing.

On one occasion when Frank was in Melleray, he heard his fellow legionary, Brendan Crowley, say that during the night he had heard strange sounds in his room. Brendan told Father Nivard, the guestmaster, about it. Fr. Nivard was startled because he had, on some former occasions, got similar reports about strange noises in the same room. Frank interjected:

"Let me stay the night in that room."

His offer was gratefully accepted by Fr. Nivard. It was considered wise though, at the time, not to tell the other visitors about it. So Frank and Brendan waited until the others had retired and then they swapped rooms. Frank retired to bed in the room of "noises." Fr. Nivard arranged to sleep in the room directly underneath.

After some time, Fr. Nivard came rushing into Frank's room.

"Are you all right?" he asked. "I heard dreadful noises and thought you were being attacked."

"Well, I must confess," said Frank, "that I had a most unpleasant feeling before I fell asleep. I did hear sounds, but as I am hard of hearing, I'm not quite sure whether it was inside or outside my head."

Melleray Revisited

So uneasy was Fr. Nivard that he called in Fr. Fintan. All was explained to him and he agreed to remain in the corridor, watching. Then at 1:00 a.m., the same terrible noises were heard. This time Fr. Fintan also heard them.

When Frank arose at 3:00 a.m., his normal rising time in Melleray, he asked Fr. Nivard if any further noises had been heard. Fr. Nivard had to admit that the same dreadful noises had been heard.

Strangely enough, the noises were never again heard in that room.

It was an indication of the high regard the monks had for Frank when Father Francis, the Prior, invited him to speak to the monks on aspects of the spiritual life. Frank was genuinely pleased at being accorded this great honor. In the monastery's long history, only three other lay people had been invited to address the monks. Two of them, Sean T. O'Kelly and Eamonn de Valera, were Presidents of Ireland. The other was Daniel O'Connell, the Liberator.

One of the highlights of the week in Melleray was the annual Legion Acies ceremony. Since the essential idea of the Legion, upon which all else is built, is that of working in union with and in dependence on Mary, its Queen, it was only natural that Frank looked forward to it as the greatest Legion event of each year. And there in the monastery chapel, he took his place in the processional queue with the other legionaries. Then, when his turn came, he placed his hand on the staff of the Legion vexillum and said in a firm voice: "I am all thine, my Queen, my Mother, and all that I have is thine." Those in the front seats always felt privileged to hear him utter these words. They were sure no one said them with more earnestness than he.

The first prayer of the Acies ceremony, as indeed of all Legion meetings, is a prayer to the Holy Spirit. Frank had been emphatic about that. It was important for legionaries to realize that their work, which is the sanctification of themselves and of other members of the Mystical Body of Christ, is dependent on the operation of the Holy Spirit and hence calls for a very close union with Him.

If we wish to achieve a really close union with the Holy Spirit and thus to become instruments of His mighty pur-

FRANK DUFF

poses then, Frank maintained, two things are essential: firstly, we must pay full attention to Him; secondly, we must enter into a spirit of union with Mary, as the Holy Spirit always works in inseparable union with her.

When reports began to come from many quarters, at home and abroad, of marvelous Legion conquests, of innumerable miracles of grace wrought through the Legion, inevitably people asked: "how can these things be?" For spirited legionaries there was joy but no unusual surprise. In their Legion handbook they could read: "The man who thus makes the Holy Spirit his helper enters into the tide of omnipotence" (Handbook, p. 134).

After Frank had given a lecture one day, a seminarian, aware that Mr. Duff had been promoting devotion to the Holy Spirit very many years before this devotion achieved general popularity in the Church, asked:

"Mr. Duff, to what do you attribute your very great devotion to the Holy Spirit?"

"To Our Lady," was the spontaneous reply. "My devotion to Our Lady has led me to an appreciation of the absolute importance of proper devotion to the Holy Spirit."

Frank often arranged that his visit to Melleray would coincide with the celebration of Pentecost. And so it was in Melleray that on one Pentecost Sunday, in the eveningtime, the thought struck him that there should be a "Promise" in the Legion system and that the Promise should be made to the Holy Spirit. He let the idea mature in his mind, he talked about it to his fellow legionaries, and then he devised a formula which was incorporated into the Legion system. Henceforward, the taking of this Legion Promise was to constitute the formal entry into the Legion of Mary.

The prayer-formula of the Legion Promise has been acknowledged as one of the great masterpieces of Christian literature on the triple theme of the Holy Spirit, Mary and the apostolic soul. Cardinal Suenens wrote concerning the Promise: "I know of few prayers in contemporary Christian literature which are of such depth and arouse such spiritual echoes" (Theology of the Apostolate: Foreword).

People who chanced to kneel close to Frank during the recitation of the Rosary were surprised to notice that on

Melleray Revisited

the reverse side of the crucifix of his rosary beads an image of the Holy Spirit was affixed. He had affixed it himself. For him, the rosary was not only a loving prayer and conversation with his Mother Mary about her Son and herself; it also celebrated the principal interventions of the Holy Spirit in the drama of Redemption.

When Fr. Declan, one of the monks who was particularly interested in the Legion, got ill, he was sent to a hospital in Dublin. Frank called to see him.

"Frank, they are very kind to me here but, as you can see, my room has no religious emblems. Can you get me a little statue of Our Lady?"

Frank was glad to oblige. When Fr. Declan regained his strength and returned to Melleray he took the statue with him. Some years later the priest again fell ill, this time with a fatal attack of pneumonia. Before he died he called the new guestmaster to his bedside.

"Father, you are new to the job of guestmaster. May I give you a little piece of advice? When the legionaries come to Melleray be patient, no matter what 'divilment' they are up to, and remember Mr. Duff's room is number 8."

And so, indeed, it was with all the monks. Not only was Frank their friend, he was their confidant. They looked forward to his coming each year. Many of them consulted him on matters of the monastic and spiritual life. He, for his part, looked affectionately on each and every one of them as loving brothers in Jesus and Mary.

Not only did most of them—perhaps all of them—become *Adjutorian members** of the Legion of Mary, but when the new public chapel was built in the monastery, a beautiful mosaic of the Legion vexillum was set into the sanctuary wall, a worthy memorial to the graces granted to the Legion and through the Legion in this holy place.

After supper each night, Frank and the brother legionaries went out to the lovely summer house in the monastery garden. There were more stories, more reminiscences and sometimes reports read from Legion envoys in far-away missions until the loud pealing of the monastery bells called a halt. Then all proceeded quietly back to the large monastery church where the monks were gathering to chant Compline. And after Compline the final hymn of the day, the

FRANK DUFF

Salve Regina, was sung enchantingly, movingly, a fond "good-night" to Her who was their life, their sweetness and their hope.

NOTE

*Adjutorian Membership is a branch of the Auxiliary Membership whose members a) recite all the prayers of the Tessera and who b) agree to attend Mass and receive Holy Communion daily as well as to recite some form of Office approved by the Church.

27 Louis from Montfort

In a tiny chapel in Iceland, the priest and five of his legionaries had gathered on the 8th of December for a special ceremony. Outside, all was enveloped in darkness and snow was falling. But inside, the candles were burning brightly. The Blessed Sacrament was exposed on the altar.

One of the legionaries, a twenty year old girl, knelt on the bare floor, a lighted candle in her right hand, a sheet of paper in her left. On the paper was written, in her own hand, a copy of de Montfort's "Consecration to Jesus through Mary." It bore the title: "Act of consecration to Jesus Christ, the Incarnate Wisdom, by the hands of Mary."

As the priest and the other legionaries stood in prayerful witness, the girl on her knees proceeded to read from her script, addressing the first two paragraphs to Jesus, the Eternal Wisdom, now before her on the altar. Then she moved a little to the left and, kneeling before a statue of the Immaculate Virgin Mary, continued to pronounce the remaining paragraphs of her consecration, renewing her baptismal promises and expressing her heartfelt desire to possess Divine Wisdom. She paused a moment, then continued: "and I give myself entirely to Jesus Christ, the Incarnate Wisdom, that I may walk in His footsteps all my life, carrying my cross. And in order that I may be more faithful to Him than I have hitherto been, I choose you today, O Mary, in the presence of the whole court of heaven, to be my Mother and my Mistress. I give and I consecrate to you, as your slave, my body and my soul, my interior and exterior possessions, and even the value of my good actions—past, present and to come."

When she had finished reading her consecration manuscript, she signed it—still on her knees, in the presence of the Sacred Host. Then the priest gave her the Benediction of the Blessed Sacrament. Her friends joined in the hymns and Legion prayers. Later, there was a little celebration supper.[1]

This simple but moving ceremony is only one of the very many indications of the far-reaching and effective spiritual influence that Frank Duff exerted around the globe. Through the Legion of Mary, countless souls have been inspired to undertake true and solid devotion to Our Lady.

Was Frank the "noble soul" that Saint Louis Marie de Montfort had prophetically in mind when, more than two hundred years ago, he wrote in his Treatise on the True Devotion: "My labour will be well rewarded if this little book falls into the hands of a noble soul, a child of God and of Mary. . . . My time will be well spent if, by the grace of the Holy Spirit, after having read this book he is convinced of the supreme value of the solid devotion to Mary I am about to describe"? St. Louis de Montfort's time was well spent.

Louis Marie de Montfort was born in Montfort, a small town in France, on the 31st of January, 1673. He was the eldest of a large family. The christian atmosphere of the home, and especially the piety of the mother, left its mark on young Louis. He was a deeply religious boy. At the age of twelve, he was sent to the Jesuit College at Rennes, where he studied for eight years. His fellow students were deeply impressed by his great charity and his assiduous attention to prayer. To be a priest and to work for souls was his greatest wish.

At the age of twenty, Louis set out on foot to walk the two hundred miles or so to Paris to enter the Seminary of Saint Sulpice. It was his choice to travel "pilgrim style," with rosary beads in hand. The money his father gave him for the journey ended up in the hands of poor beggars who met him on the road. He arrived in Paris ten days later, having begged his food on the way.

In the students' hostel beside St. Sulpice Seminary, the newly arrived seminarian read the first page of the rule: "Those whom the grace of God brings to this house will rejoice in their poverty, since Jesus has so honored it in Him-

Louis from Montfort

self and in His dearest friends. They will accordingly perform with joy the menial household tasks the worldly hold contemptible. Most of all, they will have a great devotion to the Most Holy Virgin, whom they will always honor as the Lady in charge of this house." Louis was to prove himself scrupulously faithful to that rule.

In the ensuing years, he made great strides in holiness, praying intently for long hours, undertaking difficult penances, applying himself diligently to his studies. Among his duties was the care of the library. This gave him the opportunity to read the writings of the Fathers of the Church, especially St. Bernard, and of many other spiritual authorities. He could declare later that he had read "almost all the books treating of devotion to the Blessed Virgin."

Louis Marie de Montfort was ordained a priest on June 5th, 1700. His exceptionally high standard of prayer and mortification caused some of his fellow priests to feel uncomfortable in his presence and they caused him many embarrassments and humiliations. But Father de Montfrot always looked on the cross as a great blessing and a sign of victory. And, indeed, his missionary labors were extraordinarily fruitful; hardened hearts were softened, sinners were converted and great numbers of heretics were converted to the true faith. The secret of his success? He had no secret other than the Secret of Mary. Having resolved to consecrate himself entirely to Mary, he tried to live according to the spirit of that consecration, that is, complete dependence on Mary's will after the example of Our Lord whose total obedience to Mary at Nazareth "filled angels and men with wonder and awe."

Father de Montfort loved to refer to Jesus Christ as the Eternal Wisdom. That title seemed to him to beautifully summarize both the Old and New Testaments. "Divine Wisdom is the substantial and eternal concept of the beauty of God shown to St. John the Evangelist in the wondrous ecstasy which he experienced on the Isle of Patmos, when he exclaimed: 'In the beginning was the Word' (the Son of God, Eternal Wisdom) 'and the Word was with God, and the Word was God.' "[2] To his congregation he would often repeat: "To know Jesus Christ, Eternal Wisdom, is to know enough; to know everything and not to know Him, is to know nothing."[3] On succeeding nights, he would speak lovingly on the goodness and mercy of Jesus, on His beauty and gentleness, on the unutterable sorrows which Jesus suffered for us. His sermons on the Person of Jesus were spoken with such reverence and such conviction that his hearers *knew* that he himself had a passionate love of Jesus, and that Jesus meant absolutely everything to him. They saw clearly that he was willing to suffer a thousand persecutions for the Divine Master. Indeed, Father de Montfort's most effective sermon was his own life.

When people asked him for some guidelines on how they too might obtain this wonderful love of Jesus, the Eternal Wisdom, he gave them four clear means by which such a treasure might be obtained:

Firstly, they must have an ardent desire of Divine Wisdom, but this desire must be really ardent and really sincere. Such a desire, he said, being a great grace of God, will certainly be given to anyone who faithfully keeps the commandments of God.

Secondly, persevering prayer is an absolute prerequisite. "If there is any of you who needs wisdom, he must ask God who gives to all freely and ungrudgingly; it will be given him, but he must ask with faith" (James 1:5-6). "The greater the gift, the more effort it requires to obtain it."[4] "Solomon received Wisdom only after praying for a long time and with extraordinary fervor."[5]

Thirdly, universal mortification was specified by Jesus Himself as a condition for discipleship. The Divine Wisdom seeks for persons worthy of Him. "He seeks, because there are so few, that He can scarcely find any sufficiently detached from the world, sufficiently interior and mortified to be worthy of His Person, of His riches and of union with Him."[6] "I believe," said Father de Montfort, that the Cross is the greatest secret of the King, the greatest mystery of Eternal Wisdom."[7] "By His death, the ignominies of the Cross were made so glorious, its poverty and bareness so opulent, its pains so sweet, its hardness so attractive, that it became, as it were, deified and an object of adoration for angels and men."[8] "True Wisdom has fixed His abode in the Cross so firmly that you will not find Him in this world save in the Cross."[9]

Louis from Montfort

Fourthly, "the greatest means of all, and the most wonderful of all secrets for obtaining and keeping Divine Wisdom is a tender and true devotion to the Blessed Mary. No one but Mary has had the power to conceive and give birth to Eternal Wisdom, and no one else has the power to bring Him to life, as it were, through the operation of the Holy Spirit in the souls of those chosen by Him."[10] "Here is the great advice, the admirable secret. Let us, so to speak, take Mary into our house by consecrating ourselves unreservedly to her as her servants and slaves. . . . This good Mother, who never allows herself to be outdone in liberality, will give herself to us, in an incomprehensible yet real manner, and then Eternal Wisdom will come to dwell in her as in His glorious throne room."[11]

Although he was always accepted and loved by the poor and the destitute, Father de Montfort continued to suffer humiliations at the hands of a number of priests. Sometimes he was simply dismissed, told to move on. At one stage in Paris, he was utterly alone, destitute with no fixed abode. He was fortunate to find lodgings in a poor house, and even then it was only in a rickety "storeroom" under the stairs. The only furniture was a straw mattress. Yet, in spite of all deprivations, he was intensely happy; he was sharing the Cross of Christ. And it was here that he wrote his first great book, "The Love of Eternal Wisdom," small in size but priceless in its contents. He was now writing from the fruits of his rich experience of suffering and an intense prayer-life.

A few years later, Father de Montfort set out on pilgrimage for Rome, a stick in one hand, his little statue of Our Lady as usual in the other, his great beads of fifteen decades hanging by his side. His breviary and his bible were his only luggage. Again he lived on the alms which he begged "for the love of God." He was received most graciously by the Pope, Clement XI, who gave him every encouragement to persevere in his missionary work in France. Such preaching as his was more necessary than ever to combat the heresy of Jansenism which was rife in many parts of France at that time.

He returned to France, preaching with renewed vigor and enthusiasm, and constantly invoking the help of Our

FRANK DUFF

Blessed Lady. Since the age of five, he had recited the Rosary daily with devotion. Now he found it to be a powerful instrument in his struggle with Satan for the souls of men. To his fellow priests he said: "I could tell you at great length of the grace God gave me to know by experience the effectiveness of the preaching of the Holy Rosary and of how I have seen with my own eyes the most wonderful conversions it has brought about. I assure you that the Rosary is a priceless treasure which is inspired by God."[12] And to everybody who listened to him he said: "I earnestly beg of you to say the Rosary every day. When death draws near, you will bless the day and hour when you took to heart what I told you, for, having sown the blessings of Jesus and Mary, you will reap eternal blessings in heaven."[13]

It is probably the autumn of 1712, that Father de Montfort wrote his best-known book, "True Devotion to the Blessed Virgin," the book that has undoubtedly led countless souls along the pathways of great holiness. In the concluding chapter of "The Love of Eternal Wisdom," he had written: "the greatest means of all for obtaining and keeping Divine Wisdom is a tender and true devotion to the Blessed Mary." He regarded that chapter as so important that he felt compelled to elaborate on it. The result is his book on "True Devotion to the Blessed Virgin," in which he makes a reasoned and moving plea that we should consecrate ourselves totally to Mary, so that she can mould us more perfectly into the likeness of Christ; in other words, we should consecrate ourselves to Jesus through Mary.

Frank Duff's summary account of De Montfort's treatise on the "True Devotion" is worth quoting: "De Montfort does no more than mirror the Divine idea of Mary, so vividly and unmistakenly revealed in prophecy. Likewise, the Annunciation shows her key-position. Her free decision and her faith opened up a way to God. Mary is the Mother of Christ's Mystical Body. In so far as we are members of Christ's Body, so necessarily are we children of Mary, His Mother. It is in her bosom, moulded ever more and more admirably to His likeness by her unremitting maternal care, that we grow into the perfect man who is Christ and come to the full measure of His stature. Without her, this, our sublime destiny, is not achieved; such is the Divine arrange-

Louis from Montfort

ment . . . Therefore, the soul must give to Mary a devotion *corresponding to the intensity of its dependence on her* which is a constant and an all-embracing one. The "True Devotion" is full acknowledgement of Mary's Motherhood and also—strange to say—represents the very minimum of what is due to her. Its practice is the systematic recognition of the God-assigned part of Mary in every operation of the spiritual life."[14]

The consecration to Mary, as advocated by Fr. de Montfort, requires the formal entry into a compact with Mary, whereby one gives to her one's whole self, with all its thoughts and deeds and possessions, both spiritual and temporal, past, present and future, without the reservation of the smallest, in order to belong more fully to Christ.[15] That is the first step.

The second step is to live out this consecration in one's daily life and apostolate. Frank Duff not only understood this very well but he inserted it into the very prayers of the Legion. I refer to the prayer for Apostolic Faith which Legionaries recite daily and which was taken almost verbatim from No. 214 of De Montfort's *True Devotion to Mary:* "Confer, O Lord, on us who serve beneath the standard of Mary . . . a courageous faith, which will enable us to undertake and carry out without hesitation great things for God and for the salvation of souls . . . Etc."

Father de Montfort founded three Religious Congregations, the Company of Mary (Montfort Missionaries) for priests and brothers,[16] the Daughters of Wisdom for Religious Sisters and the Brothers of St. Gabriel (teaching brothers). He died on the 28th of April, 1716. In one hand he was holding his crucifix, in the other his little statue of Our Lady.

Although he died at the early age of forty-three, Father de Montfort "evangelized seven dioceses, travelling in the course of his apostolic journeys fifteen thousand miles, always on foot. He transformed more than a hundred parishes, subduing the most rebellious hearts, inflaming the coldest, softening the hardest. He made many pilgrimages for this gift of touching hearts, and his prayers were well answered."[17]

On the 7th of September, 1838, Pope Gregory XVI be-

FRANK DUFF

stowed on Louis Marie de Montfort the title of Venerable. On the 20th of July, 1947, Pope Pius XII solemnly canonized him in St. Peter's. In his address, the Pope said of him: "The greatest force behind all his apostolic ministry and his great secret for attracting and winning souls for Jesus was his devotion to Mary."

De Montfort's treatise on "True Devotion" contains this remarkable "prophecy": "I clearly foresee that raging beasts will come in fury to tear to pieces with their diabolical teeth this little book and the one the Holy Spirit made use of to write it, or they will cause it at least to lie hidden in the darkness and silence of a chest and so prevent it from seeing the light of day . . . But no matter . . . It even gives me encouragement to hope for great success at the prospect of a mighty legion of brave and valiant soldiers of Jesus and Mary, both men and women, who will fight the devil, the world, and corrupt nature in the perilous times that are sure to come."[18] And, indeed, his "prophecy" came true. After his death, his manuscript was stored for safe keeping. Then it was forgotten, and lost. It wasn't until over a hundred years after his death that it was discovered—in an old chest!

Since that time, de Montfort's treatise on the "True Devotion" has not ceased to exercise a truly marvelous influence on souls who sincerely strive to implement its teachings. One such soul was Frank Duff. Frank wrote one noteworthy paragraph in the Legion handbook in which those who knew him can see clearly mirrored the effects that the practice of the True Devotion produced in Frank himself: "If the sum of the experiences of those who teach, and understand, and practise the True Devotion is of value, it seems unquestionable that it deepens the interior life, sealing it with the special character of unselfishness and purity of intention. There is a sense of guidance and protection: a joyful certainty that now one's life is being employed to the best advantage. There is a supernatural outlook, a definite courage, a firmer faith, which make one a mainstay of any enterprise. There is a tenderness and a wisdom which keep strength in its proper place. There is, too, the protectress of them all, a sweet humility. Graces come which one cannot but realise are out of the common. Fre-

Louis from Montfort

quently, there is a call to a great work, which is patently beyond one's merits and natural capacity. Yet with it come such helps as enable that glorious but heavy burden to be borne without faltering. In a word, in exchange for the splendid sacrifice which is made in the True Devotion by selling oneself into this species of slavery, there is gained the hundredfold which is promised to those who despoil themselves for the greater glory of God."[19]

NOTES

[1] Note: Some legionaries who make this Consecration choose to do so privately. Others prefer a more solemn form of Consecration, such as described here.

[2] "The Love of Eternal Wisdom," par. 17.

[3] ibid, par. 11.

[4] ibid, par. 184.

[5] "The Love of Eternal Wisdom," par. 184.

[6] ibid, par. 195.

[7] ibid, par. 171.

[8] ibid, par. 172.

[9] ibid, par. 180.

[10] ibid, par. 203.

[11] ibid, par. 211.

[12] "The Secret of the Rosary," ch. 1.

[13] "True Devotion to the Blessed Virgin," par. 254.

[14] "The De Montfort Way" by Frank Duff.

[15] It should be understood that a complete understanding of de Montfort's teaching can only be got by reading his books.

[16] In 1965, the Montfort Fathers and Brothers accorded Frank Duff the distinction of being the first honorary member (lay or clerical), in its two hundred and sixty-year-old history, to be admitted to their community, the Company of Mary of Montfort.

[17] "St. Louis-Marie de Montfort," pamphlet, by Monsignor Deery.

[18] "True Devotion to the Blessed Virgin" par. 114.

[19] Legion Handbook, p. 116.

28 Lough Derg Pilgrimage

Frank Duff's gaberdine coat was old and well-worn. It was patched in places but it was still serviceable and he saw no reason why he should discard it in favor of a new one. Besides, he had become attached to it. His work was very much among the poor and God had developed in him a true spirit of poverty in answer to his persevering prayer.

As his family saw it, however, his coat was not only old, it was ancient, a museum piece, and the patches on it were far too many.

"Frank, think of all the poor men down there in the Morning Star Hostel. Will you not donate your old coat to them?"

Reluctantly, he yielded, but at least, he felt, it was for a good cause.

Some time later, Frank was preparing to go on his annual pilgrimage to Lough Derg. It was then it hit him like a thunderbolt—his old gaberdine coat, how he would miss it. He wondered who was wearing it now. He met Tom Doyle, the indoor legionary brother in charge of the Morning Star Hostel.

"Tom," he said, "to tell you the truth, I'm half sorry I parted with my old gaberdine, it was quite good enough for me."

"Well, I have good news for you then," answered Tom, "none of the men in the 'Morning Star' would wear it; they said it was too dilapidated. So you can have it back."

And, indeed, back it came, to the disappointment of Frank's family. When Frank set out for Lough Derg, his old friend the gaberdine coat went with him.

Lough Derg Pilgrimage

• • • • •

Just as Mount Melleray was the monastery where Frank went to refresh his soul and spirit, and relax a little in body, so the site of the ancient monastic settlement on Lough Derg in the north-west of Ireland was the place where he chose to do penance.

Frank first heard of Lough Derg from Tom Mc Cabe who used to visit the Duff household, as he was a great friend of Frank's father. In fact, Tom was the man Frank's father had once saved from drowning. He was a very religious person and when, during his visits, he spoke of Lough Derg Frank was an eager listener.

Lough Derg in Donegal is situated in a desolate region of barrenness and bleakness with hardly a human habitation in sight. It is renowned throughout the world as a place of pilgrimage and penance. In the middle of the lake is a small island called Station Island, which was once the site of a monastic settlement. The monks have long since gone to their reward but the remnants of their stone cells and chapel remain, a stark and sacred reminder to succeeding generations that "man does not live on bread alone but on every word that proceeds from the mouth of God."

Frank's first opportunity to go to Lough Derg came in October 1915. Four young ladies from Ranelagh, Dublin, were discussing plans to go there on pilgrimage. Frank, overhearing them, asked if he might go with them. They readily agreed. The journey was long and tiring; the penitential exercises on the island were severe. Nevertheless, Frank went again the following year, this time organizing a group of twenty-one others to accompany him.

In bygone days, the Lough Derg pilgrimage had been a popular one among the Irish but by the early part of this century the numbers of pilgrims had dropped considerably, and this great penitential exercise might have been discontinued but for the faithful perseverance of the local people who kept the tradition alive. When Frank tried to reawaken interest in Lough Derg he found that very few people knew anything about it. He continued to promote it and took a group every year.

By 1922 his group had grown to fifty-seven. That partic-

FRANK DUFF

ular year, possibly due to the unsettled political situation in the country, his group was the only organized one to make the pilgrimage. When the pilgrims arrived at Pettigo, which is about four miles from Lough Derg, they found there was no mode of conveyance available for the remainder of the journey. Fortunately, they secured the services of a truck driver, and he transported the ladies and the baggage to the lakeside. The four men in the party, including Frank, set out to walk the four miles but the truck-driver, having carried out his commission to the ladies, returned and "lifted" the male pilgrims for the last mile of their journey. Local boatmen then rowed all the pilgrims to the holy island.

Year by year, knowledge of the Lough Derg pilgrimage spread. As soon as the pilgrimage had been re-established and as the number of pilgrims grew, Frank handed over the organizing of it to others. It was always his policy to delegate to others as much responsibility as he could, partly because it would give him more time to concentrate on new enterprises, and partly because he realized that there were many people who were equally competent to do these things; they simply needed encouragement. "Responsibility," he used to say, "turns sand into gold." Tom McCabe had already been organizing such pilgrimages, and Tom's fellow members in the St. Vincent de Paul Society, gave great support until, eventually, pilgrims were travelling to Lough Derg annually from all parts of Ireland. On some days there would be over a thousand pilgrims on the island.

It used to give Frank Duff particular joy to see so many young people doing the pilgrimage. He often said that young people were idealists and preferred challenging enterprises to feed their idealism rather than innocuous exercises which would not make them "feel the pinch," and he lamented that some priests presented very little challenge to young people, so that the "Catholicism" presented to them was neither stimulating nor in harmony with Christ's command: "unless you take up your cross daily and follow Me, you cannot be My disciple."

At any rate, the sight of so many people, of all ages, gathered together in this holy spot simply and solely to do penance must have been very consoling for a man whose

Lough Derg Pilgrimage

life was dedicated to raising the spiritual standards of his fellow-men. But that consolation was incidental. Frank came to Lough Derg neither to be consoled nor to be edified but simply to do penance himself.

The penitential practices of the Irish have a long tradition. When Irish monasticism was at its peak in the seventh and eighth centuries, the links between the monk and the layman were close and strong. Many of the monasteries were built in places of easy access and were central to the lives of the populace, providing them with education and even with living-accommodation as well as being religious centres. Many of the monks were, in fact, laymen and remained so. When monks from these monasteries established foundations in more desolate and remote areas, or on islands such as Skellig Rock or Lough Derg Island, their spirituality and even more ascetic way of life continued to have an extraordinary hold on the hearts and minds of the people.

Because of the large number and influence of these monasteries, it was inevitable that many of the penitential practices of monastic life should find their way into the religious life of the people.

Since that "golden age" of early Christian Ireland, the Irish have maintained a sort of kinship, a feeling, for penances; not indeed that they enjoy them, or that they have always practised these penances, but their history and their whole tradition tells them that religion is not fully genuine unless it is tested and supported by penance.

Frank found the penances of Lough Derg very hard. Yet he returned there year after year. The annual three-day pilgrimage simply became part of his life.

The great central acts of the pilgrimage are: Confession, Mass and holy Communion. But as a rose blossoms in the midst of thorns, so these great liturgical acts are set against a background of prayer and penance.

The penances are threefold. Firstly, there is the fast. The pilgrim who comes to Lough Derg must observe a total fast from the previous midnight. Only once every twenty-four hours may the fast be broken and even then, the single meal that is allowed consists of dry bread and black tea.

Secondly, the pilgrim must remain barefooted during his stay on the island, and the penitential "rounds" must be

FRANK DUFF

done barefooted. The "rounds" or stations, consist in the recital of many prayers as the pilgrim walks on the stony ground around each monastic cell, or "bed," as it is called. When the prescribed prayers of three Paters, three Aves and the Creed are completed, the pilgrim repeats them while kneeling on the sharp stones at the entrance to the "bed." After that he does the "round" inside the "bed," saying the self-same prayers. Then, finally, he repeats the prayers kneeling at the crucifix in the centre of the "bed." He has then completed his first station. There are many such "beds" or cells, or rather the remains of cells, each dedicated to a different Irish saint; each station consists in visiting many "beds" and praying there.

But there is no hurry. The pilgrim has the whole day — or rather days — in which to carry out these penitential exercises. Besides, if he is "lucky," his feet may sometimes find a smooth stone on which to rest for a brief moment!

The third penance is the all-night Vigil, which means that the pilgrim, worn out though he may be, is allowed no sleep for twenty-four hours, that is, from 10 p.m. on the day of arrival till 10 p.m. on the second day.

The four prescribed stations for the second day of the pilgrimage are said in the Basilica during the night. The performance of these stations inside the Basilica during the night hours is possibly the most trying part of the whole pilgrimage, as the battle to ward off sleep during all those prayers is a hard one indeed. Sometimes there are benevolent smiles on the faces of the more determined souls when they hear a few musical snores from the weaker-willed. But the good Lord knows all are doing their best.

On the second night, a sleep of six hours is allowed and on the third day, after some modified penances, the pilgrim may return home but must continue the strict Lough Derg fast until midnight.

For forty-nine consecutive years, Frank Duff faithfully performed the Lough Derg pilgrimage. When he was seventy-four years old, a serious illness forced him to discontinue it.

Mary Rowe, a Dublin legionary, who was often on the same pilgrimage as Frank recalled her memories of those occasions:

"When Frank did those Stations, walking around the

Lough Derg Pilgrimage

rocky beds in his bare feet, he prayed intently and was absolutely oblivious to everything going on around him. I noticed his feet never looked for a soft stone: he just kept going regardless of the sharp stones. During the Night Vigil he'd never nod or drop off to sleep. It seemed as though he had built himself up for it."

Apart from the times prescribed for doing the Stations and the Penitential Exercises, there is no "rule of silence" during the three-day pilgrimage. During the "free time" Frank would join his friends for a chat and would tell jokes and laugh heartily, as he enjoyed the "breaks" just like everybody else. As someone said of him: "There was no 'molly-coddling' about Frank Duff's spirituality; there was a healthy wholesomeness about him."

On one of the pilgrimages, the weather was most unfavourable for outdoor penitential exercises so the priest-in-charge told the pilgrims they could remain within the basilica and do the Stations there. Mary Rowe was surprised later when she looked out and saw Frank braving the weather and laboriously making his way around one of the "beds."

When she got the opportunity, she said to him:

"Mr. Duff, in your Legion handbook you stress the importance of obedience. Why, then, do you do the Stations outdoors when the priest says you should do them indoors?"

"I can't answer you that," he replied, "but I couldn't bear to do them inside."

And indeed it is likely that the priest-in-charge understood that this man who came to Lough Derg to do penance did not want any soft options.

At the conclusion of the Lough Derg pilgrimage, as the pilgrims are being ferried off the island by local boatmen, they all sing the hymn to St. Patrick.

> Hail glorious St. Patrick, dear saint of our isle,
> on us thy poor children bestow a sweet smile:
> And now thou art high in thy mansions above,
> on Erin's green valleys look down in thy love.
>
> In the war against sin, in their fight for the faith,
> dear saint, may thy children resist to the death;
> May their strength be in meekness, in penance and prayer;
> their banner the Cross which they glory to bear.

FRANK DUFF

The pilgrims are tired and hungry; nevertheless everyone leaves with a light heart and a peace that the world cannot give. They have been cleansed from all their sins; they have made atonement by three days of self denial and fasting in the manner of the early Irish monks; they have received in full measure that great gift of the Holy Spirit—joy.

At the same time, as they leave the island, they have a "sympathetic" smile for the hundreds of new pilgrims who are just arriving on the island to begin the Lough Derg pilgrimage and continue a noble tradition.

29 The Trusty Old Bike

One summer's day in 1951, four men alighted from the train at Tuam, Co. Galway, and collected their bicycles from the luggage wagon. The only thing that might have been noticed by the railway porter was that these men were rather older than the usual cycling parties that occasionally came to tour the west of Ireland on bicycles.

Frank Duff, just turned sixty, was the oldest of the four. His three companions, Brendan Crowley, Tom Doyle and Jack Nagle, may have wondered if they were wise in taking him with them on an arduous cycling holiday. He looked frail and sickly. He had lost a lot of weight in the previous couple of years. On the other hand, it was Frank who had proposed the idea.

"I'm exhausted," he had told them, "in fact I'm near breaking point; I just must get away from Dublin for a complete change."

And indeed they understood. His mother's death, especially, had had a traumatic effect on him. Other sorrows, too, weighed heavily. Just recently had come the news that a number of legionaries had been martyred in China. As well as all this, Frank's work schedule in Dublin was extremely heavy. Each new day brought new difficulties and new pressures.

• • • • •

From the moment Frank mounted his faithful old steed, the bike, outside Tuam railway station, he began to shed the cares and worries and tedium of the previous couple of

FRANK DUFF

years. The pleasant town of Tuam, where St. Jarlath founded his monastery in the sixth century, warmed Frank's heart, with its slower pace of life, its friendly helpful people, always delighted to chat with visitors who enjoy their charming brogues. The jarring sound of the telephones constantly ringing and demanding attention, the heart-breaking stories of the crushed and defeated, "the least of Christ's brethren" and the problems coming from further afield, from the other ends of the earth, were all forgotten for a while. Here were four exhilarated men, cycling along happily and not "so full of care that they had no time to stand and stare" at the wonders of God's creation.

During the succeeding week, the four legionaries cycled through the beautiful, rugged countryside of Connemara with its wild grandeur. Each evening they would seek out some small cosy guesthouse and stay for "bed and breakfast," and then continue next day through the valleys and mountain passes, enjoying the breath-taking scenery — the hills of yellow gorse, the calm lakes mirroring the blue mountains, the little waterfalls making sweet music, the white-washed thatched cottages.

When they came to some place of special beauty and seclusion, they rested and enjoyed the picnic lunch packed for them by the good lady of the guesthouse. The air was heavy with the scents of honeysuckle and wild bluebells and there was, too, the healthy smell of fresh bogs.

Frank could easily be coaxed into telling good stories. Sometimes his stories were of serious events, and could be wonderfully educative as well as entertaining. Sometimes he liked to tell about funny incidents he had witnessed, and he had a 'knack' of embellishing these to the amusement of his listeners who could usually discern the embellished parts but enjoyed more the hearty laugh of Frank as he told them.

Their route took them through Westport, on to the village of Leenane, then by Kylemore Abbey to Clifden, and Maam Cross, and Galway. The name given to this picturesque tract of mountain, glen and lake country, situated on the eastern border of Connemara and dividing it from County Mayo, is "Joyce's Country." They passed the cot-

The Trusty Old Bike

tage of the patriot, Padraig Pearse, at Rosmuck, where he wrote the beautiful stories of Losagán (The Child Jesus), Eoinín na nÉan (Eoineen of the Birds) and composed the lovely poem "The Wayfarer":

> "Sometimes my heart hath shaken
> with great joy,
> to see a leaping squirrel in a tree,
> or a red lady-bird upon a stalk,
> or little rabbits in a field at evening
> lit by a slanting sun,
> or some green hill where shadows drifted by,
> some quiet hill
> where mountainy men had sown
> and soon would reap;
> near to the gate of heaven;
> or children with bare feet
> upon the sands of some ebbed sea,
> or playing on the streets
> of little towns in Connacht."

Frank, who was nationalist and very close to the Irish leaders at the historic time of the Nation's birth, must have been moved at the sight of Pearse's white-washed cottage in lonely Rosmuck, where no sound breaks the stillness save the cry of the curlew.

Clew Bay, dotted with a hundred small islands, showed off its deep blue and green colors during the day, reserving its magic silver sheen for the sunsets. It left an indelible impression on Frank.

At Kylemore Abbey, the cyclists rested for two days. The good nuns were surprised when they learned the distances covered each day by Frank and "his merry men."

Was it too much for Frank? On the contrary, his old vitality seemed to come back to him, his appetite improved and the long daily cycle trips, tiring though they were, actually made him stronger.

It was a truly marvelous holiday and he was thrilled to find it did him so much good. He resolved he would do something similar the following year, and true enough, the following year saw him cycling through County Kerry with Sid Quinn and Jack Nagle. The cycling trips had definitely

FRANK DUFF

come to stay. It was to be an annual event for the rest of his life.

The numbers going on these cycling trips grew and, in the most remote parts of Ireland, young and old stood to stare and smile and then wave as ten or twelve "strangers" cycled leisurely and merrily on their way.

On one occasion, John Gavin, one of the cycling party, suddenly remembered he had left his glasses behind in the guesthouse where they had spent the previous night. Frank insisted on cycling back — against the wind too — to recover them, even though he was seventy years old at the time. Thoughtfulness was one of his great qualities.

Frank would never, under any circumstances, risk missing his daily Mass; sometimes travelling plans had to be restricted in order to enable the cycling party to attend Mass in a village or town. Then one summer, Frank invited a priest friend to join the cycling group. Thus the party was assured of daily Mass no matter where they found themselves. Eventually, they secured a regular cycling "chaplain" when Fr. Herman Nolan C.P. joined "the Sprocketts," as the cycling party had now come to be called.

One of Frank's hobbies was photography. He treasured a good camera that he received as a present and always took it with him on these trips. He had a great love for every square inch of his native land and wished to capture with his camera the marvelous beauty of the Irish countryside. When the winter months came, he would invite all his cycling companions to his home to show them his slides. As he presented his beautiful pictures on the screen, he would give a detailed commentary. His audience, marveling at his extraordinary memory for detail, not only enjoyed the pictures but they loved to observe the boyish delight and enthusiasm with which Frank himself relived those delightful days, as he commented on slide after slide.

His unbounded enthusiasm led him sometimes into exaggerations of which he seemed totally unaware. When he returned from any of his cycling trips, his first comment often on meeting a friend was: "It was the best ever" and, indeed, it was clear that he meant it. So no one ever liked to say to him: "But, Mr. Duff, you told us that after the last trip." Besides, those who knew him best realized that

The Trusty Old Bike

Frank's extraordinary love for the countryside and for nature in its every detail was something that was more than natural. It was a sort of mystical appreciation of God's loving, creative presence in everything that eye and ear presented to us, so that no limits could be set to either his (Frank's) appreciation of God's handiwork or to his enthusiasm in his efforts to express it.

On one occasion during a cycling trip, a legionary, observing Frank in a meditative mood as he surveyed the beautiful scenery, remarked how appropriate was the Canticle of Daniel which is so often prayed in the breviary.

"Yes," replied Frank, "that is my favourite psalm."

The reference was to chapter three of the Book of Daniel.

"And you, mountains and hills, O bless the Lord.
And you, all plants of the earth, O bless the Lord.
And you, fountains and springs, O bless the Lord.
To him be highest glory and praise for ever."
(Dan. 3:75-77)

• • • • •

"Is that Croagh Patrick in the distance?" On this occasion Frank was touring County Mayo with a priest and four legionary brothers when he saw the cone-shaped mountain rising majestically in the distance.

And indeed it was; the Grand Monarch Mountain of Erin, sometimes called the Mount Sinai of Ireland, but best known as Croagh Patrick because, according to tradition, the great St. Patrick had climbed that mountain and spent the forty days of Lent there in prayer and penance. Every year, over twenty thousand Irish pilgrims climb Croagh Patrick on the last Sunday in July to do penance and to pray. The mountain is 2,510 feet above sea level.

Frank suggested to his companions that they cycle in that direction and undertake the pilgrimage. Who could disagree with such a lofty proposal?

After about three hours of laborious climbing, they reached the summit of the "holy" mountain and said the prescribed prayers on the spot where St. Patrick had

FRANK DUFF

prayed more than fifteen hundred years before. As Frank looked out over the land he loved so dearly, he must surely have recalled the prayer St. Patrick prayed for the Irish people: "Wherefore may it never happen to me from my God that I should ever lose His people which He hath purchased at the ends of the earth" *(St. Patrick's "Confessions")*.

Frank was surprised and thrilled to meet a legionary on top of Croagh Patrick. She was a thirteen-year-old junior legionary who was on holidays from her school in Westport and had climbed the mountain with her younger sister. She was overjoyed, naturally, at meeting Frank Duff. "Incredible," she surely thought, "meeting the founder of the Legion on top of the 'holy' mountain." Her big regret was that her legionary friends back in Westport would never believe her when she told them her "incredible" story! Frank smiled. His heart went out to young people. There was nothing he wouldn't do for them. He handed his camera to one of the group and said: "Take a photo of my junior legionary and me."

The descent was dangerously swifter than the ascent. For the first three-quarter mile, the rocks were sharp and the footsteps on the shale kept causing minor landslides. Frank fell a couple of times; his leg was cut but not too seriously. By the time he had reached the bottom of the mountain, however, he was a sorry sight—cut, bruised, dishevelled but, nevertheless, none the worse for his adventure—although he was over seventy years old at that time!

And a couple of weeks later, a young schoolgirl in Mayo excitedly opened a letter which had a Dublin postmark. It was from Frank Duff. He enclosed a beautiful photograph of himself and her taken on the mountain top. Now her legionary friends would have to believe her "incredible" story.

• • • • •

Frank Duff was a true patriot in the noblest sense of the word. His patriotism derived from his two great loves—love of his religion and love of his country.

He was adamant that the Legion of Mary should never

The Trusty Old Bike

involve itself in politics but he did believe that it had a tremendous contribution to make towards the fostering of a sense of true patriotism in people. He observed that, in many countries there is a tendency by the modern State to widen its powers and arrogate to itself functions and moral obligations which Christianity had always regarded as belonging to the individual. But he also contended that this inclination on the part of the State was largely due to the inertia of the citizens. If there is serious neglect and if citizens have not got a proper sense of responsibility in regard to defects in their midst, then the State is practically forced to intervene.

The problem, as Frank saw it, was not just lack of enterprise and initiative on the part of the citizens. The bigger problem was the cynicism and scepticism that can often pervade a community and stifle resolve and action. Often, too, there was a lack of the moral courage that is necessary to tackle serious problems and to persevere in the effort. So, basically the problem is spiritual, involving a lack of "community virtues," as well as an inadequate understanding of the all-embracing role of religion.

But where is the solution? How get people to realize their responsibilities to the community? How restore to the community proper concepts of honesty and integrity in all walks of life? How enlighten people to see that their religion must be brought to bear on all aspects of living—social, cultural, educational, recreational? How inculcate the spirit of self-sacrifice and true idealism? In a word, how educate people to a proper concept of true patriotism?

"A better order," Frank said, "does not spring out of itself. There must be some force to animate it. My formula for that animating principle is a well-worked praesidium." And he outlined his ideas in a booklet which he called, "True Devotion to the Nation," possibly unmatched or unchallenged as one of the finest treatments of that subject.

Frank was convinced that love for one's country is not enough; it must be love for the right reasons and it must be understood as part of our religion. "Jesus and Mary," he pointed out, "lived the common life of their locality with perfection. It would be impossible to conceive the idea of them as being indifferent or neglectful in any respect.

FRANK DUFF

Today, the world is their country and each place is their Nazareth."

Frank knew from his wide experience that civic spirit which depends merely on enthusiasm does not last and, furthermore, that a vague appeal to Christian humanitarianism might mean little or nothing in practice. Nor can a mediocre Catholicism achieve very much in the way of idealism and service and self-sacrifice. In fact, unless the community—or at least a substantial part of it—can be brought to a reasonably sound understanding of the Mystical Body, the best intentions and the best efforts can hardly be expected to achieve substantial or lasting results. "The only root or ultimate justification which I can discover for patriotism," said Frank, "is the Christian doctrine of the Mystical Body in all its details."

And so, back to the "well-worked praesidium" which is already proposing this doctrine to its members as a motivating power, obliging them to think in terms of every person, in every place, and of all walks of life. More important still, because it requires from its members a minimum of two hours substantial work each week, it puts that doctrine into detailed and determined action. It can be the spirited nucleus in a community. Through it, with proper backing, a whole area can by degrees be brought to a proper appreciation of this central dogma of Christianity and, incidentally, to a real understanding of true patriotism.

The Legion's role in this field is put very succinctly by Fr. Thomas Flynn: "What the Legion has to offer to the temporal order is not exceptional knowledge or expertise, not outstanding skills, not even great numbers of workers —but the spiritual dynamism which has made it a world force and which can be harnessed to uplift any section of the People of God who have the insight and good sense to employ it. . . . It must realize that man has to live amid material things and that his salvation is to a large extent bound up with them" *(Legion Handbook page 37).*

30 The Miracle of South America

Frank Duff was invited to visit the College of the Irish Christian Brothers at Marino, Dublin, to speak about the Legion of Mary. The Brothers were impressed by his talk. One young trainee Brother who was deeply affected by it was Alfie Lambe, one of the Novices. Alfie, from Tullamore, Co. Offaly, had a great desire to dedicate his life to God as a Christian Brother. Because of ill health, however, he had to leave the Novitiate. His superiors in the Christian Brothers, always to the fore in promoting every good Catholic cause, and staunch supporters of the Legion of Mary, encouraged Alfie to join the Legion.

He became an enthusiastic member from the start. His ever-present smile, his gentleness, his boyish exuberance, his tender love for Our Lady all marked him out as a legionary of great potential.

He came to Dublin and lived in the Morning Star Hostel with the indoor Legion brothers. There, of course, he had close contact with Frank Duff and benefitted immensely thereby. Just as a sapling planted in moist and warm soil grows into a strong tree, Alfie's spiritual life developed and matured. Soon he was assigned to do Legion extension work around Ireland.

One of Alfie's first Legion mentors was Seamus Grace. Then one day he heard that Seamus had volunteered as Legion envoy and was being sent to the far-away Continent of South America. This announcement electrified Alfie. It was inevitable that his own mind should turn towards envoyship.

"This was what he was craving for," Frank wrote later,

FRANK DUFF

"something really big, a going somewhere into the unknown to search for souls in need and prepared to pay any price for them. Make no mistake about it; it was the idea of utter giving of himself that allured him."

Frank would always attribute such marvelous development of spirit to one's Legion membership. It never seemed to dawn on him that he himself exerted a truly remarkable influence on those around him. His ardent faith, his great determination, his dreams of world conquest for Christ, his unlimited trust in Our Lady and, above all, the utter conviction with which he spoke, all in one way or another had a profound effect on his listeners. Whenever he was speaking to an individual, or to small groups, he always spoke slowly in a gentle tone and his spirit seemed to communicate itself to receptive souls.

One such receptive soul was Alfie. It wouldn't be necessary for him to remember everything Frank said to him. It sufficed that he was able to catch something of the flame of Frank's unquenchable thirst for souls and his utter confidence in the power of the Legion.

In April, 1953 the Concilium formally appointed Seamus Grace and Alfie Lambe to be Legion envoys to South America. A period of intense preparation followed and this included a study of Spanish. Eventually, the 15th of July was fixed as the departure date. Seamus and Alfie were Carmelite Tertiaries and would, therefore, have liked to set out on the 16th, the Feast of Our Lady of Mount Carmel, but there was no plane for them on that day.

Frank Duff and many other legionaries and relatives traveled to Shannon Airport to see them off. Other travelers preparing to board the plane were probably surprised when the many legionaries suddenly raised their voices in unison to recite the Catena:

> "Who is she that comes forth as the morning rising,
> fair as the moon,
> bright as the sun,
> terrible as an army set in battle array?
> My soul magnifies the Lord. . . ."

The plane, which was scheduled to leave at 11:30 p.m., was delayed. When eventually it did leave, it was after mid-

The Miracle of South America

night. Seamus and Alfie exchanged knowing glances; they had got their wish, after all: it was the 16th of July, the Feast of Our Lady of Mount Carmel.

Many hours later, the two envoys were looking down on the vast continent of South America. When their plane landed at Bogota, the capital of Columbia, Joaquina Lucas was among those waiting to greet them. Joaquina, a legionary from the Philippine Islands, was already serving as an envoy in South America. Seamus was deemed to be sufficiently experienced to work on his own as an envoy; he was assigned to the cities. Alfie was assigned to work with Joaquina to gain further experience and to improve his Spanish. This was marvelous training for him. Together they traveled through much of the country, planting branches of the Legion, extending the Kingdom of Christ. The country was very unlike Alfie's native Ireland and he was fascinated by it—the dizzy mountain heights, the banana plantations, the huge tracts of unspoiled forest land, the wild luxurious vegetation, the exquisite coloring of the flowers.

After some months, Alfie was sufficiently experienced as an envoy to be given total responsibility for his own area. Joaquina proceeded to Brazil. Alfie was now on his own. In a letter to Dublin, he mentioned how he missed Joaquina who had been a real guardian-angel to him. Frank Duff replied: "Life is like that. Things are only given to us in order to be broken or taken away from us. But all is not taken away; the value remains."

There was a grave shortage of priests in most of the South American countries, with the result that there was widespread ignorance of religion and not so much religious practice. Alfie worked like a beaver, establishing Legion praesidia far and near, even in the remotest mountain villages. Though he worked quickly, there was nothing slip-shod about his methods. He was thorough in everything he did and his gentle and sincere manner made him acceptable everywhere.

Bishops, not only in neighbouring dioceses but also in neighbouring countries, were beginning to take notice. It was being proved in no uncertain manner, "that the Legion of Mary was able to stem the leakage from the Church, to seek out undiscovered sources of religious energy and to surround priests and religious with a band of zealous lay helpers."[1]

FRANK DUFF

In February, 1954, Alfie was directed by Concilium to move on to Ecuador where Bishop Echeverría was pleading for the introduction of the Legion. Alfie had learned from Seamus Grace the importance of recruiting and enthusing extension workers. These he trained and assigned to various outlying areas. The responsibility he gave them transformed them from being very "ordinary" legionaries into dynamic workers for the Cause of Christ. It also resulted, of course, in speeding up the growth of the Legion. Within a comparatively short time, there were four hundred praesidia in Ecuador and the Church in that country was witnessing a new Pentecost.

Alfie was besieged by urgent invitations to come to other South American countries. He moved on to Brazil. There were already three envoys there but Brazil, almost the same size as Europe, was in need of many more envoys.

Back in Dublin, Frank Duff followed every detail of Alfie's itinerary, directing, guiding, encouraging. Without ever setting foot on that continent himself, he was, nevertheless, through his envoys and through the Legion affecting the lives and destinies of thousands, perhaps millions of people.

Alfie might have remained in Brazil had the decision been left to himself. But Frank, like a skilled general on a battlefield, was expert at sizing up situations as well as persons. He recognized early that Alfie's power to influence—a power that derived from a combination of holiness and organizing ability—was truly phenomenal. Argentina needed someone of that calibre. The Concilium, prompted by Frank, instructed Alfie to proceed to Argentina and it was there he spent the remainder of his short life.

Argentina is a vast country and, once again, Alfie was covering thousands of miles on his mission work. His health, which had never been very strong, seemed to be deteriorating and he suffered from stomach ulcers. But he kept going, restless in his pursuit of souls. It is probable that when he was in the Christian Brothers' Novitiate he had learnt the prayer:

"Give me, O Lord, the grace
to fight and not to count the cost,
to toil and not to seek for rest,

The Miracle of South America

to labor and to look for no reward
except that of knowing that I do your most holy will."

That prayer was, and still is, very popular in Ireland among boys and girls who are striving after holiness. It conveys rather accurately the zeal for souls that had taken possession of Alfie. In the Legion handbook, Frank Duff had written: "The legionary must give to the utmost of his capacity. . . . Mary desires to give profusely, but she cannot do so except to the generous soul. . . . The legionary must only look to Mary to supplement, to purify, to perfect, to supernaturalize the natural; to enable weak human effort to achieve what is impossible to it. But these are mighty things. They can mean that mountains will be torn from their foundations and hurled into the sea, and the land be made plain, and the paths straightened to lead on to the Kingdom of God."[2] Alfie had well and truly assimilated those ideas. More than once, he expressed his great desire "to live the Legion." From town to town he went, from village to village, from priest to priest, offering to establish the Legion of Mary, preaching by deed as well as by word, prayerfully and in a spirit of faith and humility, accepting whatever hardships circumstances forced upon him, hardly ever relaxing, never complaining, and having an unbounded trust in Our Blessed Lady.

God blessed both his desires and his efforts. Countless bishops and priests in Argentina, as well as in a number of the other South American countries, have testified to his total giving of himself in the service of Jesus and Mary and to the extraordinary fruitfulness of his labors.

It was a great joy to Alfie to discover that the Irish Christian Brothers had a foundation in Buenos Aires. He visited them whenever he had an opportunity, wishing to show his appreciation for the invaluable spiritual guidance he had received during the few years he had spent in their Novitiate in Dublin.

The Concilium was surprised one day when a letter arrived from Alfie in which he stated that he had begun to study the Russian language. Russia held a strange fascination for him. He referred to the subject a number of times in subsequent letters and eventually asked Concilium to let

FRANK DUFF

him pay a visit to Russia. Possibly Concilium would have appointed him as envoy to Russia when he would have completed his mission to South America, assuming, of course, that Russia would be "open" to a Legion envoy.

It was not to be. Alfie was stricken with a severe and painful form of cancer. He died on the 21st of January, 1958, the feast of Saint Agnes, at the age of twenty-six. The day before he died, he had one big consolation; he got news that Noel Lynch, a young Dublin legionary, had been appointed by Concilium to assist him in Argentina. Alfie knew now that he would not live long enough to train in the new envoy as requested by Concilium but he would certainly assist him "from above."

In her book on Alfie Lambe, Hilde Firtel says: "The life of Alphonsus Lambe was like a meteor. It flashes suddenly before us, soaring to giddy heights, but hardly have we admired its splendor, than it is gone. But whereas a meteor leaves no trace, Alfie's work is thriving and flourishing in all the countries where he was active. The flame which consumed the Irishman, and which he knew how to enkindle in all those who surrounded him, has become a wildfire which has seized an entire continent."[3]

NOTES

[1] "Alfie Lambe" by Hilde Firtel, p. 36.
[2] Legion Handbook, p. 114.
[3] "Alfie Lambe" by Hilde Firtel, p. 124.

31 Nuncios and Envoys

"Mr. Duff, I have very exciting news for you."

It was Eleanor Butler, Countess of Wicklow, who had been an enthusiastic legionary.

"I have just come from Paris," she said. "There I had a long interview with the Apostolic Nuncio who expressed his great interest in the Legion of Mary. He asked me many questions about you and then gave me a message which he asked me to deliver personally to you."

Frank was eager and excited at this news. He remembered well that the same Nuncio had once written from Istanbul through his secretary, Monsignor Tom Ryan, to Legion headquarters asking for detailed information about the Legion. Later this Nuncio had been assigned to France.

Frank had himself gone to France many years previously to help sow the seeds for the Legion. By a happy "coincidence," his interview with the Cardinal Archbishop of Paris took place at the actual centenary moment of the Apparition of Our Lady of the Miraculous Medal. However, the Legion had been slow to grow in France. Some of the bishops, including the Cardinal Archbishop of Paris, were keen on it; others were not, preferring the more traditional forms of Catholic Action.

"Well, well, please sit down," said Frank to the Countess, "this is most interesting. I can hardly wait to hear what the Nuncio had to say."

"He said:" continued the Countess, "when you return to Ireland, please give my best wishes to Mr. Frank Duff and tell him that, even though the bishops of France are divided on the question of the Legion, I am not divided. I am wholeheartedly in favor of it. Its method is right. *It seeks out the individual* in the spirit of faith and love and that goes to the heart of the question."

Frank was elated. It was a great encouragement for him to hear that the Legion had won the appreciation and approval of so worthy and so important a personage.

• • • • •

Frank Duff seemed to be a man who was constantly experiencing the restlessness of the Holy Spirit. Even when things were going smoothly, he did not "rest on his oars" but was studying new situations and needs, and planning, accordingly, methods by which the Legion could help.

One such need, as he saw it, was that of developing some system of adult religious education which would be geared to cater to large numbers of people and which would present religious truths—and their application in men's lives—in a reasonably attractive way.

Frank realized only too well the sorrowful fact that Catholics, in general, did not speak about religion to those outside the Church and seldom enough to those inside it. In many cases, this was due to their not having a sufficient understanding of the doctrines of their religion and thus feeling incompetent or shy about discussing religion with others. In other cases, it was due to a false and destructive idea that religion was a completely private matter and not one for open discussion.

Frank's answer to this problem was the *Patricians.* The purpose of the Patricians, he wrote, is to build up the religious knowledge of the people, to teach them how to explain themselves and to encourage them to apostleship" *(Legion Handbook p. 167).*

Fr. P. J. Brophy succinctly describes the spirit of the Patricians: "We christians, as Christ's brothers, belong to God's family. Thinking about our faith, talking it over and discussing its application in the spirit in which Our Lord and the apostles chatted about the day's teachings at the end of a missionary day in Galilee—this is the spirit of the Patricians" *(cf. quotation in Legion Handbook p. 177).*

Nuncios and Envoys

Certainly, the chapter that Frank wrote outlining not only how the Patrician meetings are run but also—and more fundamentally—the spiritual and psychological principles on which the society is based is a most valuable contribution in the field of religious education.

• • • • •

The Legion was spreading rapidly throughout the world but there were still some areas where it was as yet unknown. Frank was looking for volunteers who would go out as envoys.

"Mr. Duff, I am willing to go as a Legion envoy if you think I am suitable."

It was young Phyllis Dowdall who was speaking. She had a reasonable amount of experience behind her and she had unbounded enthusiasm.

Frank was very pleased. She had just come at the right time; an envoy was needed for Vietnam. For various reasons, however, that project had to be postponed, so Frank proposed that she do some exploratory work among the Irish emigrants in England. The Archbishop had requested Frank to assign some legionary to that particular mission.

However, at the last moment, when Phyllis was having the required routine medical check-up, it was discovered that her health was not one hundred per cent. Instead of being an envoy on the mission, she was, three days later, a patient in the Pembroke Nursing Home, in Dublin.

Always loyal to his legionaries, and no doubt feeling he owed a special debt of gratitude to this girl who had so generously offered herself as an envoy, Frank left his busy office, mounted his bicycle and cycled out to the Nursing Home to visit her.

Phyllis was delighted and felt honored by his visit, but what joy when he came again the following week and the many weeks after that. She was indeed amazed that a man, so busy as he was with the Legion affairs of the whole world, could find time to give so much attention to one individual. Frank came to visit her every single week for the whole ten months while she was in hospital, and he would spend at least an hour with her each time.

185

FRANK DUFF

For Frank, the world was made up of individuals and each individual was another Christ to be revered and served.

Nor was his visit a solemn or a pious business. He chatted about anything and everything under the sun; he talked of his own experiences; he told anecdotes; he joked. He had his own gentle way of bringing comfort and consolation and raising the spirits of a sick person.

A patient who shared the room with Phyllis was a Mrs. Ryan, from Emly. Phyllis recruited her into auxiliary membership of the Legion. One day Mrs. Ryan was reading the Legion prayers.

"Phyllis," she said, "who composed those beautiful prayers?"

"Well, as far as I know, it was Mr. Duff" Phyllis replied.

"Indeed, he must be a marvelous man, then; surely he will be a saint."

"Well, whatever about that, you may have an opportunity to see him yourself because he comes to visit me every week."

"Won't you tell me when he's here?"

"I will indeed."

The very next day, Frank came on his weekly visit. Hanging on the end of Phyllis' bed was a long, red silk dressing-gown. Frank picked it up, put it on himself and swaggered around the room, chuckling loudly.

"Mr. Duff," said Phyllis, "what on earth are you doing?"

"I'm just trying to see what I would look like as a cardinal."

And from a nearby bed the new auxiliary, Mrs. Ryan, looked on aghast. She was gaining some new insights into the sanctity of the "holy founder"!

On the occasion of another visit, Frank opened a bottle of Guinness which had been prescribed by the doctor for Phyllis. It looked "flat." Frank, not quite expert in such matters, shook the bottle to give it a foamy "top." He produced the foam alright. It covered carpets, bedclothes and Frank himself. Not in the least disconcerted, he laughed heartily.

"What will Peg McDonnell think of me when I return to the Regina Coeli reeking with Guinness all over me?"

Nuncios and Envoys

And indeed he always enjoyed a joke at his own expense.

• • • • •

It was the 28th of October, 1958. Frank was walking into the small kitchen in the Regina Coeli where he was accustomed to having his meals with the legionary sisters. At that moment, an announcement over the intercom in the kitchen told that the College of Cardinals had just elected a new Pope. The choice of the cardinals had been rather surprising, although, judging by the great joy and excitement among the milling crowds in St. Peter's Square in Rome, it was something to shout about with recurring and sincere "Viva il Papa's."

Frank was absolutely thrilled. The news took him completely by surprise; it seemed too good to be true. But it was true. He stood up and decided that he must immediately ring up an old friend to tell her the good news; he knew she would be just as happy as he was about it. He went to the adjoining room where the phone was, but before he lifted the receiver, the phone rang. It was Eleanor Butler, Countess of Wicklow.

"Well," said Frank, "that's remarkable; I was just about to ring you; have you heard the good news?"

"I have indeed," she said, "I was ringing to tell you in case you hadn't heard."

And over the phone, they recalled that happy event of nearly ten years before when the Apostolic Nuncio of France had expressed his total confidence in the Legion of Mary. It was that same Nuncio—Cardinal Roncalli—who had just now been elected the new Pope, taking the name of Pope John XXIII.

Less than two years after his election, Pope John XXIII was to give the greatest possible approbation to the Legion when he declared: "The Legion of Mary presents the true face of the Catholic Church" *(to the legionaries of France 13th of July, 1960).*

32 "I'm Not Afraid to Die"

Reports were coming in from all over the world telling about marvelous things being achieved by the Legion of Mary. Nevertheless, there seemed to be endless problems, endless worries, tremendous strain. Frank Duff wrote a revealing letter to a nun:

"My dear Sister X,
I think that I could declare to you that the greater part of my life has been spent in the condition of fatigue. With me it has not exactly been of a nervous character as I figure it to be with you. It has been just a complete tiredness caused by the incessant and depressing labors."

In 1963, Frank underwent what was probably the greatest mental suffering he ever endured. The Regina Coeli House was threatened with closure. Those who had originally given the premises for the purpose of running the hostel were no longer in office. Those now in authority at the Department of Local Government decided that the buildings had deteriorated and were not suitable for housing people. They were not prepared to honor the commitment of their predecessors in office to carry out repairs, etc., at the expense of the Department. At best, it could be said to have been a case of grave misunderstanding. The fact was, however, that the Legion was given notice to quit the premises.

"The horror of the situation," wrote Frank shortly afterwards, "was indescribable. What faced us was the abomination that two hundred and fifty of the most helpless and vulnerable of the population were to be cast to destruction.

"I'm Not Afraid to Die"

In one minute the work, which had taken thirty-three years of desperate striving and devotion on the part of many to build up, was going to be hurled to the winds. So that it was not a question of only the two hundred and fifty but all the multitudes who would in the future be subjected to shipwreck by the taking away of the ark which could have saved them. That prospect was beyond bearing. I cannot think about it, even at the present moment, without quivering with pain."

In earlier days, all the big crises that arose had been discussed with Mr. Lalor. If he couldn't always solve the problems, at least he could, and did pour balm on Frank's troubled soul. But Mr. Lalor had long since gone to his reward. Where else could Frank go for solace? Surrender to self-pity or despair was unthinkable, and would, in any case, be totally unworthy of one dedicated to Our Lady. But there was a solution that was honorable and holy. And Frank found it. This is how he describes it:

"I sought to bury myself and my torment in Mary, to stand upright at the foot of her Son's Cross and her own—merging my pain in hers. I found it almost easy to do that by reason of the fact that it brought visible physical relief. It reduced my own position to proper perspective; my torture lessened. I held control."

In actual fact, the crisis eventually passed and the hostel was saved. The two hundred and fifty residents of the hostel came along to clasp Frank's hand and thank him in their own inimitable way: "God bless you, Mr. Duff: sure only for you where would we be?" And life resumed its normal pace once again.

We may presume that from that day forward, the large picture of Our Lady of Sorrows that graces the wall in the Regina Coeli chapel was given a glance of special affection by Frank Duff as he passed it on his way to Mass every day.

The Rosary of the Seven Dolours had always been one of his favourite daily prayers—in addition to his regular rosary. Henceforth, it would have an even greater significance for him.

● ● ● ● ●

FRANK DUFF

It is likely that the great strain caused by these worries contributed to Frank Duff's severe illness some months later. He suffered a stroke.

He was due to give a talk on a Monday morning to the Social Science students at the University. In the morning, he felt sick but insisted on going to Mass. Then he traveled across the city by bus. When he alighted from the bus he felt quite weak. Fortunately, he saw a Morning Star man whom he asked to assist him in walking. He arrived at the University and began his lecture. After a few minutes he asked to be excused for a short while. But, in fact, he was unable to resume. Blathnaid O'Broin, whose father was a great friend of Frank's, was in the audience. Alarmed at his condition she drove him straight to his home.

Next morning, he struggled out of bed and with the aid of a stick walked to the Capuchin Church in Church Street to assist at Mass. On his way home after Mass, he had just reached the Regina Coeli House when he collapsed. They lifted him gently on to a couch. Miss McDonnell, the housekeeper at that time in Regina Coeli, thought he was dead. Gradually he regained consciousness.

The phone rang in Doctor Monahan's house in Navan. The doctor, who was married to Frank's sister, received the news of his brother-in-law's condition and he drove with haste to Dublin, accompanied by his wife, Sara Geraldine. They took him to their home in Navan.

Dr. Monahan's opinion was that Frank probably had suffered a mild stroke, brought on by sheer exhaustion. He prescribed a period of complete rest and Frank spent five months at their Navan home recuperating and trying to recover some of his former strength and energy. He was seventy-five years of age.

At one stage, Dr. Monahan noticed that Frank, during his illness, was inclined to sleep for very long hours and he became rather alarmed. He thought Frank might perhaps be lapsing into a coma such as that which precedes death. He had him removed to the Mater Hospital, Dublin, where a more thorough examination could be carried out.

While in the hospital, Frank determinedly got out of his bed every morning to assist at Mass. The Mass had always been the centre of his life, the holy Communion his daily

"I'm Not Afraid to Die"

sustenance. By human calculation, it might seem that Frank would please God more by remaining in bed and giving himself a better chance to recover his health. After all, wasn't his life at stake? But Frank had long since trained himself to think on a different level, the level of faith, and he had absolutely no scruples about what he was doing. Besides, he was a fighter. He had been in many a tight corner throughout his life. With sheer faith—and nothing else—he had driven himself to the limits of endurance; he had battled his way through the various crises he had encountered. It would be inconceivable that he could change his ways now.

Providentially for him, there were some priests who were patients in the hospital at that time and these celebrated the holy Mass in the small corridor chapel. So every day Frank was able to have his Mass and holy Communion. He had just enough strength to walk to that corridor and little chapel.

While Frank was recuperating down in Navan in the home of his sister, Sara Geraldine, and her husband, Dr. Monahan, the local priest, Father Herbert, came every day with holy Communion. This was a great consolation for Frank and he was deeply appreciative.

One morning Frank was so weak that Dr. Monahan was very worried. When Father Herbert arrived and had given holy Communion to Frank, Dr. Monahan took him aside into another room and said:

"Father, Frank's condition is very weak. I think he should be anointed."

"In that case there's no point in delaying. I'll go home and come back later on with the holy oils. Does Frank know how ill he is?"

"I think not."

And in fact Frank had no idea he was so ill. When he saw Father Herbert coming for a second time on that same day he was very surprised.

Father Herbert chatted amiably for a moment or two. He wasn't quite sure how to break the news to Frank that he had come to anoint him. Very diffidently he began to explain the "new thinking" on the Sacrament of Extreme Unction, that it was a sacrament of the living and not automatically to be connected with dying.

FRANK DUFF

Slowly the light dawned on Frank. His reaction was calm and practical. He thought to himself: "so that's the way it is, so I am going to die."

To Father Herbert's great relief, Frank said: "Father, if you wish to anoint me, here I am. I am not afraid." Father Herbert expressed his happiness at such understanding and resignation.

"Mr. Duff," he said, "you know some people are a little bit afraid."

"No, not me, I'll be very pleased if I'm entitled to be anointed."

And, there and then, Father Herbert administered the Sacrament of the Anointing of the Sick. It was Holy Thursday.

When the priest had left, Frank was alone with his thoughts. Later, when he had recovered, he described his feelings of that moment:

"I was absolutely overwhelmed with happiness. I wasn't even thinking of the higher aspects of it. But I was paralyzed with joy at the thought of being reunited with my family. I could see everyone of them there waiting for me. The joy I felt was so great that after my recovery I prayed a lot that, when my time would really come to die, the occasion would be no less auspicious, that I would have no fear and that I would be filled with the same joy."

• • • • •

Frank's five-month period of recuperation in his brother-in-law's home in Navan was one of great peace and tranquility. For a long time, he was very ill and extremely weak, but his illness did not cause him great pain or distress. Dr. Monahan, in his treatment of a patient, took all aspects of the person's character into consideration. He knew well that if he were to order Frank to do absolutely no work, such an order could do more harm than good. The restlessness which would ensue would be no aid to recovery. Hence he prescribed that Frank do as much work as he wished, provided that he stayed in bed. Frank was relieved and happy about this prescription. And, in fact, he did quite an amount of work in bed—thinking, planning, writing, revising. He completed a revision of the Legion Handbook. He wrote many articles for various journals. And, of course, he said his breviary as well as his many other prayers every day. When he got tired, he simply fell asleep. So the prescription worked.

In spite of his great weakness, Frank found his stay with the Monahan family a refreshing experience. He was allowed by the doctor to get up every evening after his tea. He would then come down and join the family circle. They would talk and recall the past, as is the custom of families when they gather together, and they would watch television. They would have another cup of tea. There was leisure and relaxation and freedom from anxiety, such as Frank had never had time to experience before.

As his health gradually improved, he was allowed to get up earlier and do more exercise. Dr. Monahan would often drive him a distance of four miles, then leave him at the little bridge that spans the Boyne River and arrange to pick him up some hours later at another bridge, at the far end of the Boyne Valley. The doctor considered walking to be the best tonic of all. And Frank loved it. He had never done much walking for the simple reason that he never had time.

The Boyne Valley is one of the most picturesque places in all Ireland. It is about four miles long. Frank found it invigorating for the body and relaxing for the mind to walk along by the river bank. And he observed everything in its glorious detail. In places, the Boyne River is lazy; it is in no particular hurry and it just meanders sluggishly. In other places, its rhythm is changed by a fall in ground level or a rocky stretch; then the sleepy river comes suddenly awake and thunders angrily and impatiently over the challenging rocks. Willow trees and reeds and bulrushes on its banks dip into the cool waters and are refreshed.

As Frank ambled along the little pathway that obligingly ran parallel to the river, he found that some stretches were overgrown with that deep lush grass which is indigenous to the Irish midlands. These stretches were more tiring for the traveler, but as time was his very own just then and the weather was fine, he sat on the stump of some felled tree or in some cozy nook that nature had provided by the river

FRANK DUFF

bank, and he rested himself. And he took stock of everything, to his heart's content, and particularly of the living things, great and small, that were all around him—the cattle and sheep grazing on the far bank, the birds that flitted to and fro singing their merry songs, the insects, mighty in their own sphere on a tiny blade of grass. Occasionally, a salmon or trout jumped above the water level and, with precise accuracy, snatched a juicy dragon fly. A splash, a momentary rupture of the silence and then peace descended again. A little farther on, the river resumed its own unique song of praise to God. Clean waters, the traditional Christian symbol of life and renewal.

In later years, Frank recalled his time of convalescence in Navan as being one of the happiest periods of his life.

Frank came back to Dublin a new man and he took up where he had left off. Moreover, his enforced "holiday" had "sparked off" many new enterprising ideas in his mind. So he anticipated a busy time.

But little did he realize what an immense task and awesome responsibility lay before him. It came swiftly and unexpectedly. He recognized the official Vatican postmark. It was a summons to Rome to attend the Vatican Council as an official lay observer.

33 Lay Observer at Vatican Council

It was early afternoon on the 11th of September, 1965. At the Leonardo da Vinci airport in Rome, Bishop Crawford, O.P., and Fr. Ronan Cusack, O.P., waited for the plane from Dublin. They were expecting an important visitor who was to be their guest during his stay in Rome.

At 4 p.m. the plane landed. Bishop after bishop alighted from the aircraft and started to cross the tarmac. They were from Ireland, England, Wales and Scotland and all were arriving for the final session of the Second Vatican Council. Then from the plane emerged a lone layman, Frank Duff, his civilian clothes making him conspicuous among the exalted clerics. He was the guest for whom Bishop Crawford and Fr. Cusack had been waiting. He was to stay at their Dominican House in Rome for the three months following his arrival.

The Roman legionaries had also come to the airport to welcome Frank to the Eternal City. From the beginning he felt quite at home.

To the surprise of many, Frank had not been invited to the earlier session of the Council whereas some other laymen had been invited. The reason, most probably, was that he had not looked for an invitation. But it became increasingly clear that he had, eventually, to be invited because many of the very things that the Council Fathers were debating and promoting had been advocated by Frank as far back as 1921 and were, in fact, incorporated into the Legion system and laid down in the Legion Handbook.

Before setting out for Rome, Frank had studied the decrees that had already been issued by the Council. He must

FRANK DUFF

have been truly gratified when he read the Decree on the Dogmatic Constitution of the Church and the chapter in it concerning the role of Our Lady in the Mystery of Christ and the Church. The ideas in that chapter were remarkably similar, even in their presentation, to what he himself had written on the subject thirty years previously in a booklet which he titled "The Montfort Telescope." He would have liked, though, if the Council had elaborated further on the practical implications of the doctrine of Mary's motherhood of mankind and on the necessary connection, as he saw it, between true devotion to Mary and apostleship.

When Frank received the invitation to come to Rome for the remaining sessions of the Council, he told nobody about it. If he decided not to go—and it seems he hesitated—it is likely he would never have told anyone about it. But the Papal Nuncio in Dublin had, naturally, been informed about the invitation and had to ascertain if Frank was accepting.

Why Frank's hesitancy? He was seventy-six years old and had just recovered, more or less, from a serious illness. He was trying to get back to as much work as he was capable of doing, but he still tired easily. The doctor had told him it was overwork that had brought on this last illness. He felt that if he went to Rome to attend the Council he would die there. He confided this to a friend after he returned from the Council. It is quite certain that dying had no fears for him, but probably the thought of dying in Rome, and the inconvenience which that might cause, filled him with great apprehension. At any rate, he decided to go. An invitation from Rome was for him a summons from the Lord. When he left Dublin on that Rome-bound plane, he was quite convinced he would never come back alive.

• • • • •

On the day following his arrival in Rome, Frank visited the Coliseum and the Forum. Both places, in their respective ways, must have struck a responsive chord in his heart: the Forum because of his education in the classics, the Coliseum because it represented for him the noblest form of

Lay Observer at Vatican Council

christianity—the shedding of one's blood for the faith. It was destined to be his only sightseeing tour of Rome. From then on, his crowded days gave little scope for visiting the places that recalled the glories of ancient imperial Rome.

The Council formally reopened on the 14th of September. Frank was deeply moved by the marvelous splendor of the ceremonies. As one of the lay auditors, he was given a seat in a very good position that enabled him to follow everything with ease and satisfaction.

However, when the great Council debates began, he had difficulty in understanding. His knowledge of Latin was first-class but he had had no practice in conversations or speeches in the classical language. He would have to content himself with hearing the substance of the discussions afterwards as he made his way to the coffee bar. Very often, however, he never got as far as the coffee bar. He was "waylaid" en route. Cardinals, bishops, Religious Superiors recognized him and approached him with open arms and warm greetings. Many of these had at some time or other come to Dublin to meet Frank Duff. They had already promoted the Legion of Mary in their own dioceses and were enthusiastic about it. Other church dignitaries who didn't know him by sight would stop suddenly when they saw the gold vexillina which he wore on his lapel, and say, "Ah, you must be Frank Duff!" Frank was eternally grateful to the Ghana legionaries who had given him that vexillina.

"Oh!" he exclaimed afterwards "it was thrilling to have all those bishops from the ends of the earth greeting me eagerly because I represented the Legion."

Frank was present for the Council deliberations on "The Ministry and Life of Priests," and "The Apostolate of the Laity." He considered that these two themes were interrelated. If the layman is to be educated and trained for the apostolate, he must depend mostly on the priest for that training.

Even in his younger days, Frank could not understand the common concept of a "good priest," as "one who gave good service to his people, kept his church and parish in good shape and said his Mass and prayers well." For Frank, that was not enough. An important, even vital, ele-

FRANK DUFF

ment was missing: a priest should aim at training his people to be apostolic. At Baptism, Christians are incorporated into the Church, the Mystical Body of Christ, and thereby called to share in the mission of that Church; and "the Church," Pope Pius XI had solemnly declared, "has no other reason for its existence than to extend over the earth the Kingdom of Christ and to render all men sharers of His Saving Redemption" *(c.f. Legion Handbook, p. 245).*

For more than forty years, Frank had painstakingly and perseveringly, through the Legion of Mary and the Legion Handbook, expounded and propagated throughout the four corners of the globe that doctrine of the Mystical Body and the consequent duty of the laity to be apostolic.

What a great joy therefore it must have been to him when, at the conclusion of the Session on the Apostolate of the Laity, the Council Fathers decreed that, "In their catechetical instructions, their ministry of the word, their direction of souls, and in their other pastoral services, priests should be preoccupied with forming apostles" *(Vat. Council 2, Laity—30).* And again: "When the apostolate is one of making the gospel known and man holy, the laity must be specially formed to engage in conversation with others, believers or non-believers, in order to manifest Christ's message to all men" *(Ibid—31).*

At an appropriate moment during one of the Sessions, Cardinal Heenan of England drew the attention of the 2,500 bishops to the presence of Frank Duff in their midst. There was loud and sustained applause, a sincere gesture of appreciation from the hierarchy for what this layman had done for the Church.

Not surprisingly, each day at the end of the Council Session, Frank felt completely exhausted but his Dominican friends took him back to their San Clemente house for lunch and a little rest. Fr. Anselm, the Prior, was a long-standing friend of his and did everything possible to make his stay comfortable and enjoyable. The relaxed atmosphere in San Clemente and the hospitality of the Dominicans was a big factor in enabling Frank to survive those three tiring months.

There may have been a little supernatural aid as well, be-

Lay Observer at Vatican Council

cause Frank's work was by no means finished when the Council Sessions ended each day. In a sense, his main work only began then and was given exclusively to Legion matters. He gave no fewer than thirty-two formal addresses. Shortly after his arrival, the Irish bishops asked him to address them. Then he gave a talk to a hundred English-speaking bishops. When the French bishops and the French-speaking bishops from further afield invited him to address them, they offered to provide an interpreter. He shyly explained that he didn't need an interpreter. He went back to San Clemente, wrote out his talk in flawless French and gave his lecture at the appointed time.

He also gave talks to other groups, for example, to the Mill Hill bishops and the S.V.D. bishops as well as lecturing in the great Colleges, Seminaries and Motherhouses of the various Religious Orders.

These talks required many hours of preparation. And in his "spare" time, he wrote two hundred letters as well as several articles and memos, and he gave very many personal interviews. It is almost certain that no bishop of the Council was as busy as he during those three months.

Nor did he neglect his faithful friends in Rome, namely, the legionaries. They were extremely kind to him and he felt especially "at home" with them. He attended all their Senatus meetings and some of their praesidia meetings. He was proud of the fact that he recruited four new legionaries for them.

His greatest experience was his private audience with the Holy Father, Pope Paul VI, on the 11th of December. The Supreme Pontiff said to him: "Mr. Duff, I want to thank you for your services to the Church and also to express appreciation for all that the Legion of Mary has done."

Frank stammered words of thanks for those truly gracious remarks. Earlier that year, the same Pope had sent a remarkable letter to Frank Duff in Dublin. The specific purpose of that letter was "the praise and encouragement of the Legion of Mary." In that letter the Pope referred to the pious aims and many activities produced and developed by the Legion, "to the great advantage of the Catholic apostolate, thus proving itself to be an instrument of astonishing efficacy for the building up and spreading of God's

FRANK DUFF

Kingdom." Frank now took this opportunity to personally thank the Pope for such a marvelous tribute which was so encouraging and he assured His Holiness that the primary aim of the Legion was to keep in closest union with the Church by loyalty to the Pope and by absolute unity with the bishops and priests. Then Frank added "We look to our members to bear witness to this even to the point of martyrdom."

The Pope declared: "The Legion of Mary has served the Church faithfully, and the Church will protect the Legion."

• • • • •

There was healthy renewal within the Church following upon the Vatican Council. There were new enterprises, new policies, newly discovered responsibilities. It was inevitable, however, that some should be found who sought after change merely for the sake of change and who assumed that all pre-Vatican organizations were out of date. In some areas, greater difficulty was experienced in recruiting new members for the Legion. Some considered that, in the new "thinking," the Legion's disciplined system and its strong emphasis on prayer was too "old-fashioned" for the new generation. This saddened Frank who knew only too well that these were the very elements that had achieved such marvelous results both for the individual legionaries and for the souls for whom they worked.

Moreover, he now had a clearer picture than ever of what the Church wanted. Besides, it looked as if the Vatican Council was endorsing all that the Legion was endeavoring to do. He noted the special emphasis that the Council had given to the desired involvement of lay people in the *spiritual* mission of the Church and, in particular, its directive that lay people should be trained to speak about religion to their fellow men. The Council had repeated the plea of Christ that the Gospel, in all its fullness, should be preached to all men and that obviously meant that there must be an approach on a vast scale to the millions throughout the world who still did not know or understand the complete Revelation of Christ or the marvelous spiritual treasury which He had bequeathed to His Church.

Lay Observer at Vatican Council

Likewise, there must be a practical and genuine effort to reach out to every lapsed or careless Catholic and, indeed, to every person who was in need. Yes, more than ever, Frank realized the absolute necessity for the Legion of Mary which could, wherever it existed, provide the mechanism and the spiritual training for its members, thus enabling them to play their part as true soldiers of Christ.

Frank knew also that in some areas the priest could not be blamed if he didn't appreciate the Legion. Sadly, there were some Legion praesidia which did not portray the real Legion, or at least were only portraying it in a very imperfect way. Occasionally, reports from such praesidia indicated that the rules were not being kept, or that the local curia was not training the officers, or that senior members were confining themselves to works that could easily be done by juniors while the greater needs of the parish were not being tackled, or that praesidia were finding all sorts of excuses for not starting junior praesidia, in spite of the guidelines of the Legion handbook.

The priest might well say: "I'm not convinced by what I see." The legionaries might well reply: "If we had a priest to guide us, we could be a strong group." Not an insoluble situation!

Frank was always hopeful that the priest in such a situation would, somehow or other, look further and deeper, and see what the Legion—where it was being properly worked—was capable of achieving, whether it be in a remote rural parish or in a city parish or in the "missionfields." He liked to refer to one parish in East Africa which covered a vast territory but had only one priest. This priest sent his legionaries to organize the Legion in every village and in every settlement within the parish. To each new group was stressed the duty of extension. Soon, the priest had sixty-one praesidia which were then divided into four curia areas. By visiting a different curia each Sunday, he was able to keep in regular contact with all 244 officers. On the Sunday of his curia "visitation," he would also say Mass for his people, baptize those who had been prepared by the legionaries, solemnize marriages, etc. The harvest of souls in that area was great, and the labourers were not few. Frank would have called it an "active" parish!

FRANK DUFF

Yes, indeed, the post-Vatican era was a greater challenge than ever. The Legion would upgrade its works. It would concentrate particularly on apostolates that were of a specifically spiritual nature. Of course, if there were members to spare, they would help out also in works of service, though this was generally to be regarded as the preserve of the Junior Legion. Besides, other organizations exist to look after works of service and do so most effectively.

When Frank was asked how he felt about the role of the Legion in the years ahead, he replied: "If the Legion is allowed to retain its present complexion, then it will not only keep its vitality and its degree of success but will far improve on them. As I see things, the Legion has only now arrived at adult stature—only now. Up to the present, it has in a sense been in the cradle. Now it is a grown and armed soldier ready for the terrible fray that the next century is going to place us in the midst of."[1]

Again, Frank was asked if he thought the Legion would retain its force after his departure from it. He smiled and said: "The Legion from its first moment was in the hands of the Blessed Virgin. My departure from the scene is not going to remove it from her hands."[2]

NOTES

[1] "Frank Duff—a living Autobiography" by Mgr. C. Moss. p. 10, 11.
[2] ibid, p. 10.

34 Conquest for Christ

In 1941, Frank Duff and a group of legionaries founded the Mercier Society in Dublin. The aim of this society was to provide an opportunity and a forum for friendly dialogue between Catholics and Protestants.* Because of the historical and political factors that formed a background to Protestantism in Ireland, there was a fair share of prejudice "on both sides." As a result, there had been hitherto very little religious dialogue between persons of different religious beliefs.

Over 90% of Dublin's citizens were Catholic and these, though strong in their own faith, tended to be rather indifferent to the religious beliefs or practices of the minority. To Frank, it seemed an anomaly that thousands of Irish Catholic missionaries were preaching in far-away countries, while few offered to explain or share their religious values with their non-Catholic brethren in the homeland. Frank's own experience had shown him that there were some non-Catholics, at least, who were simply waiting to be invited into the Catholic Church. Many others, of course, though well disposed, might simply not be able to accept the Catholic faith, and their beliefs must be scrupulously respected. But surely, thought Frank, we owe it to these at least to offer to explain the teachings of the Catholic Church and we should be prepared to give them the opportunity of explaining their beliefs to us. Friendly, honest and open discussion can only do good.

Indeed, as soon as the Mercier Society (called after Cardinal Mercier, the great ecumenist) was established, its monthly meetings were well attended by both Protestants and Catholics. Apart from an occasional indiscretion, the

FRANK DUFF

atmosphere was one of sincere honesty, friendliness and good humour. It was a genuine ecumenical venture (23 years before Vatican 2) and undoubtedly great good was achieved. Prejudices gave way to mutual understanding, good-will was generated, and everybody gained a deeper understanding of the divine Truths.

The Mercier Society continued for a number of years until some ecclesiastics discovered in the Code of Canon law a regulation that seemed to restrict the holding of meetings and discussions of this kind. The Mercier Society was closed down. It seems that Frank, with his ecumenical enterprises, was "before his time."

Protestants and people of other religious persuasions who attended these Mercier Society meetings appreciated Frank's utter and sincere honesty. While he stated the Catholic truths with candor and clarity, he was never overbearing, never self-righteous. His obvious humility and genuine kindness won the hearts of those present. Canon W. Proctor, a prominent Protestant clergyman in Dublin, who attended many "dialogue" meetings with Frank, declared that even though his theological opinions were quite different from Frank's, yet this never interfered with the strong personal friendship that developed between them. And, indeed, very many Protestants who were privileged to have dealings with Frank would undoubtedly have concurred with the Canon's simple but lovely tribute: "Frank's warm handshake and friendly smile are warm memories for me."

• • • • •

Frank's early interest in ecumenism in no way distracted him from what was to become one of the great interests of his life, evangelization. For many years, he had been encouraging his legionaries to get involved in this central mission of the Church and, indeed, he must have been greatly heartened when the Second Vatican Council decreed in 1965: "In their pastoral activity, priests should stir up and preserve amid the faithful a zeal for the evangelization of the world" (Vatican 2. Missions—39).

Frank had already been greatly encouraged by letters he

Conquest for Christ

had received from legionaries in Korea. In that country, missionaries had very quickly realized the vital role of the Legion of Mary in the work of evangelization. The dynamic Columban missionary, Monsignor Harold Henry (later to become Archbishop) who introduced the Legion to Korea found only seventeen Catholics when he arrived in his first Mission. With the help of the legionaries, he achieved a veritable "Mission miracle." Before he had completed his assignment in that area, his Mission had become four parishes and could boast of having fourteen thousand apostolic Catholics.

Some months after the Vatican Council issued its decree on the Missions, Fr. Thomas O'Flynn, C.M. was appointed by the Irish Hierarchy to be the Spiritual Director of the Concilium, the supreme governing body of the Legion. Fr. O'Flynn asked Frank Duff for some guidance. Frank's reply was straightforward and comprehensive: "Urge them on to conquest for Christ."

By that year, the *Peregrinatio Pro Christo* movement had already been well established and Frank was urging it to extend its horizons and broaden its scope. The Legion *peregrinatio-pro-Christo* movement took its name from the great missionary journeys of the early Irish monks of the sixth and seventh centuries who brought the light of Christ to shine through the darkness of Europe following the barbarian invasions.

The modern Peregrinatio began with a number of legionaries from the University in Dublin devoting part of their holidays to spreading the faith abroad. It was called "holiday apostolate," then. Within a few years the number of Irish legionaries who volunteered annually for peregrinatio had grown to one thousand. They went, in teams of twelve, into all the countries of Europe, and eventually even further afield, into Africa, India, the U.S.A., Asia. The aim of these peregrini is to offer the Church in its fullness to all people and to seek their acceptance of it.

Before the teams set out each year, Frank would address them. He was not an orator; his voice was pleasant but he had no special gifts by which he might hold people's attention. And yet, in some extraordinary way, he got his message across. His faith had an infectious quality about it.

FRANK DUFF

He inspired his legionaries, raised them above themselves and imbued them with the ardent desire to do great things for God and for the salvation of souls.

Some clerics declared that legionaries were not competent to undertake that kind of missionary work, they had no theological training! Frank might have retorted: "Do you wish, then, to reduce missionary effort to a small elite and, in effect, exclude great multitudes of people from hearing the Gospel message?" Or he might have suggested that, in fact, the legionaries are not *so* incompetent, pointing out that week after week they have been studying in their Legion Handbook not only all the great doctrines of the Church (such as the Trinity, the Incarnation, the Mystical Body of Christ, the Mass, the Motherhood of Mary and so on) but also the practical application and implementation of those teachings. But Frank, knowing how such objections can sometimes arise from prejudice rather than from knowledge, preferred instead to invite the critics to come and hear for themselves the actual reports of the returned peregrini and to read the letters from priests and bishops all over the world extolling the marvelous results of the peregrinatio missions.

And indeed, wonderful things were taking place. Great numbers of people who were approached by the peregrini showed keen interest, and joined instruction classes on the Catholic faith. Many lapsed Catholics returned to the practice of their religion. A spiritual uplift was given to many a parish by the enthusiasm and example of the peregrini.

A large number of the legionaries who volunteer for peregrinatio are between the ages of sixteen and twenty. The peregrinatio has been a stimulus in their spiritual life and has also given them a deeper appreciation of their own faith, and they have revealed to young people of the parishes to which they go a challenging and attractive aspect of Catholicism that was hitherto unknown to them.

Of course, because of its short duration each year, peregrinatio has its limitations. But it has an effect similar to that of a shower of sparks. It starts fires, it spreads ideas, it stimulates others to action in the cause of Christ and His Church. "Christianity," said Frank, "truly understood, is not merely the acceptance of faith, but the accepting of it

Conquest for Christ

in such a way as to drive one forth to communicate it everywhere."

An offshoot of the peregrinatio movement was the *Viatores Christi*. Their members, aspiring by word and example to be worthy witnesses to the Catholic Church, were recruited and trained to place their talents and expertise at the service of the foreign missions. After some years, it was decided that Viatores should become an autonomous body and work side by side with the Legion rather than be directly governed by it.

Another development from peregrinatio was the movement know as "incolae Mariae." An incola is a legionary who volunteers to spend a year or so overseas in evangelization work. Frank received a letter from a priest overseas who was working with a team of incolae Mariae. In the letter, the priest said: "I am emboldened to think that Incolae Mariae may be, at least in part, the solution to one of the major problems in the Church today, namely, the dire shortage of missionaries. My reasoning is based on four factors:

"firstly, the Legion could probably supply incolae Mariae in large numbers;

"secondly, the Legion is convinced of the importance of conversion work and favors a gentle but direct approach to persons in its missionary work;

"thirdly, the Legion method, while not underestimating the value of modern techniques in training, concentrates on the Gospel essentials of faith, prayer and apostolic courage;

"fourthly, the Legion is not at this stage an experiment; it is, in the hands of Our Lady, a weapon of proven ability for sanctifying its members and winning souls for Christ — which is what mission work is all about."

One of Frank Duff's proudest boasts was the feats of the Legion in the Philippines. There had been a great shortage of priests there; many Catholics were Catholic in name but not in practice. Then the Legion was introduced and proved extraordinarily effective in winning back Catholics to a proper appreciation of their religion. Archbishop O'Dougherty of Manila wrote to Frank Duff: "Through the instrumentality of the Legion, the situation here in the

FRANK DUFF

Philippines has changed from hopeless to hopeful. I can now dream dreams and say to myself: 'this is the only Catholic nation of the Orient, why should it not convert the Orient?' "

There are now fourteen thousand praesidia of the Legion of Mary in the Philippines. Shortly before his death, Frank asked Fr. Aedan McGrath to come and see him.

"Father," he said, "It is my dearest wish that you would go to the Philippines. Tell them they are our big hope in the Orient. We are relying on them to send out incolae Mariae in large numbers to the neighbouring countries and to the multi-thousand Islands of the Pacific. With the wonderful co-operation and encouragement of their Church leaders, one can only imagine what they will accomplish."

NOTE

---

*A kindred society called "Pillar of Fire" was established for Catholic-Jewish dialogue.

35 Man, Great is Your Faith!

Frank Duff's life was such a remarkable and visible expression of faith that it is difficult to find a parallel in history.

Frank inherited the deep, strong faith of Irish Catholicism, a faith that had matured through suffering and sacrifice for many centuries. But, unlike the cautious man in the gospel story who merely kept his talent intact by burying it in the ground, he increased his faith to such a degree that it became a powerful, conquering force in his life. And this faith of his percolated through to the Legion of Mary.

When he wrote the handbook for his legionaries and told them that they ought to imitate Our Lady in all the virtues, he appealed to them to aspire especially after Our Lady's faith. That was the virtue that he recognized as the power that could conquer the world for Christ.

With St. Paul he admits that to build up one's faith one must, "persevere in running the race which lies ahead; . . . and keep our eyes fixed on Jesus, Who inspires and perfects our faith" *(Heb. Ch. 12, 1-2)*. Extensive spiritual reading, a substantial prayer life and a mind that was thoroughly honest and logical, all combined to give him a good grasp of what faith really is and of the power it can generate. He saw it as an absolute acceptance without reservation of Christ's teachings. Faith would move mountains. Christ had said so. Therefore, there could be "no two ways about it." God is faithful to His promise. But faith also

FRANK DUFF

means action, action on our part—and courage. In any good enterprise, if we do our best, we can be certain God will do the rest, even if that requires a miracle.

The keystone of Frank's faith was his understanding of the Mystical Body. The Church is the Body of Christ. It continues the personal action of Christ on earth. Christ is the head of the Body and we are the members of that Body.

People often complimented Frank on his use of very ordinary people in the Legion of Mary. For Frank there were no ordinary people. Every person was another Christ and therefore had great potentiality and was capable of heroic conduct. People of lesser faith were not enthused when he proposed tackling something that seemed to be impossible or else so full of danger that it could cause the destruction of the legionary. For Frank, nothing was impossible for Christ—working now through us. After all, we are His hands and feet. As for danger, when did Christ shrink from His mission just because of the threat of danger? He came to give His life for us. When the news reached Dublin that many legionaries were being martyred for the faith in China, Frank was deeply shocked and very sad, but at the same time he was proud that legionaries had been given the privilege of making the supreme sacrifice.

When some foreign country requested Legion headquarters in Dublin to send a Legion envoy to set up or consolidate the Legion of Mary there, Frank did not look around for someone of exceptional talent or extraordinary ability. God uses the weak things of this world to confound the strong. So he simply looked for any legionary who had a good Legion spirit. Every legionary who had made the Legion Promise was only too well aware that he or she was simply an instrument in the hands of God.

> "Most Holy Spirit, I ask of Thee
> to come upon me
> and fill me with Thyself
> so that my poor acts may be sustained by Thy power
> and become an instrument of Thy mighty purposes."
>
> (Legion Promise)

Frank once spoke to the seminarians of Thurles Seminary on the subject of the Priesthood. He began by saying:

Man, Great is Your Faith!

"I hope you will forgive me for being personal; I absolutely hate it, but if I am not to talk to you, to some extent, out of my own background, I have really no other plane on which to speak to you. The only thing which I have to point out is my considerable experience." Then he proceeded to tell them that, in so far as one can humanly judge, he had achieved most of his aims and had seemingly been successful. To what would he attribute that "success?" To his constant labor? To his long hours of daily toil? "I have," he said, "lived a long life of the most intense activity; I do not think it would be possible to live at a higher pitch of physical exertion." And yet it was not to those activities that he now pointed as the cause of whatever successes he had. No, but rather to something higher. And he explained it thus: "I have believed intensely in the spiritual order, and I have never sacrificed it to anything else. It is my conviction that anything good that emerged from my efforts has proceeded from that stressing of the supernatural. It meant that I was depending on the Lord and His Mother and not on myself."

It wasn't, therefore, simply that he prayed his breviary and his Rosary and assisted at daily Mass. It was, rather, that these daily spiritual exercises had assumed a place of paramount importance in his life and in his mission.

There were no half measures for Frank, at least as regards the demands he made on himself. If he believed a thing should be done, then all the powers on this earth couldn't stop him doing it, even if it meant dying in the attempt. At an early stage in his life, he made a decision he would never marry. Celibacy for him was not just making a voluntary sacrifice for the sake of sacrifice. It was for him an expression of his total commitment to the work he had in hand, that is, the service of God and of his fellowman. And he did not allow danger, risk or ridicule to divert him from that commitment. He once said: "On a few occasions I have risked everything that mattered to me for the sake of the Lord; I risked being completely blotted out." On another occasion, he said to a friend: "If it were God's will for me to go to hell I would do so gladly." Such a remark, made seriously, is incomprehensible, but it does illustrate how utterly and resolutely Frank sought after the

FRANK DUFF

glory of God and the will of God. Frank was undoubtedly gifted with great powers of reasoning and an extremely logical mind. But when the real test arose, or when a dilemma presented itself, then his logic became supremely simple: "Does God want this? If so, we must go ahead."

And the "going ahead" usually involved much suffering. There would be misunderstandings, rebuffs, ridicule, pangs from failure, weariness of body and spirit. Because his faith demanded that he give his utmost, he was prepared to suffer all these. Because of his late nights and his early mornings for the greater part of his life, he was constantly under severe strain, at times on the brink of exhaustion. He admitted that there were times, even, when he dreaded the dawn and what the day would bring. Opposition to the Legion was the biggest cross. He reconciled himself to opposition. "In fact," he told his legionaries, "the cross is the safest way."

This kind of faith, this total giving of himself, regardless of the cost, inevitably produced in Frank a truly heroic courage. Early on, he recognized the blighting effect that fear can have in a person's life, and so he set himself resolutely against it. For years he lived, according to his own admission, in an atmosphere of fear, and his constant struggle with it caused him much mental and even physical suffering. Nevertheless, he boldly admitted that he never remembered yielding to fear. In moments of fear, his set policy was to try to exclude every consideration but the one: "Where lies the path of duty?"

When outlining his ideas on holiness, he said: "The definition of sanctity is heroic virtue, and heroism means the defying of fear. Religion is a virile, tough thing. There must, of course, be proper proportion; there must be sweetness and gentleness; but these must be founded on and fortified by strength of character."

According as Frank responded to the inspirations and grace of God—often taking his cue from what he called the "sign language of faith"—he saw wonderful results. He saw faith in action, and bearing fruit. This emboldened him to be more daring and venturesome. One evening at a Legion meeting—the Legion had been in existence only about three months at the time—he predicted boldly: "The Legion of

Man, Great is Your Faith!

Mary will encircle the globe." And he declared it with conviction. He had absolute faith in all that the Legion stood for and he had by this time seen the effectiveness of the Legion system.

Revolutionaries, usually, are men in a hurry. They have to seize an opportune moment and try to achieve their aim quickly. Frank was not a revolutionary in that sense. True, he did have a sense of divine mission, a sense of urgency, but he was never in a hurry. He was so certain the hand of God was in the Legion, that he didn't feel the need to rush; God works slowly but surely. But, as if some relentless driving force was inside him, he pushed on inexorably, never letting up, laying solid foundations, looking on every set-back simply as delayed success, confident that there was indeed a supernatural power backing him up. He visited one particular country, hopeful of getting official approval to start the Legion. He was sadly disappointed. As he departed for home, he bade farewell to a lady who had tried to help him in his objective. He said to her: "We must obey the bishops, therefore we leave, but we do not capitulate." And, indeed, some years later he secured the necessary permissions in that country and introduced the Legion. Such delays, however—and he experienced many over the years—hurt him deeply because of the inestimable good that remained undone during the time of waiting.

In the earlier years of the Legion, Frank must have suffered acutely from a keen sense of aloneness. Few could have shared his depth of faith or his breadth of vision. In a sense, he was a man apart. But as the Legion reached maturity, he had the consolation of seeing very many souls who, through their dedicated Legion membership, had come to share his outlook and his ideals.

• • • • •

Frank's thorough knowledge of history, and especially of Church history, enabled him to see the hand of God showing itself in the various crises through which the Church passed. The Church survived all these crises. By the providence of God, some powerful defender came to the rescue, or sometimes God intervened directly, as, for example, in

FRANK DUFF

the mid-19th century when there was an acute crisis of faith due mainly to the so-called Enlightenment: atheism was spreading, all spiritual values were questioned and the authenticity of miracles was denied. Lourdes was God's answer.

Had another crisis of faith come? Frank had to consider the question. Various reports from around the globe indicated that there might, indeed, be a crisis of faith. But Frank's faith protected him from falling prey to pessimism. "Depression," he said, "is not a good stimulant towards remedy." He believed with all his heart that the Legion is a well-equipped instrument in God's hand and will be used effectively by the Church to combat whatever evils may afflict the world and to cope with whatever crises may arise.

"The Legion," he said, "stands up so well in that storm against the faith. The big reason for this is the Legion's devotion to Mary who is the torch of faith and who destroys all heresies. Another reason is the Legion's constant prayer for faith. One is emboldened to hope that the Legion is destined to play a key part in the supporting of the Church through the crisis of this spiritual winter and into a glorious spring."[1]

NOTE

[1] "The Woman of Genesis," by Frank Duff, p. 517.

36 Mother Russia

Frank Duff was puzzled. He had most readily agreed to give the interview, though he could not even guess what the purpose of a visit from this distinguished visitor might be.

At length, the expected visitor arrived and introduced himself.

"I am Dr. Victor Yarotsky, Counsellor of the Russian Embassy in London. You are Mr. Frank Duff?"

"Yes, I am Frank Duff, and I am very pleased to meet you."

After an exchange of courtesies, Dr. Yarotsky explained the purpose of his visit.

"Mr. Duff," he said, "I am representing the Soviet Government and I have a message for you."

Frank tried to conceal his excitement and his great curiosity.

"Perhaps," continued Dr. Yarotsky, "it would be more accurate for me to say 'invitation!' We would like you to come to Moscow to have discussions with our Government."

Frank had long been interested in Russia. For so many years, special prayers for Russia had been recited every Sunday in every church in Ireland. He felt, too, that the Legion was destined to play a very special role in Russia. He saw a symbolic link between the Legion of Mary and Communist Russia. The Legion was founded the very year the Constitution of Soviet Communism was approved and ratified. Frank was convinced that even the dates of both events coincided though he could not prove this conclusively. It was remarkable also that the Legion and Soviet Communism both had their roots back in 1917. That was the year the Saint Vincent de Paul moved into Myra House and the first legionaries—though they were not at that time

FRANK DUFF

called legionaries—came together to plan and work. It was then that the first meetings were held to co-ordinate and regulate their various apostolic activities. Already, the ideal and methods of the infant organization had been adopted. And, of course, 1917 was the year of the Russian Revolution which was the first step in the inauguration of Soviet Communism. In the same year, Our Lady appeared at Fatima!

Was it coincidence that both the Legion and the Soviets had—despite their diametrically different philosophies—adopted the same Latin names for their various administrative and deliberative councils, such as "praesidium," "concilium" etc.? They had even adopted the same official color—red.

It so happened that Frank didn't avail of Dr. Yarotsky's invitation to visit Moscow. He would willingly have gone, but there were circumstances which made it virtually impossible for him to go at that particular time.

However, in 1969, Russia loomed large in Frank's mind. The "Iron Curtain" was being drawn aside somewhat and Russia was inviting tourists to visit the U.S.S.R. By now, Frank was eighty years old and was disinclined to travel overseas. But he was full of enthusiasm and hope as he addressed a group of legionaries in Dublin and encouraged them to go on a peregrinatio to Russia. Some observers considered that such a venture was too daring. Others expressed the view that the Legion should have nothing to do with the Communists.

But Frank was all things to all men. He could never, of course, accept the ideology of communism, but he did believe in dialogue. "What can be lost," he said, "by talking to people?"

And, so, in the summer of that year, a group of Irish legionaries flew to Moscow, feeling a little apprehensive, perhaps, at venturing into the unknown but strengthened in spirit by the talk Frank had given them prior to their departure.

"Remember," he had said, "you are going in a spirit of faith. You are few in number and the U.S.S.R. numbers 262 million people. But it is Our Blessed Lady who is sending you there; you are her emissaries. And be careful that you don't involve yourselves in any way with politics. Politics is not our business."

Mother Russia

When the Legion group arrived in Russia and had settled in, they found themselves quite overawed by the sheer magnitude of things—great panoramas of land and mountains and forests; and then Moscow with its eight million people; a city steeped in history; its gleaming golden-domed churches—many of them now, unfortunately, used as museums; and Leningrad, undoubtedly one of the most beautiful cities in all the world, reveling in the sheer poetry of its gorgeous squares and parks and boulevards.

It was a pleasant surprise to find that a sizeable proportion of the people could speak English, and they were so gentle, so friendly, so courteous.

The legionaries were so well received, that soon the "Russian trip" became an annual enterprise. Frank took a keen interest in every detail and, in fact, Russia became one of his absorbing interests for the remainder of his life. Every summer, as the Legion party got ready to set out for the U.S.S.R., he would come along to counsel and encourage them, reminding them constantly that theirs was a step in faith, under the mantle of Our Lady.

Courtesy calls were paid to representatives of the Soviet Government in Moscow and in other Russian cities. It was nice to discover that the Soviet officials already knew a good deal about the Legion of Mary and its mission throughout the world, and even appreciated certain of its values. Probably, also, they were aware that in a number of countries where the Governments do not favor the Catholic Church, for example, Burma, Ceylon, Egypt and Sudan, the Legion, nevertheless, was given full freedom to carry on its work, evidently because those Governments recognized that the Legion possesses advantages from their point of view, and no doubt they appreciated also the official policy of the Legion not to involve itself in politics.

In September 1978, Frank wrote a letter to Mr. Leonid Brezhnev, President of the U.S.S.R., asking that the Government look favorably on the proposal to have the Legion of Mary introduced into Russia. It was a lengthy letter, courteous and humble, outlining in the main what the Legion of Mary has to offer the State as well as the Church in Russia.

"In writing to you," Frank said in the letter, "may I specially stress the aspect of the Legion's utility to the State?

FRANK DUFF

The Legion is primarily built on the Christian principle that the individual has the duty of helping his neighbour in every way. This principle requires to be organized. Otherwise it will not be honored in practice. The Legion method has proved to be successful among people of every race and condition, advanced or primitive, even illiterate. To each legionary is assigned a weekly task of not less than two hours duration. . . .

"The legionaries learn the simpler aspects of administration. They learn also how to face up to problems. They survey the social situation and attempt to deal with its needs. It will be realized that even a small proportion of the community, if so animated, would affect the total body, and would add up to patriotism for the whole country."

Frank, on one occasion, asked some of the legionary team if they had any difficulty in getting a place to have their Mass while in Russia.

"Oh no, Mr. Duff, we have no difficulty about that. Our priests are given every facility to say Mass in one of the hotel rooms every morning. Of course, we are a bit crushed because the rooms aren't very large, but we are so happy to have our Mass in one of those rooms high up near the top storey. We call it the 'Upper Room.' "

Since I was one of the priests on the team, Frank said to me: "Father Bradshaw, I possess a nice small Mass chalice that was given to me some years ago. Please take it to Russia with you for your Mass. I will feel privileged if you do so."

"Thank you, Mr. Duff," I said, "I will be very glad to have it for our Mass."

And, indeed, every year after that, wherever the team went, Frank's chalice went with us, and as it traveled from town to town throughout the U.S.S.R., it not only served its proper function in the offering of the holy Sacrifice but it was also a constant reminder to the team that Frank was with them in spirit in the lap of Mother Russia.

• • • • •

Frank had a great love for the Russian Orthodox Church and appreciated its unique role in Russian history. He

Mother Russia

looked on it as a sister Catholic Church. It had its own wonderful traditions, faithfully preserving its spirit, its discipline, its rich liturgy. It had been somewhat bruised and shaken in the recent past but it had survived and was surely destined to play a major part in the conservation and strengthening of religion in the U.S.S.R.

But Frank sensed a new danger for the Orthodox Church, this time from without. Many of the Protestant denominations, availing themselves of an increasing measure of religious liberty in Russia, were "cashing in" on the situation and were attracting great numbers of Russians whose connecting links with the Orthodox Church were rather weak. For example, within a few years, the Baptists alone had gained half a million registered members. And that trend seemed likely to continue—to the detriment of the Orthodox Church.

Frank was convinced that the Orthodox Church would benefit immensely if they adopted the Legion of Mary. He had already sought and obtained permission from the Vatican authorities to propose the Legion to the Orthodox Church Authorities. He had expressed the willingness of the Concilium to hand over to the Orthodox Church all authority over the Legion in its area. It was also made clear that there would be no efforts to westernize any of the Orthodox elements of devotion. The Vatican expressed its intention to respect the traditions of the Orthodox Church, and the Legion would be faithful to that commitment.

Frank, therefore, corresponded with the Russian Orthodox Authorities on all these points, and it was only natural that each year when the Legion team went to Russia, Fr. Moriarty and Fr. Bradshaw (and sometimes Fr. Kenny or Fr. Kennedy) should visit the Russian Orthodox Bishops and have dialogue with them. Everywhere, they were received by the bishops with great courtesy and friendliness. Lengthy audiences were readily granted.

In Leningrad, Metropolitan Nikodim invited the two priests to participate in the great Liturgical Celebrations in the Orthodox Cathedral and they were given places of honor in the sanctuary. The Cathedral was packed to capacity with young and old. Everybody in the congregation, absolutely everybody, participated in the liturgical chanting and

FRANK DUFF

three choirs added beauty and solemnity to the ceremonies which lasted three and a half hours.

When the time came for exchanging the sign of peace, the Metropolitan said to his two priest-guests: "It is remarkable that your visit to me has coincided with this day. You have come in the name of the Legion of Mary; Mary is your Patroness. But this very day is our feast-day of Our Lady; it is the feast of Our Lady of Kazan. Surely there is a sign from heaven in this." And indeed until then, the priests had not known that it was the feast of Our Lady of Kazan.

Then the Metropolitan showed them the beautiful gilt crucifix he was wearing.

"It was Pope Paul VI," he said, "who gave it to me. I must also tell you that I am looking forward to reunion with Rome."

It was, indeed, remarkable that Metropolitan Nikodim died in Rome a few years later while he was actually having an audience with Pope Paul VI's successor, Pope John Paul I. Could not this, too, be linked with the sign-language of faith?

One of the most revered gifts that Frank Duff ever received was Metropolitan Nikodim's prayer-beads—rather like the Catholic rosary beads—which the Metropolitan's successor gave as a loving memento of one who had been a great friend of the Legion.

The P.P.C. trip over the years brought the legionaries to towns all over the U.S.S.R.—Kharkov, Odessa, Volgograd, Batumi, Rostov-on-Don, Zaporozhye and so on. Everywhere, the Russian Orthodox bishops and priests welcomed them warmly and showed a great willingness to hear about the Legion of Mary.

On a visit to one town, Fr. Moriarty and Fr. Bradshaw were invited by the bishop to visit him at his summer house in the country.

It was an old-fasioned timber house set in a garden of rambling-bushes and trees which were a protection from the torrid heat of the summer sun. The bishop and his two guests were seated on the veranda-type balcony at the front of the house. On the small table, was the traditional Russian samovar and a dish of fruit. Tea and cakes were served while the priests explained to their gracious host the ideals and methods of the Legion of Mary.

In a town in the south of Russia, the Russian Orthodox bishops invited the "Legion" priests to visit the rural villages in his diocese, an invitation that was gratefully accepted. They were driven in the bishop's car on a tour that included visits to seven remote villages.

The southern parts of Russia are more mountainous and more scenic than the northern areas. The drive took them along winding roads through fruit orchards and wooded terrain. The little houses by the wayside were mostly made of timber, and were older and poorer than in the cities but there was an old-world quaintness about them that was fascinating and attractive. There was an abundance of fruit trees—peach, apple and cherry.

At each of the seven villages, a group of Russian peasants had come with their local priest to the village church to meet the visitors. The little congregation consisted mostly of elderly people; all the women wore colored scarfs. Their tanned, weather-beaten faces and toil-worn hands betokened a life-style of rustic simplicity and manual labor in the fields. Their demeanor and reverence indicated a deep faith.

In these remote areas of Russia, neither the Orthodox priest nor any of his flock had ever met a Roman Catholic priest before and they showed deep appreciation for the visits. The welcoming speeches indicated a genuine desire for Church Unity. Huge bouquets of flowers were presented to the visitors but the most significant gesture, however, was when the peasants presented the priests with a loaf of home-baked bread and salt. This, the traditional Russian symbol of sustenance and life, was offered now as a warm gesture of genuine love and welcome.

Back in Dublin, Frank Duff listened with avid interest to the Russian reports. Most especially, he was thrilled to hear of the truly marvelous devotion that the Orthodox believers in Russia had to Our Blessed Lady. He prayed fervently that, sooner or later—God willing—the Legion would be established even in the remotest parts of that vast country. He was greatly encouraged by the remark of a priest-professor in one of Russia's seminaries: "The important thing," the professor said, "is the spirit of the Legion of Mary which would seem to appeal to the hearts of the Orthodox believers."

37 Golden Jubilee

In Dublin, the Golden Jubilee celebrations of the Legion of Mary were scheduled for Sunday, September 7th, 1971. A magnificent timber altar was being erected in a wide spacious field not far from Legion headquarters. Everybody was extremely busy and enthusiastic. One could have expected that Frank Duff would be eagerly looking forward to the big day. In fact he was not. He was quite nervous and uneasy. On the Saturday night before the "big day," he paced up and down his room. It was very late. From time to time, he looked out into the darkness, as if he expected to see something. Then, from weariness, he fell asleep.

Later, Frank confided to a friend that he had feared that the Jubilee altar would go up in flames that night. He thought that, in some way or another, the devil would contrive to bring that about. His long experience and his many struggles against the powers of evil had convinced him that the devil does not easily concede defeat. Frank still shuddered at the thought of his bone-chilling experience the night before the Morning Star Hostel was opened.

However, Sunday morning came and with it came relief. Nothing untoward had happened to the altar. Instead, all was joy and peace that day. The sun shone brilliantly from an azure sky. The crowds numbered in the thousands. Some of them were legionaries of long standing. Rose Dingley, for instance, had joined the Legion very soon after it had been founded. She took pen in hand and wrote a brief letter of congratulations to Mr. Duff. In her letter, she marveled at the extraordinary growth of the Legion which had spread all over the world. It was, by this time, in practically every country except in countries behind the "iron curtain." Who, even the most sanguine, could have imagined it would have blossomed so fully and helped so

Golden Jubilee

many souls everywhere? Rose had not met Mr. Duff for some years and she knew he would be pleased to hear from her.

There were great numbers of young legionaries also. To many of them, Frank Duff was just a name. But they were legionaries and so it was their day as well as the veterans' day. They came in their brightest colors. Their excitement was moderated by their spirit of piety and reverence.

The Most Rev. John Charles McQuaid, the Archbishop of Dublin, was the chief concelebrant at the Solemn High Mass of the Jubilee. Concelebrating with him were many Legion Spiritual Directors. His Excellency, Archbishop Alibrandi, the Papal Nuncio, presided. It was indeed a day of heartfelt gratitude for the many blessings bestowed by God on the Legion and through the Legion during its fifty years.

After the religious ceremonies, it was an occasion for chatting, for remembering, for renewing old friendships, for meeting legionaries from far and near. Bill Thompson, a Legion representative from the U.S.A., exclaimed: "Gee, what a beautiful day." Smiles all around and fresh hope for the future.

Everybody wanted to meet Frank Duff and shake his hand. He was embarrassed by all this but accepted it humbly. When he got tired, they provided him with a small table and a chair and he willingly gave his autograph to all who sought it.

In the afternoon, Fr. McMahon, the Archbishop's secretary, approached Frank:

"Mr. Duff, we have some of the sacred hosts left over after the Mass. As your house is the most convenient, would you be good enough to let us use one of your rooms as a temporary chapel in which to keep the consecrated hosts for the moment?"

"Oh, most certainly, that would be a great privilege for me."

And indeed it was a great privilege, but with eyes of faith, Frank saw even a bit further. "Oh! how inexpressibly gracious," he thought, "that the Lord should come in person to visit my house on the Jubilee day." And he often spoke about this afterwards.

FRANK DUFF

Some days after the Jubilee, Rose Dingley received a letter. It was from Frank Duff. In it, he thanked her for her letter and her felicitations. She must have smiled as she read on: "But, Rose, you express surprise at the wonderful way the Legion has developed and spread over the years. You say 'little could we have imagined that such could ever come to pass from such small beginnings.' But do you not remember, Rose, that at our very first meeting we placed everything in the hands of Our Lady? Whenever you commit things into Our Lady's hands, don't be surprised at anything that happens."

A footnote added: "When are you going to rejoin the Legion, Rose?" Rose, then over 80 years, rejoined the following Friday.

• • • • •

Of the thousands of congratulatory letters that Frank received from all corners of the globe on the occasion of the Legion's Golden Jubilee, the one that surely gave him greatest joy was the gracious letter he received from the Bishops of his native land:

Dear Mr. Duff,

The fiftieth anniversary of the foundation of the Legion of Mary is a cause of joy, not only to Dublin, its place of origin, but also to Ireland and even to the Catholic world.

We, the Bishops of Ireland, express to you our glad congratulations that, having nurtured the Legion from its earliest moments, you have been allowed by God to witness the marvelous expansion of this unique association of lay apostles.

The origins of the Legion of Mary are marked by obscurity, poverty and even hostility, that are seen at the outset of Our Divine Saviour's life in Bethlehem and Nazareth. Yet, in the plan of God, the supernatural faith and courage of the founding members have merited the grace not only of survival, through every kind of human vicissitude, but also of diffusion throughout the countries of the world.

Nor has the Legion relaxed its discipline of prayer and activity in the varying circumstances of climate or peoples or cultures. We praise you for the steadfastness with which

Golden Jubilee

you have conserved the basic constitution sanctioned by thousands of Bishops and approved by the supreme authority of the Holy See.

No other power than that of God, no other inspiration than that of the Holy Spirit, no other protection than that of the Mother of God can adequately explain the supernatural constancy of the Legion of Mary.

With great fruit of holiness has the Legion emphasized from its earliest days the unique function of the Mother of God in dispensing grace. It is by the union of will and suffering between Jesus Christ and Mary, that she has merited to become the dispenser of all the gifts that Our Divine Saviour purchased for us by His death alone on the cross. Who that examines the Legion of Mary can deny that the primary grace which her intercession has won for its members is a deeply interior love of Jesus Christ, her Son?

In the courage of that divine love we must find the source of the immense outpouring of the Legion's works of charity, particularly those that are concerned with the most abandoned and helpless types of mankind.

We pray that Our Divine Lord, in His indulgent mercy, may be pleased at the unceasing prayer of His Blessed Mother, to preserve her Legion through the coming years in the spirit of prayer that has been the character of its members, since they first knelt on the 7th of September, 1921, to recite the Rosary before the statue of the Immaculate Virgin.

And may God be pleased to grant you in the years of life that yet remain to you the consolation and reward of presiding over a Legion unbroken in its spirit of supernatural holiness.

Very sincerely yours,
+ John McCormack
+ Eugene O'Doherty
Secretaries to the Bishops.

Frank replied to the Bishops' letter and expressed his deep appreciation of their kind and encouraging remarks. In the concluding sentences of his letter to them, he wrote:

> "It forms a happy retrospect that the Legion has not failed notably in its duty of love and obedience to authority. May that feature ever continue in its special mark. Without it, may the Legion perish."

FRANK DUFF

• • • • •

By normal standards, Frank Duff would by this time have been regarded as old. He was over eighty years of age. Yet no one thought of him as being old. His voice, his manner, his hearty laugh, his action-packed days, all conveyed the impression of perpetual youthfulness.

When his sister, Sara Geraldine, died in 1975, he was the only surviving member of his family. Although he had innumerable Legion friends and was engrossed in so many Legion activities, he admitted, nevertheless, that he missed his family very much. Every night at 11:00 p.m., when the Legion offices "closed down" for the night, Frank walked alone to his home a little further up the avenue. Sometimes the other legionaries felt sorry for him. They wondered if, perhaps, he suffered from loneliness going home to an empty house. On the other hand, he used to say to Nellie Jessop, the faithful and loyal legionary who looked after him:

"Nellie, you have no idea how wonderful I feel when I get in home every night and close the door after me. And to know that nobody will come looking for me, and I have such peace."

And, indeed, when he got to his room he found that, invariably, Nellie had left a flask of hot tea for him.

"What I like about Mr. Duff," Nellie used to say, "is that, although he may get a little angry sometimes, yet he is so gracious and so gentle. He appreciates every little thing you do for him."

And, indeed, Frank always appreciated it when one or the other of the legionaries would invite him to their home for an informal social evening. In Jimmy and Doreen Cummins' home, he enjoyed showing his slides and he laughed hilariously at Jimmy's talented mimicking of him. Other times, Enda and Marie Dunleavy would take him for a drive into the country. He loved to hold their baby in his arms. Marie, knowing his tastes, packed some egg-and-tomato sandwiches and some fruit for their picnic. Then in the evening, when they returned to the Dunleavy home, she made pancakes and potato cakes for him. He did not have a very good appetite but it was so nice to see him enjoying the same delicacies that his mother used to prepare for him

Golden Jubilee

in bygone days. The Kennedys, the O'Broins and others also had regular visits from Frank.

Frank still cycled to Mass every morning. He dictated very many letters to all corners of the globe. He gave talks and lectures and addressed Congresses. He attended curia functions and reunions. He even composed and conducted the music for an operetta which he called "Moscow Moments," holding rehearsals in his own home, encouraging the most "ordinary" legionaries to discover and develop their God-given talents for music or drama or poetry.

With such groups as these, Frank felt very much "at home." With them he was utterly relaxed. He could scold them if they started a song on a false note. He could get impatient if somebody arrived late. He could get annoyed if somebody forgot to bring something as promised. And yet they loved him. They forgave him even if he was sometimes cross with them. He was so human, so natural, without affectation or guile. They were willing, too, to tolerate his stubbornness, and he could be stubborn at times. If, for instance, he had made up his mind about taking some course of action, he found it difficult to accept another's view that it was the wrong line to take.

But the moment the rehearsal or performance would actually start, a lovely smile would light up his face, a smile that betrayed real pleasure and perhaps also a joy that he had helped his fellow legionaries to develop their dormant talents. And, of course, Frank loved music. He was particularly keen that the old classical songs should not be lost. Possibly, too, it brought back memories of his boyhood days when his mother sat at the piano and taught the children those lovely old Irish songs.

He still enjoyed his annual cycling holiday with some of his fellow legionaries, amazing everybody with his energy and enthusiasm. Of course, the distances traveled were not so long as heretofore but his ingenious co-cyclists managed to make the journeys seem longer than they really were.

Mount Melleray Abbey was another "must" for him every year. The monks welcomed him as one of their own. He had received so much from Melleray over the years. It was there he got his first theological understanding of Our Blessed Lady. It was there he had been inspired to write

FRANK DUFF

the Legion Promise to the Holy Spirit. It was there that he first got his proper appreciation of the wonders of the Mass. In the quiet and peace of Melleray, his ideas had the proper atmosphere in which to mature and be developed. And the monks, for their part, had benefitted from his presence. Over the years many of them had approached him for counsel and advice.

Some years previously, Frank had stepped down from the governing body of the Legion, the Concilium, of which he was an officer. He believed younger heads should be given plenty of responsibilities. But he still continued to attend Concilium in the capacity of Counsellor. Whenever there was a delicate situation, or some very serious problem had to be tackled, he was invaluable for his advice. Overseas visitors were amazed at his insights and understanding of religious problems in far-away lands.

Those closer to home were not so amazed, as they had been well aware of his sagacity over the years. But one and all were astonished at the wisdom of his answers. He seemed to draw not only from his long experience and his natural genius but also, indeed, from his close contact with the Holy Spirit. Even though he could be dogmatic by nature, he sought always to outline a case or a problem in pure logical terms, so that the solution, in the end, seemed obvious enough.

• • • • •

Frank had a couple of illnesses late in life. On one occasion, four vandals broke into his house with the intention of stealing. When they demanded money from him, he grabbed a big stick which was by his bedside and struck out at them. They fled in terror from the house. At a later date, however, they returned and struck him a severe blow on the head. He was taken to the hospital where he made a slow but good recovery.

In the early part of 1979, he was again rather seriously ill. This time, Doctor Michael McGuinness attended him. Frank was very consoled by this because Dr. McGuinness was not only a great doctor but he was also a very close friend and a legionary.

Golden Jubilee

True to form, Dr. McGuinness treated Frank with great understanding. He prescribed no radical treatment, but he did say gently one day to Frank:

"Mr. Duff, if I can get you a bed in a small private Nursing Home out near my home, will you take it?"

Frank had utter confidence in his doctor. He replied simply:

"Michael, I suppose I would be a fool not to."

Over the next couple of weeks Dr. McGuinness and another friend, Dr. O'Leary, kept a watchful eye on Frank and slowly he recovered his strength. Absolute rest was prescribed for him. No visitors. But there was one happy exception. Frank must have smiled at the remarkable turn of events when she came to see him. It was Phyllis, the young lady who, some years previously, had come to him to offer herself for envoyship and whom he had subsequently visited every week for ten months when she was hospitalized. She was now Dr. McGuinness's wife.

On one of her visits to the nursing home, Phyllis said to Frank:

"Mr. Duff, I know you are anxious to attend the Acies ceremony. Well, the doctors have agreed to let you out for it, so I'll come and drive you there."

Frank was thrilled to be able to attend the Acies. It meant so much to him. Besides, it was a break for him to get away from the hospital even for a few hours. He absolutely hated being in hospital, though only his close friends knew that, because in the hospital he never betrayed this great distaste. In fact, he was a model patient, taking without a murmur whatever medicine was prescribed, doing everything he was told to do, and doing it readily and with his usual gentle smile.

When the Acies ceremony was over, Phyllis drove him back to the nursing home again. As she said good-bye, her heart went out to him. It had been like driving a lonely little boy back to school after his holidays.

When Frank was discharged from the nursing home, he readily accepted an invitation from the McGuinnesses to spend a few days with them. It would give him a chance to "get on his feet." And indeed, those few days were a real tonic for him. Susan McGuinness, the only child in the

FRANK DUFF

family, was now ten years old. Frank, who loved children, was very fond of Susan. He chatted with her, played with her, teased her. She was "at home" in his company and he in hers.

Then Frank returned to his own home in Morning Star Avenue. There was work to be done. He was eighty-eight years old at this time but his mind was as keen and alert as ever. Even though he was never robust during the few years that were left to him, he was, nevertheless, able to do a pretty full day's work every day. His appetite was poor now but Mrs. Jessop, his housekeeper in the Regina Coeli, took good care of him and provided him with some little dainties and sweet dishes that tempted his appetite.

His bicycle was once again brought out of storage and he resumed his daily cycling trips to Mass and elsewhere around the city. When the summer came, he surprised everyone by declaring his intent to go, as he had always done, on his cycling holidays. And he was true to his word.

One of his friends said to him:

"Frank, you're a born fighter, you don't easily give in." And Frank answered with a long, hearty laugh.

•••••

On the 10th of August 1979, five Americans arrived at Dublin Airport. Their accents, their business-like gait, their accoutrements and heavy luggage inevitably attracted attention.

Monsignor Charles Moss, Walter Brown, Bill Peffley, Al Norrell and Beatrice Flanagan, five well-known legionaries from the Senatus of Philadelphia, had come to make a series of video cassette recordings of Frank Duff. Frank was now ninety years old and Monsignor Moss thought, "Let's not wait too long!"

Mr. Duff was the ideal performer on T.V. To quote Monsignor Moss: "As a T.V. personage, Mr. Duff was truly amazing. He would sit under the lights and patiently endure our half-hour of testing each day and then continue under those lights for another hour or two or even three and never complain. He was convinced of the value of these recordings for the future good of the Legion. For a

Golden Jubilee

man of ninety, he was amazingly spry. The day after we concluded our videotaping, he went on a cycling trip to the west of Ireland!"

Within a few years, the same inimitable Monsignor Moss had distributed copies of these invaluable recordings throughout many countries where thousands of legionaries (and others) who had never had the privilege of meeting Mr. Duff in person could now hear the truly extraordinary words of wisdom fall from his lips and witness the indomitable yet gentle spirit that built the Legion of Mary into the beautiful and powerful force that it is in the world today.

38 Twilight

It was Thursday, May 10th, 1979. Shortly after 6:00 a.m. a taxi was winding its way through the beautiful gardens of the Vatican. Frank Duff and three other Dublin legionaries, Enda Dunleavy, Lily Lynch and Jimmy Cummins, were on their way to assist at the Pope's Mass in his private chapel. They had received a special invitation from the Holy Father.

The chapel was very small. Pope John Paul II was kneeling on a prie-dieu facing the altar. After a long prayerful preparation, he vested for Mass, assisted by Father Magee, his secretary. During the Mass, three Polish nuns, standing at the entrance door, sang beautiful hymns. The four legionaries received Communion from the hands of the Holy Father himself.

Frank was so overwhelmed by the great privilege granted them, that he found it difficult to concentrate on his prayers.

After Mass and thanksgiving, the Holy Father came forward to clasp Frank's hand, greeting him warmly. A like greeting for Enda, Lily, and Jimmy. Then, ushering them into another room, the Holy Father said: "And now you are in the Pope's kitchen." An Irish breakfast was provided by the Pope's housekeeper for the occasion.

During the breakfast the conversation was, naturally, about the Legion of Mary. The Holy Father spoke about the contacts he had had with the Legion, first when he was in Paris, then in Belgium, and later in Poland. He told them also about his meetings with legionaries in parishes in Rome itself. He then asked for more information regarding the progress of the Legion throughout the world. Enda Dunleavy said later: "We covered the entire surface of the globe for him. We found ourselves marveling at the informality of the occasion. It was as if a general had called in

Twilight

some of his officers for consultation concerning a great campaign. The Pope gave every possible encouragement to all our Legion undertakings."

Then his Holiness said:

"I must tell you a story. When Cardinal Hlond of Warsaw was dying, a young priest knelt by his bedside. There had been great difficulties, not only in Poland but also in many other countries as well. The Cardinal, as if leaving a last testament, said: "Victory will come through Mary." Then His Holiness added: "and that is my message to the Legion of Mary—'Victory will come through Mary.' " And a thrilling message it was.

One of the legionaries said to the Holy Father:

"Your Holiness, Mr. Duff will be 90 years old in a few weeks' time."

The Holy Father turned again to Frank and said: "Well, you can consider yourself young until 90."

Strangely enough, Frank Duff took those words very seriously. Perhaps for him it was a sign. At any rate when the Legion party left the Vatican he said: "I know now my time is very short."

Before the Holy Father said his final farewell he said again:

"Remember the words 'Victory comes through Mary.' "

● ● ● ● ●

In their lovely bungalow in Thurles, Co. Tipperary, David O'Keeffe and his wife Mary were dusting and polishing everything in sight. And they were excited. It was June 1980. Frank Duff was coming to spend his ninety-first birthday in their home.

The occasion for the visit was Michael Kennedy's Ordination to the Priesthood. It was Michael who had started the Legion of Mary in Maynooth College six years previously with the encouragement of the then President, Monsignor (later Cardinal) Tomás O'Fiach. Frank was deeply appreciative and was now pleased to be able to accept Michael's invitation to his Ordination in the beautiful Cathedral in Thurles. It was also an opportunity for Frank to renew his acquaintance with Archbishop Thomas Morris

FRANK DUFF

who had given such generous support to the Legion at home and abroad. Frank often said that the Archbishop's seminary in Thurles was the one he mostly recommended to young men wishing to study for the priesthood.

Frank obliged the local legionaries and the local Presentation, Ursuline and Mercy Communities (who had regularly supplied Spiritual Directresses to Legion praesidia), by coming to Thurles early on the previous evening to give a talk on True Devotion to Mary. He greatly appreciated the very important role which nuns were playing in Legion activities in many lands. He had a deep respect for nuns both because of their exalted vocation and because of their power for spiritually uplifting the world. "The nun," he said, "can send powerful evangelistic and charitable impulses moving through the people, the ultimate consequences of which no man can foresee."

The nuns made a cake for him, with ninety-one candles on it. And they sang for him, even though it was only the eve of his birthday. He was very happy. Then because, of course, it was past their own bedtime, they said:"Mr. Duff, you should get to bed early tonight; you have a full day ahead of you tomorrow."

For the young O'Keeffe couple it was, indeed, an honor that Frank accepted their offer of overnight accommodation. At ten o'clock, a priest friend of the O'Keeffes arrived at their home. He had just returned from overseas for the occasion. "Father," said David O'Keeffe, "Mr. Duff has just this minute retired to his room; go and say 'hello' to him." The priest tapped on Frank's door, then peeped in. What a beautiful sight! An elderly man of God kneeling, like a child, at the side of his bed saying his prayers. The priest hadn't the heart to disturb him.

Frank was up early the following morning and was thrilled to be able to assist at a Mass concelebrated in the O'Keeffe home by the "overseas" priest and by Fr. Hermann, a long-time friend. Then, after a hearty breakfast provided by Mary O'Keeffe, all set out for the Ordinations at the Cathedral.

What a moving and sanctifying experience that Ordination ceremony must have been for Frank. How he loved the Priesthood. True, during his lifetime, he had suffered

Twilight

greatly from the persistent opposition of some priests, especially when the Legion of Mary was in its infancy. Nevertheless, priests were God's anointed. In the Legion handbook, Frank transcribed a quotation from Benson: "Devotion and reverence towards the priest is a direct homage to the Eternal Priesthood of which the human minister is a partaker." And, of course, Frank was deeply appreciative of the thousands of priests who did understand the Legion and who promoted it. He knew, too, that their own priestly lives had been enriched by it.

There are very few ceremonies that are as impressive as the Liturgy of an Ordination Mass. And when the Ordination Mass had ended that morning in Thurles, Frank remarked that he had been tremendously uplifted by the whole occasion—so solemn, so beautiful, so holy.

It had been known that Frank's health had been deteriorating slowly over the previous couple of years. Therefore, everybody was pleasantly surprised when they saw him in such marvelous form as he chatted to all and sundry after the Mass. He was so fresh, so cheerful, so healthy looking. It really did seem that the Lord had given him a new vitality to enable him to enjoy that very special occasion.

And he knelt humbly, to receive Fr. Michael's blessing. It had been a wonderful ninety-first birthday.

• • • • •

When Frank returned to Dublin, he resumed his regular routine of work. He addressed a team of legionaries who were setting out on peregrinatio to Russia. He also spoke to groups of legionaries going to many other countries. He was available always to help representatives of Legion councils overseas who came to Dublin for his guidance and encouragement. He dealt with a huge correspondence. And he was glad to be able to attend another Ordination; this time it was the Ordination of Terry McGuckian, a former Legion envoy.

But he was slowing down. Those close to him thought he looked tired. He was finding it increasingly difficult to get rid of the colds that used to bother him. But, stubborn to the last, he battled on gamely like an old warrior enjoying

FRANK DUFF

the fray, taking an intense interest in everything, willing to give of himself to the utmost of his ability. He still cycled to his daily Mass, was ever faithful to his battered but beloved breviary and could be found, after his supper each evening, in the front pew of the Regina Coeli chapel, relaxed and prayerful before the Blessed Sacrament.

On the 25th of October, just two weeks before he died, came the "grand finale," the Halloween Peregrinatio Pro Christo Conference. Legionaries came in large numbers from all over Ireland, and representatives came from the Legion in many foreign countries. There were marvelous reports from far and near, stories of the awakening of new life in sleepy parishes, conversions of "hopeless" cases, miracles of grace. As one visiting priest expressed it, it was reminiscent of the Acts of the Apostles. And, indeed, it was obvious that the Holy Spirit was present with His mighty power. Equally noticeable in all those happenings was the touch of Our Lady's hand.

The highlight of the Conference was Frank Duff's concluding address. Did he sense that it was to be his last public address? Remarkable that he should bring the minds of his audience back to the very origins of the Legion and to the ideals on which it was built. At the very first Legion meeting in 1921, the members had turned to Mary and said: "Lead us." "And thus," he said, "began the campaign that was to take them into every country in the world." He spoke of what had already been achieved through the Legion. He spoke of faith and courage and vision. Legionaries must strive for even greater conquests for Christ. "The prospects are unending if we are hand in hand with Mary."

His concluding sentence, spoken in a strong, firm voice and with utter conviction, was his final testament to the Legion of Mary. "So we must think," he said, "in terms of the apparently impossible: the conquest of the world of souls. Mary will make the dream come true."

● ● ● ● ●

Frank Duff died on the afternoon of Friday, November 7th, 1980 at the age of ninety-one. The news stunned the world. Though he had not enjoyed the best of health dur-

Twilight

ing that year, he appeared to be reasonably well. Those nearest to him, however, thought that he seemed rather weak and even, at times, exhausted.

But Frank never surrendered easily, not even to exhaustion. With his iron will-power, he kept driving himself on. Even on the day of his death he went to two Masses. As Mrs. Nellie Jessop, his housekeeper, knew that he planned to attend the second Mass, she concluded he wouldn't be coming home for breakfast, so at 7:15 that morning she brought a nice light breakfast to his bedroom—a little bowl of porridge, a cup of coffee and some toast. He was most grateful. Then Sid Quinn drove Frank and Mrs. Jessop to the 9:00 o'clock Mass in the Capuchin Church. It was a special morning for Frank, because it was the First Friday of the month, and he had a wonderful devotion to the Sacred Heart and the First Friday devotions.

The morning was very cold. After the Mass, Jack McNamara collected Frank and drove him to Our Lady's Hospice for the second Mass. It was the funeral Mass for Joan Cronin, the great Legion envoy, who had died a couple of days previously. Joan had given seventeen full years of her life extending and consolidating the Legion in many countries. There was a great gathering of legionaries at the Mass and the interment. For many of them, it was an opportunity to meet once again the beloved founder of their organization, and exchange a few words with him. He was most amiable and willing to chat to all who approached him. Little did they realize that it was goodbye. Mr. Duff was very sick.

Jack McNamara drove him straight home. Jack and Frank had been close friends for over 50 years. Before they parted, Frank said:

"Jack, I'm not feeling too well. Will you ask Mrs. Jessop to come up to me."

Mrs. Jessop hurried up straightway. She found him sitting on the bed. "Nellie, I don't feel well at all."

"Right enough, Mr. Duff, you don't look too well."

She helped him remove his shoes and stockings. She had, for some time past, insisted on putting an electric blanket in his bed and he hadn't protested. He felt the cold a lot, and the heated bed helped him to get some necessary sleep.

FRANK DUFF

Fortunately, the electric blanket was still on. When he had got into bed she came to fix the blankets.

"Ah, Nellie, it's lovely to get into the lovely hot bed. I won't come down to any lunch today."

"Don't, Mr. Duff, I'll bring you a cup of tea about 4 o'clock." When she was going out the door, he called after her: "Nellie, don't ring Doctor O'Leary. You know how I hate hospitals."

When Mrs. Jessop brought up the cup of tea that afternoon, Frank Duff was dead.

"I went up with the cup of tea. When I opened the door, I knew he was gone. I saw him sitting with his arms folded across his breast. I think he was staring at that picture of the Sacred Heart. The picture was right opposite him. I just closed his eyes and I ran down to get help."

Just about the same time, a young priest, Father Michael Ross S.D.B., was approached in a different part of the city by a "down-and-out" man seeking an alms. The man was a "resident" of the Morning Star Hostel, so Father Ross drove him to the hostel. The Indoor Legion of Mary Brothers at the hostel invited Father Ross to have a cup of tea. He had just begun to drink it when the phone rang; the caller gave the brief urgent message: "Mr. Duff is dead, get a priest quickly." Frank's house was only a couple of doors away, so within a minute Father Ross was at the bedside to give a blessing and Conditional Absolution. Father Mulligan, the local curate, came soon after and administered the holy Anointing.

Frank had always taken Christ at his word when He said: "As long as you did it to one of these my least brethren, you did it to me." Surely in this poor "down-and-out" man of the Morning Star Hostel, we can see the Person of Christ Himself bringing His priest to bless His good and faithful servant, now that he had finished the work He had given him to do.

The Legion prayers were recited at the bedside. As the legionaries knelt there, they knew well that Frank had died in the manner he would have desired—quietly and without any fuss. Probably they were wondering what the last few moments of his life had been like. What were his last prayers, his last thoughts? Had he been contemplating the

Twilight

wonderful reunion with his own family which he had often spoken about and ardently longed for? Or the welcome that awaited him from his larger family, the many thousands of brother and sister legionaries who had gone before him? Was he rejoicing that the good Lord was calling him home on the First Friday, the day of the Sacred Heart? — he had always been so passionately devoted to the Sacred Heart of Jesus. Was he wondering how exactly our Blessed Lady was going to greet her "old reliable"? He knew her immaculate and glorified beauty would be immeasurably greater than anything the human mind could ever imagine. Oh, the unspeakable joy of it!

As a young man, Frank had composed a beautiful prayer for souls striving for sanctity. How significant and how lovely it seemed in retrospect:

> "Oh, my God, I do not ask for the big things — the life of the missionary or the monk, or those others I see around me so full of accomplishment.
> I do not ask for any of these; but simply set my face to follow out unswervingly, untiringly, the common life which day by day stretches out before me,
> satisfied if in it I love You, and try to make You loved. Nature rebels against this life with its never-ending round of trivial tasks and full of the temptation to take relief in amusement or change.
> It seems so hard to be great in small things, to be heroic in the doing of the commonplace; but still this life is Your will for me.
> There must be a great destiny in it.
> And so I am content.
> And then to crown the rest, dear Jesus,
> I beg of you to give me this . . . fidelity to the end, to be at my post when the final call comes,
> and to take my last, weary breath in your embrace.
> A valiant life . . . and faithful to the end.
> A short wish, dearest Jesus, but it covers all."[1]

NOTE

[1] "Can we be Saints?" by Frank Duff.

39 Farewell

Frank's body was brought to lie in state in the Regina Coeli Hostel Chapel. What more fitting resting place for the mortal remains of one whose whole life was centered around this very chapel and its environs? It was here he had prayed his breviary daily; —pure communication with God, he had called it. It was here he had assisted at so many Masses, had been nourished and strengthened so often by Holy Communion, had prayed so many rosaries. His co-pilgrims, as he did the "round of the beads," were for the most part the poor women whom he and his fellow legionaries had rescued from homelessness and destitution. They were his beloved hostel "residents." Their respect for him was somewhat akin to reverence, but his meekness and humanity were such that they could—and did—approach him with that sort of brusque familiarity which is at its noblest among the poorer classes. Indeed, they had no qualms about interrupting him at his prayers to ask: "Won't you pray for me, Mr. Duff?"

Frank had usually knelt in the front pew, his rosary beads slipping gracefully through his fingers, his lips moving ever so slowly. When he wasn't praying his breviary or his rosary, he would just sit there, motionless, his gaze rivetted on the tabernacle. Yes, Frank had dearly loved this little chapel. It was quiet, peaceful; it provided a refuge from the hustle and bustle of life, an oasis for refreshment, a little bit of heaven on earth.

Now he had come for his final visit. They carried his coffin gently, out of reverence and because of the privilege, and placed it at the gospel side of the altar. Near the coffin, the legionary sisters arranged a small Legion altar. It seemed so appropriate; Frank had always looked on the Legion altar as the symbol of Our Lady's presence.

Farewell

Many years previously, Frank wrote a beautiful paragraph in the Legion handbook about our deceased legionaries. Unwittingly, he was writing his own epitaph:

> "The end of the campaigning has come and a legionary lies nobly dead. Now at last he is confirmed in legionary service. Through all eternity he will be a legionary, for the Legion has shaped that eternity for him. It has been the fibre and the mould of his spiritual life."[1]

Father Ahearne said Mass in the presence of the great number of grief-stricken legionaries who had quickly gathered. Other priests, too, came to say their Masses there. During the next few days, many thousands of legionaries filed past the coffin in quiet prayer. Among the moving crowds were Government Ministers, bishops, priests, nuns and Religious. There were rich and poor. There were nurses from the hospitals in their white uniforms. There were schoolboys and schoolgirls. And there were Frank's own beloved friends—the poor women and children from the Regina Coeli and the "residents" from the Morning Star.

On Wednesday, November 12th, the remains were removed to St. Andrew's Church where the most Rev. James Kavanagh, Auxiliary Bishop of Dublin, concelebrated Mass with a large group of Spiritual Directors. Canon Francis Ripley, a lifelong friend of Frank's, preached a moving homily.

The following morning, Solemn Requiem Mass was concelebrated in the same church by his Eminence, Cardinal Tomás O'Fiaich, Most Rev. Dermot Ryan, Archbishop of Dublin, Most Rev. Thomas Morris, Archbishop of Cashel and Emly, Most Rev. Joseph Cunnane, Archbishop of Tuam and many other bishops and Legion Spiritual Directors. Cardinal O'Fiaich preached the funeral sermon.

The crowds were so great that it was impossible for very many people to gain entrance to the church. When Holy Communion was being distributed to the members of the congregation, four extra deacons were required to distribute Holy Communion to the crowds who lined the streets outside.

With a State escort, the funeral proceeded to Glasnevin

FRANK DUFF

Cemetery where the remains were laid to rest in the family grave.

Truly, a noble soul had gone from our midst.

FUNERAL SERMON by Cardinal O'Fiaich

Dear brothers and sisters in Jesus Christ: In the Legion of Mary everyone is a brother or a sister; so today, gathered around the mortal remains of the man who was not only its founder but for almost 60 years its great spiritual guide and philosopher, we all feel in a special way brothers and sisters in Christ.

We mourn Frank Duff today as a brother who has gone before us. "It is accomplished." We mourn him as a man of deep humility, who was the friend and adviser of Popes and prelates, but never lost the simplicity and naturalness of the true Dubliner; a man who was constantly in correspondence with all parts of the globe, yet had time to listen to everyone who called on him here at home and whose closest friends were to be found among the poor; a man who was honoured by a Papal Decoration in 1961 and a Doctorate of our National University in 1968, yet whose favourite dress was his well-battered suit and whose favourite conveyance was his trusty bicycle; a man of great kindness and personal charm, of self-effacing modesty, of absolute integrity, of unflinching courage, of frail body but unquenchable spirit, of godliness and of prayer. "Never embark on any action without prayer" he used to say, "especially prayer through the intercession of Mary." "Mother, this is your Son; Son, this is your Mother."

And yet this humble singleminded Dubliner has been described as "the man who made the greatest contribution to the life of the Catholic Church in this century." What was the secret of his amazing spiritual influence throughout the world? Surely it began with his own personal sanctity, his infectious faith, his complete trust in God, his dependence on the help of Our Blessed Lady, his consciousness of the Church as Christ's Mystical Body, years before this doctrine became the subject of Papal Encyclicals, his insatiable desire to reach out to every person as a brother and sister and to help them along the road to heaven, his belief that

Farewell

ordinary men and women will do heroic things for Christ if they are shown the way, his conviction that no one is so bad that he can't be helped or so good that he doesn't need help. And so, aided by his outstanding qualities as an organizer and his profound understanding of human psychology, by his utter dedication to the promotion of his organization and the unselfish labours of a heroic band of envoys and helpers, no less dedicated than himself, the Legion of Mary encircled the globe until it conquered millions for Christ through its secret weapon of *personal contact*. "With God on our side, who can be against us?"

It was not surprising that Frank Duff was invited by the Pope to attend the Second Vatican Council, for in many respects the Legion of Mary had been propagating the ideas of Vatican II decades before the Council was called. Frank Duff was truly a man before his time in challenging complacency in the Church and calling for a new awakening, in emphasizing that everyone is his brother's keeper and that the Church is not merely a collection of individuals: he was almost a radical in stressing the need to involve the laity in the work of evangelization, in giving women a predominant role in his organization—from the saintly and indefatigable Edel Quinn as envoy to the humblest member of the most remote Praesidium—in promoting ecumenical discussions with Protestants and Jews, in the need which he saw to increase the knowledge of the faith possessed by adult Catholics through a movement such as the Patricians, in the extra care which he lavished on special groups in society—the young, the sick, the lonely, the foreign student, the street-girl, the non-practicing, the down and out. For him, as for St. Paul in today's Second Reading, all these demanded a share in the "Love of God made visible in Christ Jesus Our Lord."

The amazing spread of the Legion of Mary during its own founder's life must seem to us today little short of miraculous, but Frank Duff never waited for miracles to happen—he went out and made them happen. For him the growth of the Legion meant the hard slog of unremitting labour—full time for nearly half a century—seeking to overcome the indifference of the laity and the reluctance of the clergy, fighting for admission to new territories abroad

FRANK DUFF

and for wider acceptance at home but always fighting with a great sense of obedience and loyalty to the Church. One of his greatest joys during the past decade was to see the Legion return to Russia when young men and women from Ireland visited the Soviet Union every Summer and spoke of the things of God to many who had been brought up in unbelief. One of his last ambitions, which he did not live to see fulfilled alas, was the return of the Legion to China where a few thousand of its members were martyred in the 1950s.

For all these special tasks, for selection as envoys to foreign lands and for going on *Peregrinatio* abroad during the Summer holidays, the Legion of Mary depended particularly on young Irish men and women. For while Frank Duff had a global outlook on Church matters, he was a great lover of his native land, of the friendliness of its people, of the beauty of its landscape. St. Patrick was no less his spiritual guide than St. Louis Marie de Montfort and much of his inspiration came from the early Irish missionaries in Europe, whose work he wished to emulate in the Legion of Mary. His book entitled *True Devotion to the Nation* provides a handbook of practical patriotism in which work for our fellow Irishmen and women is given a spiritual dimension. He was quick to see the potential of a cultural organization like *An Réalt* and the value of having it closely linked to the Legion. Is iomaí Gaeilgeoir a tarraingeadh isteach sa Légiún de bharr obair *An Réalt* agus leathnaigh *An Réalt* eolas agus meas ar fud na hÉireann ar oidhreacht spioradálta ár dtíre.

In 1976 Frank Duff was awarded an "Irishman of the Year" Award but politely declined it. Perhaps the day may come soon when the Church will declare him "Irishman of the Century." We pray fervently today for his eternal reward as we repeat as his epitaph the gracious words of Our Holy Father Pope John Paul II in his telegram of sympathy.

Telegram from the Holy Father

The Legion of Mary throughout the world mourns the death of its founder, Frank Duff. I join with the members

Farewell

in praying for the eternal repose of his soul. The association that he founded has made countless lay catholics aware of their indispensable role in evangelization and sanctification and has enabled them to fulfill that role zealously and effectively. To all legionaries I impart the Apostolic Blessing and comfort in their loss and encouragement in their future task.

John Paul II

NOTE

[1] Legion Handbook, p. 103.

40 Magnifier of Mary

Undoubtedly, Frank Duff's great contribution to the Church was that he focussed world-wide attention on the real greatness of the Blessed Virgin and on Her role in the lives of the faithful.

Frank's aim was to bring the great masses of people to a reasonable understanding of the doctrines of Our Lady and induce them to practice a devotion to her that would be worthy of these doctrines. And in particular, he advocated that a true and genuine devotion to Our Lady must in some way involve service to Her. To serve Christ, Her Son, in our fellow-men would be the ideal way of letting our love for Her overflow into action. Therefore, Mary must be presented in the context of the doctrine of the Mystical Body of Christ.

The Legion of Mary, which is founded on the twin doctrines of the Mystical Body and True Devotion to Mary, was Frank's way of introducing these doctrines into the everyday lives of the people and demonstrating to them the absolute need for a great lay apostolate without which millions of souls could be lost forever; in the Legion he showed them how attractive and challenging and adventurous the life of a lay apostle could be.

When Frank introduced the title, "Our Lady Mediatrix of all Graces," into the Legion handbook and into the Legion prayers, some theologians protested that they did not consider it to be certain doctrine. Frank was not content with quoting papal documents and the Tradition of the Church; he explained these documents and the traditional teaching of the Church. Then, with masterly logic and step by step, he outlined the precise position of Our Lady with-

Magnifier of Mary

in the Mystical Body and the role assigned to Her from all eternity: Mary is inevitably and necessarily, under God's plan, the Mediatrix of all Graces.

He published in article or book form his lectures on this subject and challenged all who found fault with his arguments to debate the issue honestly and sincerely. Today eleven million active and auxiliary members of the Legion throughout the world invoke Our Lady every day under the title of "Our Lady, Mediatrix of All Graces."

De Montfort's book was Frank's starting point in regard to Our Lady. But it was so important, that Frank felt that it must be amplified, it must be explained to a wider public. Although Montfort himself says that he is writing for "the poor and simple, who being of good will, and having more faith than the common run of scholars, believe more simply and more meritoriously" (T.D. No. 26), nevertheless he senses the need to explain more in detail some of the theological implications of his Marian Christo-centric spirituality. Likewise, Frank Duff, in the Handbook, supplies the necessary doctrinal background and, in such a way as to be understood by the ordinary people.

Furthermore, he devised the unique but simple Legion "system" whereby True Devotion to Mary could be attractively and effectively linked with service to one's neighbour. The Legion system involves: (1) a weekly meeting—it has been called a "meeting with a difference," (2) a weekly assignment of some substantial apostolic work, and (3) all to be linked with the twin doctrines of the Mystical Body and Mary's Motherhood.

Frank's efforts have resulted in countless people throughout the world practicing De Montfort's True Devotion to Mary and practicing it in an enlightened manner; we might say, in an ecclesial manner.

Doubtless it was, to a great extent, through the practice of this devotion that thousands of legionaries were inspired and fortified to give their lives as martyrs in China, Vietnam, Zaire and elsewhere; that people like Edel Quinn and Alfie Lambe and, indeed, many other legionaries rose to heights of heroic sanctity; that many ailing parishes have become healthy again and even missionary; that in remote parishes of Ireland, in isolated leper villages of India, in

FRANK DUFF

busy city parishes of all countries, parishioners are giving more than a mere lip service to Our Lady and are showing themselves worthy members of the Body of Christ. Vast numbers, through prayer and service, are magnifying the Lord, with and through Mary.

But the connoisseur of diamonds is more pleased with one pure gem than with countless sparkling stones of lesser quality. Surely, Our Lady saw in Frank Duff's own soul a gem of rare quality. By his deep and tender devotion, Frank magnified Our Lady to a degree that can only be known in heaven. And his faith, his charity, his humility, his zeal for souls were all brought into play to intensify and enhance that devotion.

To the unspiritual, it may seem that the secret of Frank's success in building up the Legion was his genius and his intellectual brilliance and his organizing abilities. He certainly had these talents in abundance. But these were not the secret of his success. He used these talents but only to demonstrate where the real power came from—Our Lady. As Fr. Marius MacAuliffe pointed out, "God raised up this man to beat the world at its own game."

For Frank, Our Lady was the personification of true humility. Through his intense prayer life, he came to appreciate the importance of humility. He realized that the lack of grace in a soul is the result not only of sin but also of subtle selfishness. So his prayer life was not simply the saying of prayers but striving to discover and acknowledge his own nothingness, struggling to conquer self and selfishness, making himself absolutely and unreservedly available to God and to the workings of grace. Part of the Secret of Mary that he discovered from De Montfort was that humility comes through Mary. Later, when, by the slow, painful process of experience, he had begun more fully to appreciate its worth, he elaborated on it in the Legion handbook: "The legionary's battle for souls must begin in the heart of the individual legionary . . . determinedly conquering in his heart the spirit of pride and self. This terrible struggle . . . how exhausting it is. It is the battle of a lifetime. . . . In the faithful practice of the spirit of dependence upon Mary will be found a supreme, simple, comprehensive way of humility" (Handbook P. 108).

Magnifier of Mary

Humility, for Frank, was no "soft" commodity. Rather it was a tough, virile thing, a sort of ruthless honesty with oneself. It was simply the stark realization of the utter uselessness of man's powers, unless they are aided by the supernatural. He saw vividly that if he ever attributed any real power to himself, God would cease to work through him. In a conversation with a friend, he said: "I wouldn't for a moment suggest that I'm not prone to the customary petty temptations regarding the little things. For instance, I am very sensitive; I am easily hurt; I have been "walked on" often during my life and I have felt it very much; I can't claim that I ever rejoiced in those hurts, as you read in the lives of the saints. But as regards the big things, I have been saved from vulgar pride, and that's because I have depended on the Lord and His Mother and not on myself. So when anything worthwhile happened, when there was development, I was not tempted to ascribe it to my own abilities: it could hardly even cross my mind to claim any credit. No, I realize my position; if, for one minute I claimed any of the credit for myself, I'd soon be flattened to the ground."

Frank was, of course, proud of the Legion, not because of his involvement in it but because of what it was doing for Mary, and when people praised or admired the Legion he was very pleased. The trouble was, however, that quite often well-meaning people lauded Frank, even sometimes during public gatherings. It was an agony for him. It pained him but he had to bear it in silence. Once, a colleague said to him, "Frank I could see how embarrassed you were when Father X was praising you in his speech; I suppose you can say that's a bit of your purgatory over for you." "I can tell you," replied Frank gravely, "that *is* my purgatory."

On another occasion, a legionary noticed Frank chuckling over a newspaper. The legionary approached to discover the cause of his merriment and saw a large paragraph in the paper about Frank. Frank explained his "chuckling." "I have learned," he said, "when I come across things about myself, to look at myself in the third person; then I find it very funny."

In a discussion on true devotion to Mary, Frank was asked if he himself constantly adverted to Mary's presence.

FRANK DUFF

He replied that it would be impossible for anybody to be explicitly adverting to Our Lady all the time. "But," he said, "when you understand what her motherhood is all about, you just know she's there, she's always close by, she's interested in absolutely everything you do and is ever willing to help you."

Frank had the good fortune to experience in a marvelous way the maternal solicitude of his own earthly mother. He knew his mother would do anything for him. She catered patiently and lovingly to all his needs, no matter how irregularly he came and went. She concerned herself with all his activities. If he suffered, she felt it too. And there remained permanently in his mind the remark she had once made, when she was taking him as a young boy to the hospital for a minor operation: "Frank, I wish I could undergo this in place of you."

These happy ideas of motherhood stood him in good stead when he got to know his heavenly Mother. He knew that all the wonderful qualities of Mamma Duff would be found in Our Lady. But he also knew that no earthly mother's love could compare with that of Our heavenly Mother, Mary. His familiarity with Our Lady had grown and developed to a very great degree. He looked on her as always being close to him, ever ready to help him, loving him tenderly. He could depend on her absolutely. And he, on his part, would be a loyal son, an "old reliable."

When Fr. Declan died in Melleray, the monks, knowing the great regard he had for Frank Duff, looked for something to give Frank as a keepsake. They decided to give him Fr. Declan's small statue of Our Lady, not realizing it had once belonged to Frank. Frank surely smiled at the manner in which the statue came back to him. Ever afterwards, he kept it as a prized possession. It was a small statue, but he made good use of it by keeping it constantly by his side in his sitting room where he did much of his work. It wasn't so much that he needed, at this stage, a reminder of Our Lady's presence; she had been "walking side by side" with him now for many years and he was well aware of that. But he was anxious to express in some visible way to Our Lady that he wished to bring her into everything he did. When he used his dictaphone, that little statue was

Magnifier of Mary

perched on top of it; when he was writing articles, it was by the edge of his notebook; when he opened his morning mail, it was right in the middle of the envelopes and letters; when he went on a cycling holiday, the little statue reposed in his pocket or in his bag. His attachment to it was no childish devotion, it was the symbol of his intimate union with his heavenly Mother. One sensed that they were on "first-name" terms.

De Montfort, in his book on consecration to Mary, suggests that devotees of Our Lady might consider wearing a chain as a sign of their total dependence on Mary. A chain can represent slavery, but in the case of consecration to Mary it is a voluntary "slavery," a willing, loving service, a total trust and commitment. It is most likely Frank did not wear any such chain. It may be that he feared it would some day be discovered, as he knew it had been in the case of Matt Talbot, and Frank had a real dread of being considered special in any way. At any rate he had, in effect, a chain of a different kind, a chain that was far more binding than any iron chain, and that was the Legion of Mary. The Legion was, for him, the chain that linked him with Mary for the greater part of his long life. It was his discipline, it was his work, his vocation, his joy and, at times, his cross. It was, in fact, his life, and the burdens of that life were made easier to bear by his conviction that the Legion was, as it were, the presence of Mary, always there at his side, helping him along the rugged path to that heavenly home where she would show herself in all her beauty and present him to her Divine Son. Yes, it was worth all the labor.

In the early days of the organization, all the members had been asked to propose a suitable name for the infant organization. Frank gave it much thought. It was extremely difficult to find a name that was most suitable. Then, one day, he stood and looked at a beautiful picture that hung on the wall of his home. It depicted Our Lady as the "Morning Star." Suddenly the name 'Legion of Mary" flashed through his mind. "In that instant," he later said, "I knew with absolute certainty that this was the name we had been seeking."

God had created Mary out of nothing; she was His greatest masterpiece. Out of love, God redeemed her; out

FRANK DUFF

of tenderness, He chose her to be His mother. Everything she had, everything she did, reflected the glory of the Almighty. To praise her was to praise and honor God's wonderful power and goodness. To magnify Mary was to magnify the Lord. And that was the work of Frank's life.

• • • • •

In December, 1956, Frank was invited to the U.S.A. to receive from the University of Dayton, Ohio, "the highest honor within her power to bestow—THE MARIANIST AWARD." En route, he stopped off at New York City to address a large gathering of legionaries in the Cathedral High School Auditorium. Monsignor Rothlauf, Spiritual Director of the New York Senatus of the Legion, rose to welcome Frank and introduce him to the legionaries. "I understand," he said, "that it would not be quite accurate to call Mr. Duff the founder of the Legion, since we have been told so often that it was Our Lady herself who took the initiative on that first Legion of Mary night, gathering her first legionaries around her and summoning them to apostleship. Therefore, I would like to introduce Mr. Frank Duff to you with a different title, namely, the "Magnifier of Mary."

There was thunderous applause from the audience. Frank Duff smiled beautifully but blushed with embarrassment.

Later, in the University of Dayton, when he received the Marianist Award, he said: "There is no saying that could be addressed to me that would give me greater pleasure than to tell me I have served Our Lady."

When Frank returned to Dublin, he dutifully related all, including Monsignor Rothlauf's remarks. And as he told about his new title, "Magnifier of Mary," he betrayed his embarrassment again by blushing, and again the beautiful smile lit up his face. And those who listened and watched felt very happy for Frank. They knew the indescribable joy that must have flooded his soul at that remark. They knew that, for him, the very thought that in some little way, during his lifetime, he had helped to make Our Blessed Lady better known and loved would, in itself, have been adequate reward for his incessant labors on her behalf.

The photos in this pictorial section were culled at random and are intended to present the man, Frank Duff, at various stages of his life.

Taken at the turn of the century, this photo of the six Duff children shows Frank, the oldest, with his youngest sister, Ailis, standing in front of him.

254

Photo right, detail and close-up of photo at left, reveals the serious and mature side of the young Frank Duff and his life-long attachment to his "favorite" sister, Ailis.

"When he was just 21 years, he invented a system of calculus which attracted the attention of the principal officers of his branch of the Department. As a result, he was invited to London to demonstrate his system to the officials of the London Treasury. The Department subsequently adopted his new system."

"On the whole, the young Mr. Duff was having a very pleasant and exhilarating time. A number of his friends belonged to the 'upper-crust' society and he acted as best man at many fashionable weddings."

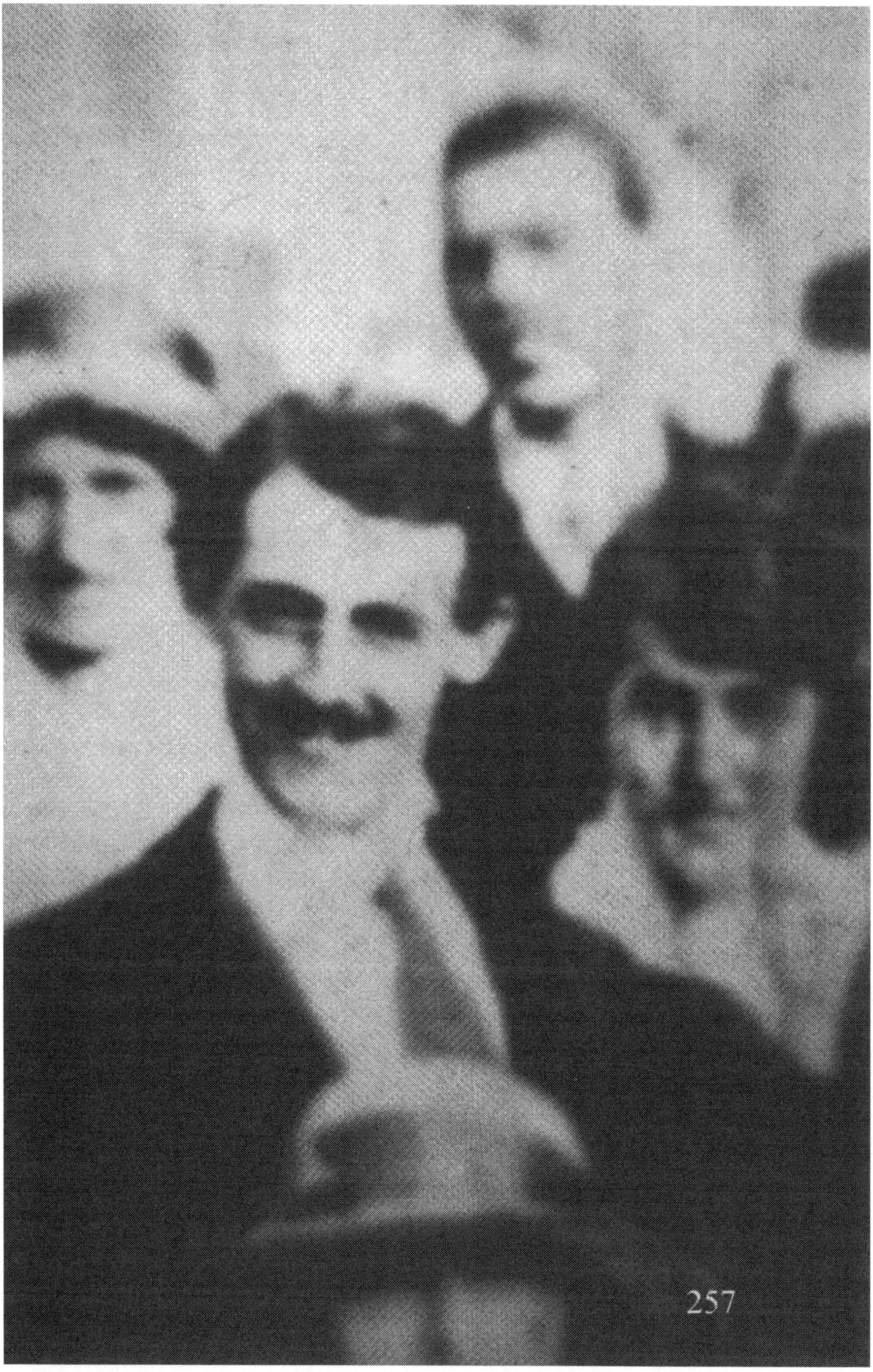

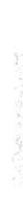

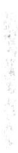

258

Frank Duff poses with a few children who lived in the home for unwed mothers — a home constructed by the Legion of Mary on the grounds of their headquarters, in Dublin.

"Brother Duff," who until the end of his life was to remain the Legion of Mary's guiding light, addresses a meeting of the world governing body, the "Concilium," in Dublin.

In his lighter moments Frank Duff could clown as well as any and, in typical Irish fashion, he could spin a yarn or two to the delight of his hearers.

In his more serious moments, Frank could be seen spending long hours before the Blessed Sacrament. Photo right was taken at Trappist Monastery Chapel, during his yearly retreat in Mount Melleray Abbey.

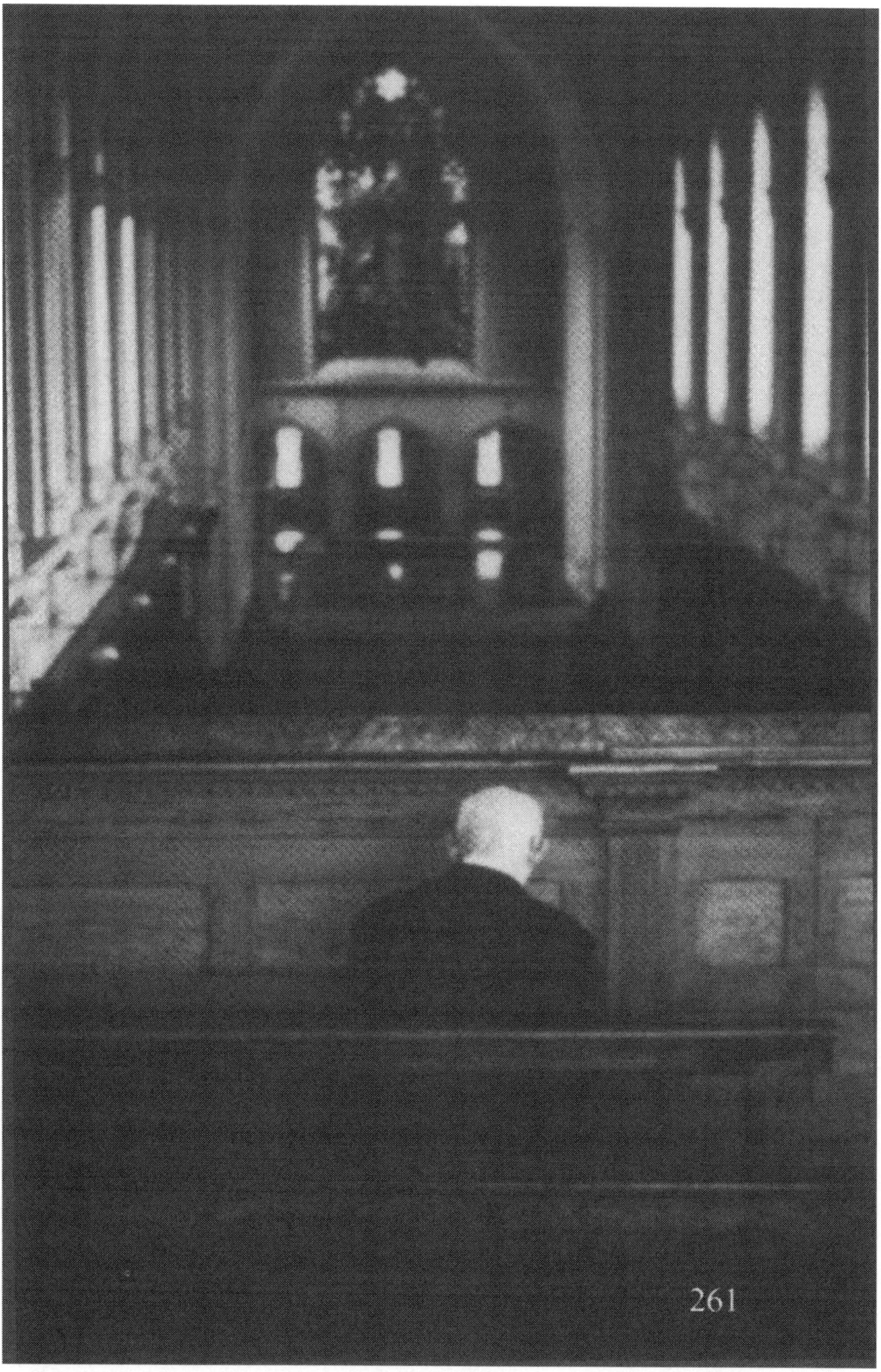

A biography of Frank Duff would be incomplete without reference to the profound influence of Edel Quinn on "Brother Duff" and his world-wide Legion of Mary apostolate.

In a friendly atmosphere, Frank Duff enjoys a good laugh with Archbishop Gaetano Alibrandi, Apostolic Nuncio to Ireland.

"Of all the outdoor activities that he enjoyed, cycling undoubtedly took pride of place . . . his 'bike' became his travelling companion . . ."

And he was to cycle right up until the day he died — truly a remarkable feat for a man who lived 91 years. . . .

Thru the

1889 7th June. Born in Dublin. Lived at Drumcondra.

1899 Family moved to Dun Laoghaire. Frank enrolled as a pupil in Blackrock College. Received First Holy Communion.

1907 Took up a post in the Civil Service. Spare time given to sports and athletics.

1911 Began to take a serious interest in reading books on spirituality, especially books on the lives of the saints.

1913 Joined the Saint Vincent de Paul Society. Turned more and more to religion.

1914 Made his first enclosed Retreat. Decided to attend daily Mass for Lent, and then for life. Joined the Pioneer Total Abstinence Association. Undertook private apostolate to lapsed and careless Catholics.

1915 Joined the Third Order of the Carmelites. Began the daily praying of the Little Office of Our Lady. Made his first pilgrimage to Lough Derg.

1916 His first booklet, "Can we be Saints?" was published by the Catholic Truth Society of Ireland.

1917 Discovered De Montfort's "True Devotion to the Blessed Virgin."

1919 His first visit to Mount Melleray Abbey.

1920 When Irish delegates were invited to London to discuss terms for the Anglo-Irish Treaty, Frank was chosen to accompany them as manager on their second trip.

1921 7th September. Birth of the Legion of Mary.

1922 Sancta Maria Hostel was established.

1927 Morning Star Hostel was opened.

1928 The Legion spreads its wings overseas . . . Scotland.

1930 Regina Coeli Hostel was opened. (Much of Frank's life revolved around the three hostels.)

1931 Frank's first visit to Rome. Pope Pius XI's blessing on the Legion.

years

1931- Rapid expansion of the Legion throughout the world.
1933

1937 Edel Quinn assigned as Legion envoy to East Africa.

1951 Frank, weighed down with great stress, decided to take a "bicycle holiday."

1953 Seamus Grace and Alfie Lambe were appointed Legion envoys to South America.

1963- Frank spent "five long months" recuperating from a seri-
1964 ous illness.

1965 Lay observer at Vatican Council.

1969 First peregrinatio pro Christo team goes to Russia.

1971 Golden Jubilee celebrations.

1979 Frank visits Pope John Paul II.

1980 Frank celebrates his 91st birthday by attending an Ordination Ceremony in Thurles.

1980 7th November. Frank Duff died at his home in Dublin.

Printed in Poland
by Amazon Fulfillment
Poland Sp. z o.o., Wrocław